Visible Saints

Puritanism, believing itself quick with the seed of religious liberty, laid, without knowing it, the egg of democracy.

James Russell Lowell

Cover photo by Bryan Page

Visible Saints

West Haven, Connecticut, 1648 - 1798

PETER J. MALIA

THE
CONNECTICUT
PRESS

Inquiries should be addressed to:
The Connecticut Press
135 Church Street
Monroe, CT 06468
www.connecticutpress.com

First Edition

Cataloging-in-Publication Data
Malia, Peter J.
    Visible Saints: West Haven, Connecticut, 1648 - 1798.
    Illustrated, includes annotations, bibliography, appendix and index.
    ISBN 978-0-9825468-1-9 (hardcover)

    1. West Haven (CT) – History – Colonial – 1648 - 1798   2. New
    Haven (CT) – History – Colonial – 1648 - 1798   3. Connecticut –
    History – Colonial – 1648 - 1798   3. New England – History –
    Colonial – 1648 - 1798   4. Puritans – History – 1648   - 1798
    5. United States – History – Colonial – 1648 - 1798   6. United States
    – History – Revolution – 1775 - 1783
    I. Malia, Peter J., 1951 -   II. Visible Saints
    ISBN 978-0-9825468-1-9
    LC Shelving No.   974.6   2009908525

THE
CONNECTICUT
PRESS

Printed in the United States of America

To My Parents
and All Who Made This History Possible

Contents

Illustrations

Preface

My first encounter with West Haven history occurred while walking to St. Lawrence Grammar School a half century ago. Along Main Street across from the old West Haven High School, there was an ancient house I passed every morning. It looked run down and abandoned. I remember how surprised I was one day to see an army of workers carefully disassembling that house piece by piece like some giant jigsaw puzzle.

Every day for a week or so, the old place slowly disappeared. Its huge framing timbers were carefully numbered and stacked. Windows were neatly piled next to fireplace mantels, and finally the staircases and roofing timbers were all carefully collected outside. And as quickly as they appeared, they were gone with just a hole in the ground remaining. People told me it was the Thomas Painter House. That didn't mean much to me at the time. I was eight years old. But seeing that old house being taken down piece by piece stayed with me through the years. I don't know what I missed more – watching the crews dismantle the place or simply rummaging around that hole in the ground where a piece of West Haven's history once stood.

Years later I learned the fate of the Painter House, which resides in Litchfield on the site of the former Lyman Beecher home. By then I was a graduate student writing a thesis on the colonial history of West Haven at Trinity College. Afterwards, I often thought about turning that study into a book, but I never seemed to find the time to do so. When I recently came across that thesis cleaning out a bookcase the image of the old Painter House became crystal clear. What a shame to see a town's history packed up and carted off like some Lincoln log set, I thought. So I decided to revisit, rewrite and finally publish the history of early West Haven. A half century after walking by that old house, I realize I owe it a debt of gratitude for not letting me forget West Haven's past.

Many people have helped bring this book to life over the years. Foremost among them was a charming and gracious West Havener named Edward Chase, late historian of the First Congregational Church of West Haven and a longtime resident of the city. His willingness to open the church archives and share his thoughts in many long conversations helped me to better understand the evolution of Congregationalism as it played out in this small New England village.

Through the expert guidance of the late Dr. Glenn Weaver, Professor Emeritus of American Colonial History at Trinity College, Hartford, and Editor of the Connecticut Bicentennial Series, that understanding became more focused on the unique nature of West Haven's past. His patient and seasoned advice improved this study immeasurably, and his friendship and encouragement will never be forgotten.

To my father, the late Donald J. Malia, Sr., I owe a special mention. Long before computers, he served as typist, proofreader, editor and fellow learner on a journey he loved as much as its author.

Finally to my wife, Celeste, I owe a debt of gratitude beyond which words fail to convey. She has been a faithful and supportive companion on our many jaunts through old graveyards, dusty archives and on our long walks along the West Haven shoreline.

Peter J. Malia
Monroe, CT
2009

Introduction

The subject of colonial West Haven is largely unknown to Connecticut history. Overshadowed by neighboring New Haven, the village across the West River has long been considered an appendage of its larger, more influential neighbor. Despite being one of the earliest settlements in Connecticut, it is also the last to be incorporated as a town in 1921.

Therein lies the irony of West Haven's past. Dismissing its history as merely an add-on to New Haven is an opportunity lost in witnessing the growth of independence in microcosm. One of the first Connecticut villages to challenge Puritan religious authority, West Haven nurtured maverick principles that ran undercurrent prevailing Puritan restraint. Impatient with the slow pace of a theocratic government, the village thrived on repeatedly pushing traditional authority to its limits. Constantly on the edge of financial insolvency and often on the brink of social and religious unrest, West Haven's founding families unwittingly cast the mold for momentous changes in the cultural and social makeup of the village and, inevitably, the colony. Eventually, their example set in motion a process that placed a high value on speaking one's mind, challenging Connecticut's legendary Standing Order and ultimately seeking political independence from Great Britain itself. In many respects, the story of West Haven proves that the road to revolution was as much a local affair as it was national movement.

As unique as West Haven history may be, its residents faced the same issues that steered a course toward independence for all of colonial America. To better understand how this small community responded to the challenges of living in a new world — inventing many of its social and political institutions as it moved forward into the unknown — also helps to explain America's subtle transition from colonial outpost to independent nation.

Paramount among the lessons learned in this study are what it reveals about early American society and its evolving sense of self-awareness. It is the story of a people in transition, who first came to this place as religious zealots intent on founding a new Eden. Out of their necessity to survive in primitive circumstances, their original dreams were first altered, then replaced altogether, by the realities of eking out an existence in a new world where one's wit and resourcefulness spelled the difference between life and death. By virtue of their self-sufficiency, inventiveness, common sense and downright true grit, these transplanted Europeans simply did what we all would have likely have done to meet the circumstances of their evolving community. Call it governing by trial and error, these visible saints, as they liked to think of themselves, proved to be all too much the stuff of flesh and blood. Driven as much by human passions and emotions to succeed as they were by their religious fervor, their story is our story and a timeless tale of ordinary people rising up, time and again, to face extraordinary events. Dynamic, turbulent, even raucous at times, the history of colonial West Haven is the story of the Puritan experiment in practise on a local level. In many ways, it is America's birth story.

Finally, whatever faults this history may inadvertently present are solely those introduced by the author. Future historians will hopefully regard his efforts with a sympathetic eye.

Peter J. Malia
Monroe, CT

CHAPTER ONE

Original Settlers

I ts first inhabitants called it Quinnipeokke, or long-water land. It was
here that the Mishimayaget, or great trail, from Shawmut (Boston)
to Manhattan converged with two other Native trails leading inland
into the vast forests of the Northeast. The first of these trails led east to
Mattabesec (Middletown) and the other led off into the forestlands towards Sicoag, or what is now Hartford. Near these crossroads in present-
day East Haven was the Grand Council of the Quinnipiac, or Quiripi,
who had tribal and blood ties to an indigenous nation that extended from
the Hudson River on the west to Cape Cod on the east, into modern Massachusetts to the north and included parts of Long Island to the south.[1]

Three miles to the west of the Quinnipiac's Grand Council site is
the opposite bank of a deep water port and what is today known as West
Haven. To the Native peoples, it was more like their warm-weather haven. Even before recorded time the area's accessible coastline has always
been a source of sustenance, easy transportation and prosperity. But its
normally calm waters also mask its unpredictable nature. Devastating
storms, disease and hostile armies have all swept ashore on its tides to
weave their threads of dashed dreams and disaster into the tapestry of
the region's history.

For the area's original settlers those threads proved to be their
eventual undoing. Part of the Algonquian family of American Native
people, the Quinnipiac and their ancestors resided along the Connecticut
shoreline for thousands of years before the first European explorers set

foot in the New World. As glacial ice receded northward, Paleo-Indian hunters roamed through New England's forests from 11,000 to 9,000 years ago. Through the archaic period Indian hunters became familiar with the southern New England shoreline and its bounty.[2]

The discovery of making ceramics, mastering new agricultural techniques and the craft of weaving propelled these native tribes into the Woodland Age (700 B.C. to A.D. 1600). Combining their traditional reliance upon hunting, fishing and gathering with their newly acquired farming skills, the New England tribes developed a vibrant economy based on squash, beans and corn, known as the "three sisters," as their staple crops. What was not eaten immediately was dried or ground into meal for bread, cakes and porridge or stored for winter when the coastal tribes moved inland into the protection of the forest near present-day Middletown.[3]

Native men typically attended to tribal politics, trade, hunting and occasional warfare. From burned out, then hand-hewn, trees they built canoes, or mishoonash, for fishing, transport and trade. Among their primary commodities was the manufacture of wampumpeague, or shell

Despite its primitive appearance, the Native roundhouse proved every bit as cozy as the best settler's cabin.

money, hewn from clam and oyster shells that were crafted into finished beads and used as currency. Another commodity was copper, which the Quinnipiacs mined from West Rock as large nuggets that were then worked into beads, amulets, knives and axes.[4]

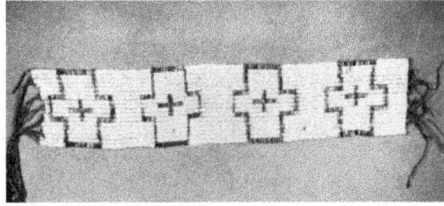

Example of a Sun wampum sash, crafted from seashells in red, white, and purple beads of cylindrical shape, drilled in the center, and used as both a form of currency and to commemorate significant events.

Native women and children tended the fields. They also made most of the clothing and fishing nets, dressed game and wove baskets and mats that were used for gathering, bedding or were fastened to roundhouses as outer walls. Fashioned from a circle of poles bent and tied to form a dome, these shelters were reinforced by weaving vines horizontally through the structure. The framework was then covered with bark, mats and skins, leaving only a smoke hole at the top. Despite their crude appearance roundhouses proved the equal to any settler's cabin in offering protection from the elements for as many as 10 or more inhabitants. They also had an added benefit — portability.[5]

New England Natives flourished in the woodland period because of the region's plentiful resources and adequate growing season. By the beginning of the 17th century it is estimated that their numbers swelled to as many as 144,000 inhabitants throughout what is now lower New England.[6]

Far from their portrayal as nomads, the New England tribes were primarily agriculturalists living in a complex, hierarchical society. They lived in a highly defined culture that was developed through count-

Above is a photo of the remains of an Native dugout canoe. Measuring nearly 11 feet by two feet, the vessel was hollowed out by fire, stone and shells. Others were much larger, holding 20-plus men.

less generations of religious experiences and ceremonies, political dealings and treaties, intermarriages among tribes, diplomacy and, when all else failed, occasional warfare.[7]

Underpinning every aspect of Native society was a deep sense of spiritualism and respect for the land. For Native Americans, the land was alive with spirits, or manitos. There were spirits for men, women, warriors and children, the sun, moon, tides, seasons and even the game they hunted. One contemporary English observer accounted for no fewer than three dozen such spirits, good and bad, who controlled all the forces of Nature in a complex world of interdependence among Natives and their environment.[8]

Paying homage to these spirits was no small task and took the form of regularly staged ceremonies called nickommo.[9] Planting and harvesting, marriages, deaths, famine, drought, war or pestilence were all reasons for ritual gatherings. Dancing was the predominant form of expression at these ceremonies, but trials by ordeal, hallucinogenic experiences and storytelling by powwow and pniese, or tribal shaman, also played a vitally important role in Native rituals.[10] Although accounts of these events are scant, they also had their lighter side when the Natives partook in sporting events, games and contests ranging from marksmanship, footraces and swimming to

Sleeping Giant in Hamden (above), and Thanksgiving Rock, located on the East Shore of New Haven, where the Quinnipiac held annual harvest festivals and councils, were both sacred to the Native people.

a precursor of modern lacrosse. According to Roger Williams, this last endeavor was often a spectacular event involving dozens and sometimes hundreds of participants with the respective goals set as much as a mile apart and played over a period of days.[11]

In stark contrast to their European counterparts, the Quinnipiacs' religious pantheon was centered around Manitou, or the belief that spirits dwelt among them in all things both living and inanimate.

Among the strongest of these deities were two mythical giants, Maushop, known for his good deeds, and Hobbamock, whose name was originally associated with death and darkness. Native lore noted that after Maushop tragically drowned, his burial mound became West Rock. Quinnipiac legend also tells of Hobbamock being slain by mighty thunderbirds and his body and the land that covered it becoming the Sleeping Giant in Hamden. Both sites are sacred to Native people.[12]

One thing the Quinnipiac could neither fight off by reason or ritual was disease. European explorers and settlers carried with them not only a foreign culture but its Old World blights, such as plague, measles and smallpox for which the Native inhabitants had no immunity. By the dawn of the 17th century these diseases became so prevalent throughout New England that they decimated some New England tribes entirely and reduced many others by as much as 80 to 90 percent.[13] By 1637, for example, the Quinnipiac numbered no more than 250 with only 47 adult males surviving the effects of European-born disease or their own internecine warfare.[14]

Organized into clans, the Quinnipiac adhered to the same social structure as other Northeastern Algonquian tribes. They were led by a sachem, or chief, who could be either male or female depending upon the absence of a male heir. In either case, sachems wielded considerable authority over tribal affairs by virtue of their own persuasive powers, their sense of generosity and their blood ties to other tribal leaders. Most important of all, they provided leadership in times of diplomacy and war.[15]

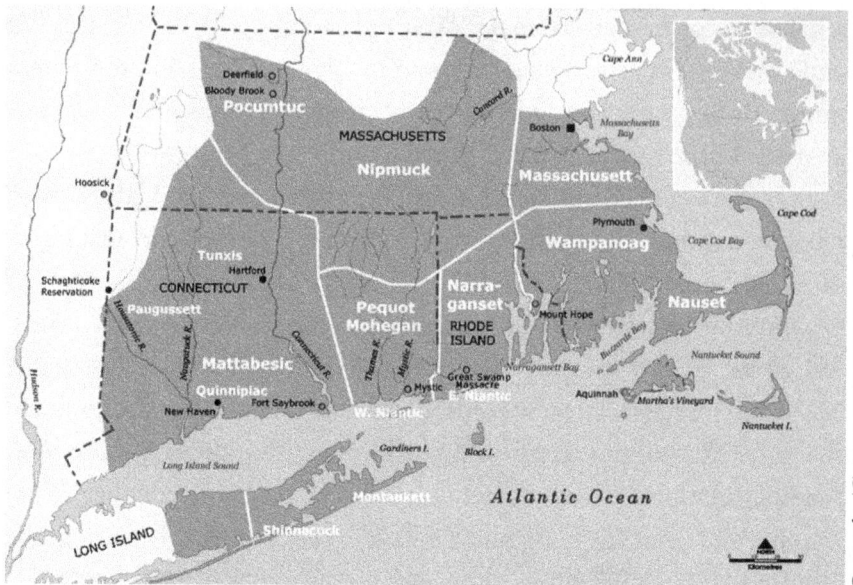

The above map depicts the tribal territories of the Southern New England Native peoples at the time of the Puritan arrival in the early 17th century.

In the case of the Quinnipiac, the tribe's diminished numbers only heightened their sachems' need to hone their diplomatic skills. Ruling families often intermarried to strengthen ties and alliances between independent sachems from other tribes. Eventually, a Native hierarchy developed with each band having a chief sachem assisted by lesser sachems who met in council. Inevitably, the more powerful sachems imposed their authority over the lesser tribes of New England.

Three of the most feared of these powerful groups were the Mohawk, Pequot and Mohican. The last two traced their origins to the same source, but they separated over a bitter leadership dispute. Despite their dislike of each other, all three tribes subjected the other shoreline Natives to a subservient state, extorting annual tribute in the form of food, skins and trade goods. To enforce their demands the Pequot from the East and the Mohican and Mohawk from the West occasionally visited the Quinnipiac to exact their toll. Failure to meet their demands often resulted in terror tactics ranging from simple intimidation to kidnapping, torture and occasionally even murder.[16]

As fearful as these tribes were along the Connecticut shoreline, a more forceful presence was about to reveal itself. It would soon hurl the Quinnipiac and all Native Americans into an era of unprecedented change and eventually near extinction.

II

Although Europeans were aware of the Quinnipiac region through the exploits of Verrazzano in 1524, actual contact with its inhabitants was not made until 1614, when Adrian Block, a Dutchman, sailed into Quinnipiac harbor to explore the surrounding area. Impressed by the reddish hues of East and West rocks, he christened the area Roodeberg, or red hills.[17]

For the next quarter century the New Amsterdam Dutch frequented Quinnipiac harbor, even constructing a small trading post at Branford to barter with the Natives for furs. In return, the Dutch revolutionized the Quinnipiacs' lifestyle, providing them with weapons, tools and new modes of carrying on trade, warfare and diplomacy. Receptive to what the Dutch had to offer, the Quinnipiac began the practice of coast watching, or signaling passing ships in hopes of attracting visitors to shore. With bonfires as the established means of contact, trade with the Natives remained a Dutch monopoly until early June 1637, a date that nearly spelled an end to the Quinnipiac tribe.[18]

Since their arrival in the Hartford area in 1635, English settlers had struck up an uneasy peace with their Pequot neighbors along the Connecticut shoreline. While the Pequots wanted European trade goods they considered the English a threat to their own security and way of life. Relations were strained from the start and open warfare seemed inevitable between these two diametrically opposed cultures.

Center Church on the Green

From 1634 - 1637 10 English settlers were killed in various encounters with the Pequots. The Natives were then subjected to brutal retaliatory raids by the English. One last raid pushed both sides over the edge. On April 23, 1637, a Pequot raiding party murdered nine Wethersfield settlers and kidnapped two young women who were later released unharmed.[19]

Intent on retribution, the colonists raised a small army of 90 men under the command of Captain John Mason. A seasoned veteran of European wars, Mason proved intent on carrying out his orders "not to do this work of the Lord's revenge slackly."[20]

Designed by Tiffany & Company, The Davenport window in Center Church New Haven, depicts the first religious service held in New Haven.

With the help of the Pequots' arch enemies, the Mohicans, Mason and his Puritan-Indian army targeted the Pequot stronghold at Mystic for annihilation. Using the element of surprise and superior firepower,

Mason's forces burned the fortress and massacred between 600 - 700 men, women and children on May 26, 1637. The stunned survivors escaped westward toward the Hudson River along the great path through Quinnipiac land. The Puritan army and their Indian allies, now augmented by 120 Massachusetts troops, were determined to exterminate the Pequots and pursued the fleeing survivors along the Connecticut shoreline.[21]

As Mason's army approached what is now Branford, the advance guard spotted a huge bonfire, mistaking the Quinnipiac council fire as a Pequot encampment. Fortunately for the Quinnipiac, the Puritan army realized its mistake before any hostilities ensued.

The Rev. Mr. John Davenport (1597 - 1670), from an engraving based on a portrait owned by Yale University Art Gallery.

http://www.havelshouseofhistory.com

No friends of the fleeing Pequots, and undoubtedly fearful for their own lives, the Quinnipiac agreed to assist the English. Scouts pushed ahead to locate the Pequot stragglers in what is now Fairfield. Eventually the English-Native force killed all but about 200 of the Pequot tribe, only to sell off the survivors into slavery to the Mohicans, Mohawk and the West Indies.[22]

While the scouts reconnoitered the Pequot stragglers the bulk of the Puritan army encamped by Quinnipiac harbor for two days to explore the surrounding area. The troops were impressed by what they saw. As news of Quinnipiac's discovery traveled back to Boston, a recently arrived party of self-exiled English Puritans led by the Reverend John Davenport and wealthy London merchant Theophilus Eaton was searching for a permanent home in the New World. Davenport had been the vicar

Courtesy of bumpusgenealogy.org

Reproduction of the Mayflower is typical of the English vessels used in transatlantic voyages in the early 17h century.

of St. Stephen's Church on Coleman Street in London, and he was interested in establishing a strict Puritan haven for his followers. Eaton shared Davenport's vision of a religious oasis, but he also wanted to insure its prosperity by settling in a location where he and several other prosperous merchants in the party could resume their substantial mercantile careers. Together with about 200 other followers, mostly from London, but others from Kent, Hertfordshire and Yorkshire, the group arrived in Boston in June 1637 aboard the *Hector* and a sister ship whose name has not survived.[23]

Realizing the value of counting these wealthy settlers among their own numbers, Bay Colony leaders wasted little time courting the newcomers with offers of settlement anywhere in Massachusetts. Davenport and Eaton were not interested. They had left England to practice their own brand of religion unfettered by the views of the Massachusetts Bay Colony or anyone else. Graciously refusing the Bay Colony's offer, they decided to bide their time in search of the right opportunity. That came with the returning troops from Connecticut, who spoke of the Quinnipiac region in such glowing terms that the Davenport and Eaton Company decided to investigate the area for itself. On the last day of August 1637 Eaton and a small party of men sailed from Boston to survey this place called Quinnipiac.

What the Eaton party found in early September exceeded their expectations. Surveying its lush forests, a natural port and abundant land, Eaton left seven men behind under the command of Joshua Atwater to spend what turned out to be a harsh winter that claimed the life of its first English victim, John Beecher. Eaton, meanwhile, returned to Boston to persuade Davenport and his followers that he had found their new haven along the southern Connecticut shoreline.[24]

With their numbers now swelled by additional religious dissenters, some 400 men, women and children set sail for their new home in March 1638.[25]

What they found on their arrival on April 24, 1638 startled them. Despite the beauty and abundance they saw as they entered the harbor, once on land the newcomers heard grim stories of the brutally cold

A QUINNIPIAC INDIAN
FAMILY WALKS TO THE
HARBOR TO MEET THE ENGLISH
NEWCOMERS - APRIL 24, 1638
AS THEIR WAY OF LIFE
CHANGES FOREVER

MONTOWESE SAWSEUNEK MOMAUGIN SUGCOGISIN QUESAQUAUSH CARROUCHOOD WEESAUCUCK SHAUMPISUH

Fort Nathan Hale Park, New Haven, Connecticut

*Erected in 2000 on the one-time site of their reservation (now Fort Hale Park), The Quin-
nipiac Memorial Monument in New Haven commemorates the major contributions made
by these Native people and assistance they gave to the first English settlers in establishing
New Haven.*

winter. Had it not been for the kindness of the local Quinnipiac, the survivors claimed, they would have surely perished.

But the settlers were not easily dissuaded from their dream of creating a Christian utopia. Despite lacking any royal authority to actually settle in the region, the Puritans soon undertook negotiations with the Quinnipiac to purchase the land. It was a lopsided affair. The concept of land ownership was so completely foreign to the Natives they likely did not fully grasp the settlers' insistence on paying for something that was always considered a communal asset.

To the Puritans, however, land ownership was the traditional building block of a civilized society, and they pursed it with a passion. In November and December of 1638, and augmented with still another purchase in 1645, the settlers secured title to lands extending to present-day Branford and North Branford to the east, Cheshire, Meriden and Prospect to the north and West Haven, Orange, Woodbridge and Bethany to the west. In return, the Quinnipiac received the pledge of English protection, hunting privileges, the right to keep their Branford council grounds and a potpourri of trade goods ranging from knives and cloth to hoes.[26] Both sides initially seemed content with the deal.

Their land now secured, the settlers set to work establishing what they planned to be a great commercial seaport. Surveying their fine harbor, inland rivers and their own sizable fortunes – considered to be among the richest in the New World – they had every reason to believe that their dreams would soon become reality.

It took nine years before the failure of additional arrivals, the disaffection of many original settlers and the loss of the "Great Shippe" forced the remaining New Haveners to realize that their dream had turned into a nightmare. In one last great commercial effort New Haveners built and outfitted a 150-ton vessel. They gathered together their dwindling fortunes in trade goods and with many of their principal citizens aboard, the ship set sail for England in January 1647. Cutting a path through the harbor's ice, the ship's captain

Original Settlers

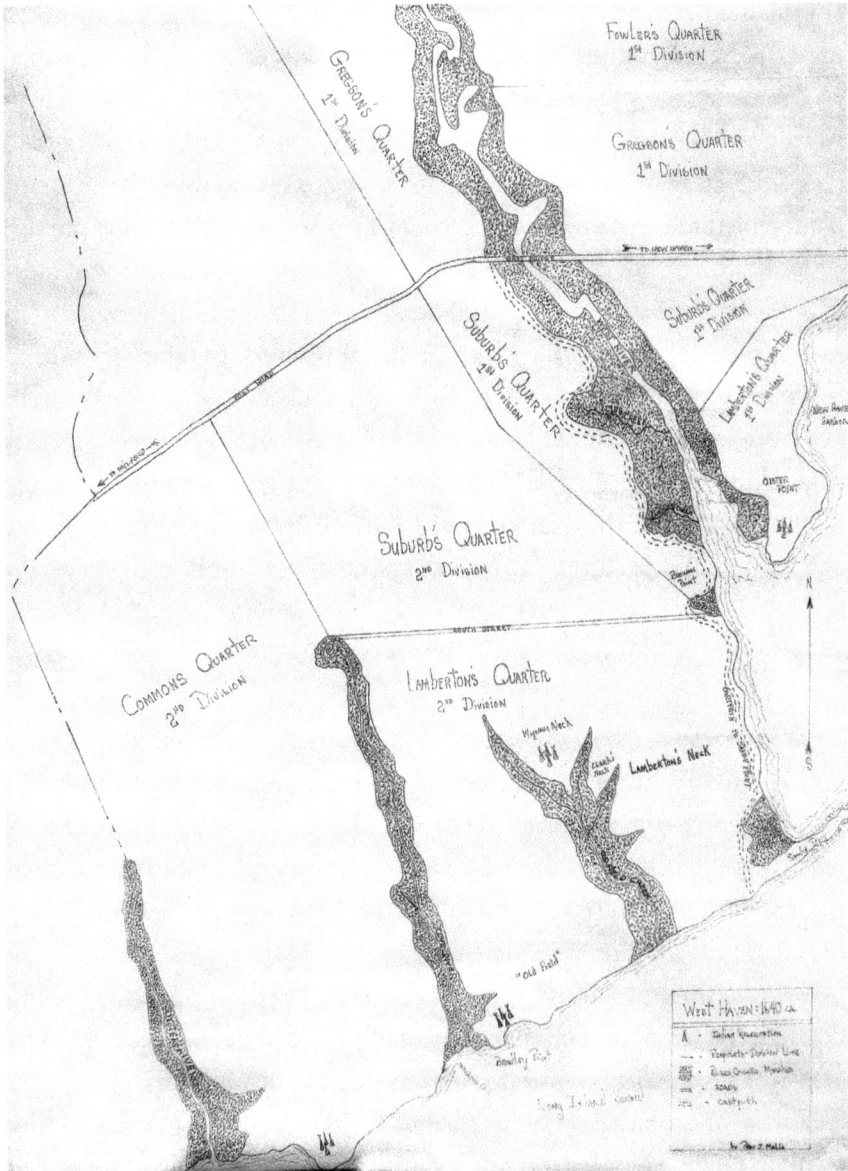

Map of West Haven, ca. 1648, drawn by the author from information contained in the Ancient Records of New Haven *as well as land-record details contained in the Harry Ives Thompson Working Papers, Connecticut State Library. At the extreme left of the map is Oyster River and the border between West Haven and Milford.*

13

complained that it was overloaded and would be their grave. If nothing else, he proved prophetic. The ship was never heard from again.[27]

Most of the original settlers who remained behind in New Haven were now reduced to near poverty. While New Haveners launched two smaller vessels over the next three years to establish some semblance of trade, necessity forced them into the less glamorous pursuit of agriculture. It was an avocation that many of these former merchants and landed gentry frankly knew little or nothing about. In an ironic twist of fate those who did know something about working the land suddenly grew in stature as did the value of property itself. For the Qunnipiac people, who had shared so freely their agricultural skills with their new neighbors, Puritan gratitude proved fleeting. Increasingly, the Natives were looked upon as heathens, devils and impediments to the Puritan mission of creating heaven on earth.

III

As early as 1640 the lands surrounding New Haven proper were divided among the townspeople. The first division dispensed land on the eastern side of West River. The second division officially opened lands on the West Haven side to settlement and required the erection of a cart bridge, which the New Haven General Court ordered built on January 25, 1641.[28]

Consisting of salt marshes, meadows and dense woodlands rolling down to the sea, West Haven was originally divided by the General Court of New Haven Colony into four large sections or Quarters.

The first of these Quarters, and by far the largest, was held by Captain George Lamberton, the wealthy merchant mariner and ill-fated captain of the "Great Shippe." With lands bounded east and south by the sea, north by a cart path (presently Main Street) and west by the Cove River, Lamberton's Quarter was one of the largest plantations in New Haven Colony.[29]

"Fording of the West River to Settle West Haven," oil on canvas by Elizabeth Shannon Phillips, is an idyllic depiction of West Haven's first families painted in 1938 as part of the New Deal/ WPA project. The mural is located in the U.S. Post Office on Campbell Avenue.

Northwest of Lamberton's plantation was the Suburbs Quarter then in possession of 10 men who figured prominently as shareholders in the original Davenport and Eaton Company.[30]

Extending across West River to the north of the Suburbs were the Gregson and Fowler quarters, encompassing approximately three hundred acres and used exclusively as farming and grazing lands.[31]

The remaining West Haven parcels were divided among the lesser planters or retained as common acreage for livestock. Between 1675 and 1704 most of these common lands would pass into private ownership, as New Haven ordered a third and fourth division of property by public lottery.[32]

IV

Most of the land development undertaken during the first decade of West Haven's existence was agricultural in nature. Lot sizes were determined by a man's standing in the community and were based on the size of his estate and what he contributed to founding the town. The second determinant was family size and the last was his social position. If a planter happened to draw an especially difficult lot to work, the town allowed for "sizing," where the lot's size was increased to compensate for poor soil or its distance from the owner's home.[33] Fields were then cleared of trees and rocks and soon sprouted corn, beans, hops, rye and some tobacco. Fences bounded the fields to keep livestock from ruining crops. Roads were also constructed to facilitate easier access to the farms. By 1648, however, only three roads were completed. One ran from the West Bridge to Sandy Point, another to the West Meadows and a third ran the northern breadth of West Haven to Milford, a rival town founded in 1639.

Further road building took place in the latter part of the 17th-century as Pent Road (now First Avenue and then a toll road), North Street (Elm Street) and South Street (Main Street) were in operation by 1684. Sabin Street (now Savin Avenue and likely the victim of misspelling rather than indicative of red cedar trees), Cove River Road (Platt Avenue), Sawmill Road, Meloy Road, Benham Hill Road and Kings Highway (Jones Hill Road) were all completed by 1700. By authority of the town's selectmen, roads were built by right of eminent domain. To ensure their maintenance every adult male age 16 to 60 was also obligated to work on the roads a given number of days each year or pay a fine for negligence.[34]

By 1648 West Haven had all the earmarks of a thriving community but one, there were no permanent residents. Planters continued to travel the four to six miles from New Haven to their outlying farms each day. It was a tedious journey under the best of conditions. When roads turned muddy or the weather grew cold, the route between New Haven and the West Farms became a penance that even the Puritans were not willing to pay.

Necessity and convenience encouraged adventurers. First one, then a handful and finally a community of planters accepted the risks of settling at their farms. By 1670 the number of permanent residents in the village of West Haven had increased to nearly 100 inhabitants.[35]

CHAPTER TWO

In the Shadows of New Haven

Throughout the first half century of its settlement the village of West Haven was considered a vital appendage of New Haven proper. Being so closely aligned with their parent community West Haven residents were fully expected to adhere to both New Haven's civil and religious authority.

There was, in fact, little difference between the two. New Haven's civil organization closely paralleled that of the Congregational Church itself. Government existed to perpetuate New Haven's brand of Congregationalism and both sought guidance from the Scriptures as the primary source of law.[1]

The basic building block of this church-state was the family. As the center of religious and moral training families were required to teach their children to at least "read the Inglish tounge and Capitall Lawes" of the colony.[2] They did far better than that. Puritan families read the Bible so often most children could quote it chapter and verse by the time they were teenagers. Virtually everyone was conversant in even the minutiae of his or her religion and how it applied to their daily lives, slaves and bonded servants included.

One universally shared belief was that salvation could only be achieved through a conversion experience or a personal metamorphosis to a state of grace. The clearest path to that end was to model yourself after those who were already saved. For early West Haveners that ideally meant your parents and village elders. Armed with the knowledge that they were already among God's Elect, Puritan families were both paternalistic and extended in nature with eight to 12 members being the norm. It was not unusual for a first wife to deliver a number of children in rapid succession. Since one in six colonial women died in childbirth, subsequent marriages and a proliferation of step-families were commonplace.[3]

Family responsibilities also extended beyond blood lines to include servants, apprentices and even slaves, a number of whom were in the New Haven area since its founding. Slavery was not abolished in Connecticut until well after the Revolution, and slaves were among the village's earliest residents with about one in 10 families owning a slave.[4]

Courtesy National Museum of American History, Smithsonian Institute

In return for their labor, extended family members received room and board, religious instruction and the opportunity to learn a trade or profession. Girls, meanwhile, learned to spin flax, weave, cook, sew and care for their younger siblings in what amounted to on-the-job training for eventual marriage.[5]

Boys were expected perform the manual chores. They chopped wood, fed the farm animals and worked the fields or in a shop. By the time they reached their teens, boys were often bound out

View of a colonial sampler by Sarah Prince Fenn (1763 - 1790) of Milford. Mastering the art of sewing provided young girls with the chance to gain a critical skill qs well as meeting the Puritan passion for teaching their children both their numbers and alphabet.

Interior view of the Thomas Painter House built in the late 17th century was typical of homes of the period. The house was located on Main Street, West Haven and eventually moved to Litchfield.

as apprentices to learn a trade or profession. In doing so they would become extended members of their master's households for as many as seven years or until they reached the age of 21.[6]

Marriage for young women normally came in their early twenties. Men married a bit later, with their average age being about 25. In West Haven's earliest years, many men remained bachelors into their thirties. It was not by choice. Men simply outnumbered eligible young women by more than three to one.[7]

Married or not, everyone was expected to abide by New Haven's strict civil and religious codes. Church attendance and religious training were mandatory. Nonconformists were never welcomed and sometimes persecuted. Those judged negligent in their civic or religious responsibilities met with swift Puritan justice. Thomas Trowbridge, for example, alledgedly abandoned his West Haven family and returned to England. In truth, he may have been lost at sea. Whatever the reason, the law called for the same solution. His family was disbanded and the Trowbridge children were sent to Sergeant Jeffery's so "they may be well educated and nurtured in the fear of God."[8]

While the Trowbridges' fate seemed harsh, it was also rare. The cohesiveness of Puritan families and their pursuit of learning were legendary. It was a matter of personal pride and part of the social compact to watch out for the well being of others, family members and neighbors alike. In such a tightly knit society Christian piety was the true measure of a individual's worth. No one could afford a tarnished reputation and expect to reside among the "visible saints," as early New Haveners cared to think of themselves. You either complied with the letter of the law or you moved elsewhere.[9]

Many did just that. Among the original English settlers of New Haven the majority were young, single men seeking out their fortunes. What they found was backbreaking labor and little chance for quick riches. When new arrivals, especially single women, slowed to a trickle in the 1640s, nearly a quarter of New Haven's population moved elsewhere or returned to England.[10]

Those remaining had reason to stay. They were generally older with established families, which provided them with a readily available work force to keep a house and farm. Unlike their younger counterparts, most of those who remained also had a profession or skill to fall back on, even if it was simply knowing how to farm. Most important of all was their sense of religious conviction. These were the resolute Puritans. They had risked everything to follow the Reverend Mr. Davenport and his brand of religious idealism across the Atlantic and into the wilderness. When early adversity forced the less committed to leave, these settlers never wavered from what brought them to New Haven in the first place — the right to worship and live their religious convictions as they saw fit.

Another essential part of that Puritan sense of mission was civic responsibility. The two, in fact, were inseparable. As members of a religious state, West Haveners were expected to attend town meetings held in New Haven proper once or twice each month. Serving as the legislative branch of government, the assembled townspeople voted on all issues concerning the town, including the election of officials. It was democracy by acclamation among the saints.

In order to vote, however, individuals had to be male (there were a few exceptions of propertied women voting in place of their deceased husbands), be at least 21 years old, have property valued at 40 shillings or more and have received "honest man" status. That determination was made by the minister and put to a vote at the town meeting. If the majority accepted the candidate, he earned the local franchise. To vote in colonial elections residents needed "freeman" status, which few original West Haveners attained because of its higher property restrictions.[11]

Since most colonial offices were town-oriented, a large number of West Haveners did hold public office at one time or another. The most respected of these officers were the Deputies to the Connecticut General Assembly and the seven selectmen, who served as the executive branch of town government. Also elected were the town clerk, tax listers and collectors, constables and deputies, overseers of the poor, tithingmen, who dealt with church delinquents and taxes, surveyors of highways, branders, haywards, who regulated access to common lands, fenceviewers, sealers of weights and measures, packers, who supervised the proper packaging of meat and fish, justices of the peace and keykeepers.[12]

All of these positions were part-time and effective for one year. Once elected inhabitants served their term or paid a fine. Not surprisingly, most served multiple terms and there was a wide range of people holding public office in what amounted to a rough-hewn democracy on the local level.

As home and property owners, West Haveners were also obliged to respect their neighbor's welfare and observe several ordinances to ensure that end. Among the most important of these laws was prompt payment of property taxes.

By 1642 the town selectmen ordered every planter holding land grants in West Haven to pay an annual rate of 2d. per acre in order to fund a public treasury. Payments were due in May and October. Delays met with fines. Repeated delinquency, or failure to pay taxes, resulted in foreclosure.[13]

Next to taxes in importance came public safety and the preservation of private property. At home, that meant fire protection in the form of a clean chimney. With nothing but a bucket brigade to fight fires, prevention was the only cure. Consequently, homeowners were required to keep ladders beside their homes for monthly chimney inspections and as a fire fighting protection measure. Failure to keep chimneys clean risked serious consequences and heavy fines. The village abounded in agricultural fields, which were both highly valued and flammable. Errant embers from a dirty chimney could quickly destroy a season's crops and jeopardize lives. To prevent that from occurring a town chimney sweep conducted regular inspections and set his cleaning rates based on a chimney's height, normally 2d. for a one-story home and 4d. for anything higher.[14]

While fires threatened devastation, roving farm animals, especially pigs, proved to be a more common nuisance. With the exception of harvest time, hogs were allowed to roam freely to eat wild berries and nuts in the woodlands, thus costing the settlers little or nothing to raise. But hogs could also make quick work of a farmer's crops. Fencing of fields became an essential task and a New England tradition that defined good neighbors. Not only did they keep livestock off neighbors' property and the wolves away from sheep and cattle, they conveniently delineated property lines in a society that defined success by land ownership. If disputes occurred or livestock caused property damage, a fenceviewer would be summoned. As a town official, the fenceviewer could levy fines and award damages, keeping a portion of the settlement in payment for his services.[15]

Still another critical public responsibility was military service to the colony. Throughout West Haven's first half century a succession of wars with the Dutch, Indians and the French placed the village in a near constant state of military alert, and the town, itself, resembled a walled fortress.

With no provisions for a standing army, the colonies relied on the local militia for protection. As early as 1642, New Haven's General Court ordered that a militia be formed and required all able-bodied males, black and white, ages 16 to 60, to attend six training days each year. As a further precaution the town ordered each male inhabitant to have at constant readiness a workable gun, a sword, four pounds of pistol shot, a pound of gunpowder, matches for a match lock and six good flints. Those failing to attend training sessions or lacking proper equipment were fined up to 10 shillings.[16]

Whether or not West Haveners could actually mount any kind of organized or sustained military campaign is questionable. Officers were usually elected based on community prestige and popularity rather than on any real military experience. Discipline was also lax, and defective equipment was commonplace. In one instance, John Down was fined two shillings sixpence for missing a squadron meeting. Robert Meaker was fined two shillings for too short a sword and for lacking both powder and shot. Peter Browne and John Benham were both fined two shillings for owning defective guns. None of these charges was isolated. Throughout the early years of the town, residents were constantly cited for a number of such infractions that may seem humorous today, but were matters of life and death in the 17th century.[17]

That is not to suggest that most men within the village did not take their military duties seriously. Robert Seeley, for example, served as the West Haven unit's first lieutenant and proved to be an able solider. John Clark, Thomas Jeffrey and Robert Alling were appointed sergeants, and all of these men acquitted themselves with honor in battle during the Indian wars.[18]

As for military training it was a mix of muster and frivolity. Depending upon the severity of the pending threat, training days varied from weekly to only a few days a year in peacetime. In either case drilling, cudgel contests, broad jumping, turkey shoots, wrestling, fencing and games added to the festivities of what became more like family outings than serious military exercises.[19]

II

That all changed with the outbreak of King Philip's War in 1675 - 1676. Philip was the powerful sachem of the Wampanoags of Rhode Island. Through deft leadership he formed a powerful Native confederacy bent on exterminating the English settlements following his brother's death in English captivity. The war was short-lived and brutal with a 10-percent casualty rate on both sides. Philip destroyed several Massachusetts' settlements and thousands lost their lives. Among the 70 Connecticut men lost in a single battle was Robert Seeley's son, Nathaniel, who was killed leading his troops in an attack on the Narragansett stronghold at South Kingston, Rhode Island, in December 1675.[20]

While the war largely spared

Metacomet (1639?- 1676), also known as King Philip, was war chief of the Wampanoag. After suffering the encroachment of his tribal lands due to English expansion, Metacomet finally led an uprising against his one-time allies in 1675, vowing to rid the continent of the English.

24

Illustration of the Great Swamp Battle near South Kingston, R.I., November 2, 1675. Over 1,000 colonists felled trees to approach the fort from less defended swampy areas. During the battle, West Haven's Lieutenant Robert Seeley was among the 70 colonists killed.

Connecticut from direct attacks, stories of atrocities to the north and east made West Haveners nervous and neighboring Native tribes suspect. Increasingly, local Natives were subjected to even tighter restrictions, including a prohibition on their coming into town unannounced, in groups or bearing arms at all. Residents were also told not to wander into the woods alone. Petrified by rumors of Native-led atrocities, colonists fortified their homes and a night watch patrolled the farms. If they encountered trouble, they sounded the alarm. In West Haven's earliest years that was a drum, and John Benham was the first village drummer, probably because he owned one. Benham was succeeded by fellow West Havener Nathaniel Kimberly in 1672. In addition to summoning and discharging the watch, the village drummer also provided cadence for military training drills and sounded the call to village meetings and Sunday services.[21]

A decade barely passed before West Haven was again on high alert with the outbreak of King William's War (1689 - 1697). As hostilities began against the French and their Indian allies New Haveners took matters into their own hands even before the official declaration of the General Assembly in April 1690, which ordered that "the present occasion do call for us to put ourselves in a posture of war."[22] With the night watch resumed throughout the town, increased precautions were taken and armed riders patrolled the surrounding woods. West Haven homes were also garrisoned in case of a possible attack.[23]

One of many depictions of the death of Wampanoag Chief Metacomet in 1676, his passing ended King Philip's War. Matacomet's head was placed on a pike at the entrance to Fort Plimouth as a warning to the Native peoples.

www.nativeamericandeeds.

Once again, the area escaped direct hostilities. But living in a state of near constant war preparedness took its toll on West Haven. Contingents of village militia fought against both the French and their Native American allies in several abortive assaults on Canada in various wars, and their losses over the years proved to be significant. Out of their sense of duty to the colony — but more likely in search of adventure, wealth and the promise of generous land grants in return for their military service — generations of West Haven men marched off to war. Many never returned.[24]

III

By 1760 West Haveners had suffered through five colonial wars since their settlement in the New World. For better or worse warfare, or the threat of it, had become a way of life in colonial America. The colonists had grown accustomed to being in a state of perpetual readiness. Native Americans, meanwhile, were increasingly fearful of genocide spurred on by the racial prejudices and fears of the visible saints. In such a volatile environment of distrust confrontations were inevitable, frequent and usually favored the English.[25]

Thus armed and reasonably effective when it came to protecting their own rights, liberties and homes, the colonials grew overly confident of their military prowess, and they increasingly saw no real need for British regulars to be stationed in the colonies to protect them.[26]

The British Home Government thought differently. Throughout the 150 years of its American colonial experience, Great Britain viewed the militia system with growing uneasiness and disappointment. Protecting one's home with a citizen-led army was all well and good. Against limited, well-defined objectives the colonial militia performed reasonably well in staving off attacks and putting down rebellious colonists and Indians. To mount an organized, sustained campaign against the French, Spanish and their Native allies, however, required a level of discipline, coordination and expertise that the colonial militias simply lacked. The economic value of the American colonies called for a professional, permanent army to protect British interests anywhere in its colonies. Crises could not wait on provincial actions nor could local militias be expected to defend the empire. Considering New England's anti-redcoat traditions, however, such imperial thinking was bound to eventually cause much trouble.[27]

CHAPTER THREE

The Rise of Self-Sufficiency

In many respects West Haven owes its existence to the unraveling of a Puritan dream. That dream envisioned the New Haven Colony at the epicenter of a vast Puritan enterprise that spread across Long Island Sound and extended as far south as the Delaware River Valley. Drawing upon its considerable wealth, mercantile experience and its apparent readiness to take up arms to achieve its ends, the New Haven Colony was intent on building itself into a major force in colonial America.[1]

Initially all went according to plan. In 1640 New Haveners settled Greenwich and Stamford bordering on, or if the Dutch were to be believed, violating Dutch territory. More New Haven transplants moved across the Sound to Long Island in violation of another Dutch land grant. Still more New Haveners attempted settlements along the Delaware River Valley, this time violating land titles held by both the Dutch and Swedes. Dutch protests did little to temper New Haven's expansionist appetite. When the Dutch finally dug in their heels and chased the New Haveners back home, New Haven turned to its sister colonies of Connecticut and Massachusetts for help. A combined attack on New Amsterdam, New Haven argued, would clear the way for unhindered development of Puritan interests. Although not fond of the Dutch, both colonies declined, leaving the New Haven to pursue its own designs alone.[2]

For nearly 20 years the New Haven Colony demonstrated no lack of imagination in its war of words and settlement schemes to possess the Delaware River Valley. When New Netherland finally did fall to the English in 1664, victory came too late for New Haven. In that same year the New Haven Colony was absorbed into Connecticut.[3]

Unsuccessful in its efforts to expand by land, New Haven's great wealth was slowly being sapped away. It hit critical mass with the sinking of the "Great Shippe" in 1647. In the wake of that tragedy's staggering loss of life and personal fortunes, New Haven was left poorer, perhaps a bit wiser and definitely at a crossroads.[4]

Fearing its leaders had steered them on a course towards financial ruin some New Haveners called for moving the town to the Caribbean, Mexico or Ireland, where they felt they could enjoy the fruits of their labors instead of struggling for their lives in the hostile environment of New England.[5] Throughout the 1650s up to a quarter of New Haven residents abandoned the colony. Some returned home on news of the Puritans' Glorious Revolution that brought Oliver Cromwell to power in England. Most expatriates, however, were young men who cared little about their spiritual well being and even less for their present state languishing in New Haven. With the economy stagnated, there were few jobs to be had, fewer available young women to marry and no chance at all to make quick fortunes. All that remained was a stubborn determination to survive in a place that William Hooke, a principal assistant to the Reverend John Davenport before deciding to return to England, described as being "straited, the sea lying before us and a rocky rude desert, unfit for culture and destitute of commodity, behind our backs."[6]

Hooke's harsh assessment of New Haven was heartfelt but overblown. The tragic loss of the "Great Shippe," in fact, actually produced a leveling effect in the colony. While it hit either end of the economic strata hardest, the majority of New Haveners remained among the "middling sort," or middle class. With the failure of the colony's mercantile schemes, the makings of a local aristocracy based on wealth or birth

Ironclad plows pulled by oxen were needed to clear the rocky land of West Haven, no doubt giving rise to many a rock wall.

now seemed less likely. Out of necessity average citizens would have equal say in shaping New Haven's future.[7]

No matter what their station, residents clearly understood that their survival required closer attention to fields, farms and self-sufficiency. It was no coincidence that only two years separated the loss of the "Great Shippe" from West Haven's permanent settlement as a farming community. New Haveners moved there because their lives now depended upon it.

Averaging 70 acres West Haven farms were large enough to provide for a family and raise some additional crops for sale. Local markets consumed beans, corn, wheat, rye, hops, beef, mutton, poultry and pork. While some flax, hemp and tobacco were cultivated for export markets, the early colonists lacked the agricultural expertise needed to produce those export crops in any great quantity for resale.[8]

A more prosperous endeavor was lumbering. The demand for good lumber and wood products was insatiable both at home and abroad, with ready markets in the West Indies, the Canaries and Europe. And at least for the first generations of West Haveners a marketable stand of trees stood ready to harvest and mill into ships' masts, planks, shingles, tar, turpentine and big profits. Lumber was also needed for pipe staves in barrel making for trade goods. Even the stumps were burned and converted into potash used in soap. With little more than an axe, saw and team of oxen, this homegrown industry provided a healthy income for many early West Haveners.[9]

But it was backbreaking work. In a good year the average farmer could reasonably clear no more than four or five acres using a four-pound English axe. In cold weather its brittle iron often cracked, and under any conditions its steel blade required frequent sharpening. Tree stumps also had to be removed the old-fashioned way, taken out by hand, shovel and grub axe.[10]

Courtesy of Plimoth Plantation

The 17th-century saw pit was backbreaking but effective in processing the abundant raw timber available in the New Haven area into usable, plank lumber.

When it came to felling trees, West Haveners were an industrious lot. Apparently too much so. Depleting their own lands of usable timber by 1650, they began chopping and sawing their way through the commons. Settlers denuded such vast tracts throughout the colony within the first 20 years of settlement, New Haven officials were forced to order "that no man shall fell any trees within the bounds of the common without leave from some magistrate and then shall have but for his particular trade or necessity."[11]

One such necessity was the construction of a home. During the first few winters in New Haven, settlers resorted to living in cellars until they could build the infrastructure to mill wood. In West Haven that all-important business was located on South Street west of the common. One of the area's earliest forms of manufacturing, the sawmill was owned and operated by the Downs family. In return for their services, sawyers normally received a portion of what they produced for resale.[12]

Then, as now, home styles dictated design with some accommodations being made to better cope with New England's colder environment. Balloon-style framing so common in today's homes was unheard of in the 17th century. Heavy timber notched with grooves and held together by wooden pegs were the preferred building materials. While they made for some substantial and durable homes, such as the Ward-Heitman house on present-day Elm Street, they also required tons of lumber and much labor to build. Pieced together on the ground, the heavy framing was lifted into place with the help of friends and neighbors in what became known as a "raising." Because of New England's harsh climate, settlers insulated walls with bricks, horse hair, clay and straw. They designed bigger fireplaces to stay warm, and they imbibed in the luxury of siding their homes not with English clay as they were accustomed but with wood, considered an extravagant luxury in timber-starved England. Among other Old World luxuries commonplace in West Haven and throughout New England were big barns and, yes, outhouses.[13]

Closely related to the timber industry was shipbuilding and the sea trades. Highly valued as a source of food and useful products, such as fish oil and lime made from burned seashells, Long Island Sound was early exploited as a means of aquaculture, transport and local trade. Prior to 1700 New York merchants evaluated West Haven's potential as a maritime port. As in the earlier case of New Haven the surrounding waters were found to be too shallow for shipping on any large scale and their plans for the village were abandoned.

Although that decision struck a major blow to West Haven's future as a major seaport it by no means discouraged the building of small shipyards on the eastern ends of North and South streets.

Shipbuilding and shipping, in fact, employed a considerable number of West Haveners throughout the colonial years. Most were either shipwrights or among ships' crews on small coastal traders and fishing vessels. Others thrived in the export of ship's masts and barrel staves. And a handful of West Haveners even built seafaring ships of their own and prospered through their efforts. A century separated two such men. Philip Alcock established a respectable exporting business along the coast by 1681. Thomas Painter was captain of the

The Ward-Heitman House (circa 1684) on Elm Street (above) is one the oldest remaining homes in West Haven, and is a registered historic landmark as well as home to the West Haven Historical Society. Other examples of early homes also remain on what is now First Avenue, formerly known as Pent Road. At right is an example of the heavy timber framing used in the construction of original colonial homes and barns.

Courtesy The Ward-Heitman House

sloop *Hannah* after the American Revolution and enjoyed a prosperous trade with the West Indies and beyond.[14]

Since no one individual could afford to build and maintain a ship alone, owners' shares in the vessel were normally sold to local merchants, planters and business investors both large and small. Depending upon the ship's fate, investors stood to either gain handsomely from profitable voyages or potentially lose everything they invested if the ship floundered at sea, as occurred in 1647 with the so-called "Great Shippe."[15] Either way, the stories of West Haven and the sea have always been intertwined.

II

By the beginning of the 18th century the majority of West Haveners were third generation or younger. Prosperity had returned, and the religious zealotry of the original founders had dimmed considerably. In its place was an increasingly diverse and growing economy filled with promising opportunities for the industrious at heart. Even casual observers could not help but notice the change sweeping over New Haven.

In 1704 Sarah Kemble Knight of Boston jotted a brief but telling entry about New Haven into her diary. "I find the people of New Haven sociable, religious, but a little too independent in their principles," she confided to her journal, "as I have been told, [they] were formerly very rigid in their administrations towards their laws."[16]

Madame Knight should not have been so surprised. By now three of five West Haveners counted themselves among the "middling sort," the equivalent of today's middle class. Most adults owned some land and were self-employed as farmers, tradesmen, merchants or seamen. With expectations rising above their parents' and grandparents' desire to primarily build a church-state, these younger Puritans seemed just as concerned with their well-being in the here-and-now. As early as 1665 the friction between old and new manifested itself in two all-encompassing areas: religion and commerce.

West Haven's original settlers adhered to a restrictive church membership that was limited to what they called the visible saints. These church members believed that they not only acted as God's elect but had actually experienced a conversion — or personal metamorphosis — allowing them into a special state of grace with God. The initial roster of visible saints was conveniently almost all-inclusive. As the community grew into its third generation, however, so did the number of the unconverted who were denied full church membership. Predictably the younger Puritans grew restless with their exclusion from full religious and political participation. Nearly a half century in the wilderness taught them that not every accomplishment was left in the hands of divine providence. Ambition and hard work on their part also helped to build their new haven. They reasoned that human enterprise deserved God's blessing too, and they demanded to be heard as a new generation of visible saints.

No one saw this Puritan dilemma clearer than the Presbyterian clergy itself. To preserve the established church into the future, they recognized that the covenant of grace and the issue of church membership was in need of serious updating. Their solution was the Half-Way Covenant, aptly named for having one foot in the Puritan past and the other tentatively exploring its way into a new age. In short, the Half-Way Covenant allowed partial church membership to all baptized children thus eliminating the conversion requirement. That unique experience was now reserved for those who wished to receive all of the Church's sacraments.[17]

If the Church was beginning to come to grips with a changing society, the Puritan elders had a far more difficult time coping with the worldliness of their own offspring. Not unlike every passing generation, the Puritan elders mourned the loss of what guided them through life. Their sense of religious mission and communal cooperation, which proved so essential to their early survival, no longer seemed that important. In its place they detected what they felt was a poisonous atmosphere in which competition, secular pleasures and outright bickering among the saints had become commonplace. No longer so sure of their own place in the world, some church elders predicted that the Puritan mission was doomed. Others saw it as the devil at work.[18]

They did not have far to look for apparent proof. When several pigs belonging to West Havener Thomas Mulliner allegedly died "in a strange way..." he thought them bewitched and quickly accused his neighbor, Thomas Meaker, of practicing black magic. With the

Although West Haven was not a deep-water port a number of residents made their living as shipwrights, fishermen and sailors. The scene above provides some idea of what shipbuilding entailed for the colonials.

town's officials a willing audience, Mulliner, who was as often before the magistrates himself on any number of petty charges, commanded a rare moment of authority when he cut the tail and ears off a sow and burned them in an exhibition that supposedly would prove Meaker guilty. It did not, and cooler heads prevailed. Mulliner was forced to admit that he lied and Meaker was released. Three other New Haveners were not so fortunate. Declared guilty of witchcraft two were executed and one was imprisoned.[19]

What happened to this society of saints that now required the ferreting out of devils and witches among them? Psychiatry might classify it as a form of repressed aggression. Certainly there was reason for pent-up emotions. Competition among neighbors had become so fierce that it created relationships that were "often tense and downright abrasive."[20]

The Puritan mind had a simpler solution than modern psychiatry. Superstitions provided a potent response to life's many unknowns, and people were quick to interpret the hidden meanings behind natural events in supernatural terms. A simple toothache, the mysterious death of a pig, a violent storm — all carried supernatural messages if only one listened intently enough to hear the voices of Nature speaking.

The Reverend Cotton Mather heard them loud and clear. "The

"Examination of a Witch" by Thompkins H. Matteson, 1853. Although this scene depicts the search of Quaker missionary Mary Fisher for "the devil's mark" in 1655 Massachusetts, it represents the hysteria that also gripped Connecticut in the 17th century. Forty-two Connecticut men and women were accused of witchcraft between 1647 - 1697, and 10 were executed.

wilderness thro' which we are passing to the Promised Land is over fill'd with Firey flying serpents," wrote the renowned Massachusetts cleric in describing the state of New England in 1692. "All our way to Heaven, ... there are incredible droves of Devils in our way." For New Haveners there were now three less devils blocking their path.[21]

Interwoven into the religious controversies of the times was an equally fervent debate over growing secularization. Older Puritans believed that their commercial interests served to pay homage to God as part of what they called the covenant of works. Besides the conversion experience that proved one's state of grace, they reasoned, material self-improvement was the worldly mark of God's elect. With the ascendancy of the second and third Puritan generations, however, the quest for worldly goods became an end unto itself.[22]

Alarmed by the rise of secularism in New Haven, officials took swift action at a town meeting in May 1692:

> Recommended to the authorities, town officers, and heads
> of families to take the utmost care they can to prevent
> all disorders, especially on lecture days, and particularly
> that there be no horse racing on such days, it being a
> great disorder.... The town unanimously voted the above
> written as their mind and desired their hardy thanks to be
> returned to the reverend elders for their pious and great
> care to father religion and reformation among us in these
> declining times.[23]

New Haven's "declining times" were by no means unique. Throughout New England there was a noticeable deterioration in spiritual values. In his ground-breaking study *Wayward Puritans* Kai T. Erikson argues that the original Puritan experiment was drawing to a not-so-successful close. No longer the great religious adventurers striking out into the wilderness, New Englanders were only beginning to cope with the realization that "They were just themselves, living alone in a remote corner of the world, and this seemed a modest end for a crusade that had begun with such high expectations."[24]

Connecticut's leaders would not have agreed. Fearing the consequences of losing control over growing secularization, the Colonial Assembly took a bold step forward. It summoned representatives of the 41 Congregational societies in Connecticut to meet in Saybrook. The agenda was clear: fashion a platform upon which they could all effectively cope with common problems and the rising disenchantment of a growing population clamoring for full membership in this church-state.

The result of this meeting was the Saybrook Platform of 1708, considered a master stroke in religious diplomacy. In reality, the Saybrook

Platform was more of a capitulation to the forces of progress. Amid proposals to promote religious cohesiveness and education throughout Connecticut, it also called for the formation of new ecclesiastical societies. Puritanism would no longer be so exclusive and that was music to the ears of West Haveners.[25]

In fact New Haven's outlying villagers wasted little time in pressing for more representation. No sooner had the ink dried on the Saybrook Platform than a New Haven town meeting raised the question of creating new congregations within the expansive town:

> "Voted that the livers within the bounds of said villages be
> forever free from paying rates to the ministry and school
> in New Haven and therefore we understand, freed from
> said rates if they uphold the ministry and school in the
> said villages."[26]

All across Connecticut the Saybrook Platform led to a stampede of communities anxious to establish their own churches. One such community was West Haven. For the better part of 75 years West Haveners traveled along the crude roads to New Haven proper and church services held on the central green. Now, "God has been pleased to increase our number so that we find it a great burden to come to the public worship of God with yourselves," read West Haven's petition of 1712. As if to reassure the town fathers that its request was no bid for independence the petition bluntly continued, "we would not have you think we desire in any way to be separate from you only as a ministry, and as to that, not for any dislike we have for our worthy pastor, nor distaste against any of you ...."[27]

Despite such reassurances, the West Haven petition initially fell on deaf ears. Three years passed before New Haven decided upon the issue of a West Haven parish. In April 1715 a special town meeting was called to grant West Haven's petition. In doing so, the town devised a parish boundary that retained all of the taxable property it thought was needed to support its own church and school. Instead of making use of the natural divisions between New Haven and West Haven, the town decidedly stacked the ecclesiastical deck in its favor.[28]

In protest West Haveners appointed Samuel Browne, Samuel Burwell, Daniel Bristol and Samuel Smith as a committee to redress the boundary issue with New Haven. Failing that the West Haven committee brought its case before the Connecticut General Assembly on May 10, 1715.[29]

As the proceedings progressed, it was discovered that New Haven had only begrudgingly consented to West Haven's request for a parish. New Haven elders argued that many West Haveners were anxious to remain a part of the town's current congregation. They also feared their property values would decline significantly if they were aligned with a new church. Contrary to promoting the Gospel, argued New Haven's defense, a West Haven parish would cause irreparable damage to its parent ministry in New Haven. With a much reduced tax base, New Haveners complained that they would be left with "a very poor and barren soil which will bear little else but men and children affording very little for their support or the support of the ministry."[30]

The Connecticut General Assembly would hear none of New Haven's argument. It likely even bore a certain prejudice against such pleas. As the co-capital of the colony, New Haven was well known to the Deputies as a prosperous town that could well afford the support of its ministry and school, West Haven parish or not. To break away one of its important appendages might even help serve another end: weaken the ultraconservative brand of New Haven Puritanism that the rest of Connecticut found overly restrictive. The Assembly thus dismissed the town's charges as unwarranted. West Haven's boundaries were extended, and the parish of West Haven became a reality that the Assembly would soon regret.[31]

CHAPTER FOUR

Challenge To Permanence

T he dawning of a new century takes on added significance for anyone who happens to experience it.
Inevitably, comparisons are drawn between the past and present, as if to measure our collective progress or decline. By the year 1700,
doom sayers and visionaries alike had much to contemplate about the
Puritan dilemma in Connecticut.

Quite simply, New Haven was no longer what its founders envisioned. Geography, human nature and political intrigue saw to that.
Their great seaport never materialized. Their separate identity as a colony
was wiped away with the stroke of a pen. Most troubling of all were their
fledgling efforts to carve out a Puritan utopia in the wilderness. They had
pushed the vast frontier hundreds of miles to the west. But when they
surveyed their handiwork of more than a half a century in the New World,
they saw bustling communities that had strayed far from John Winthrop's
envisioned "city upon a hill." Self-conscious by nature, and now preparing
to pass the administration of public affairs on to their offspring, many
Puritan elders worried that they had wandered onto a wayward path.[1]

They had reason for concern. A new generation was already hard
at work in reshaping the Puritan experience, pushing old ideas and
doctrines aside to better accommodate their own views of what was and
was not socially and spiritually acceptable. The children of the original
Puritan experiment were themselves experimenting with self-identity
and self-government.[2]

No longer a patchwork quilt of outlying farms, West Haven was a growing community by 1700. With more than 50 families in permanent residence, the villagers never lacked ambition. Years before winning their fight for a separate parish, West Haveners were already thinking ahead. In 1710 a village committee negotiated with Eliphalet Bristol for title to seven acres of land located in what would become the center of village life, the West Haven Green. Bristol regarded the property as useless. It was primarily wetlands overgrown with bramble bushes that posed a threat to livestock. The village committee saw things differently. It was determined to see its plans through to convert this land into the central green and site of West Haven's First Congregational Church.[3]

Seven years followed the date of exchange between Bristol and the committee before West Haveners opened the doors to their own meetinghouse located on the northeastern part of the green.[4] During these intervening years, the villagers continued to worship in New Haven and town records indicate they were paying ministerial rates to the church there. By 1717 West Haven parish seems to have been functioning independently, as "John Sherman was chosen collector of the rate on the West Side to be used for settlement of its own minister."[5]

Regarded as the center of community life, the West Haven meetinghouse hosted a number of religious and civil functions. As a place of worship, the meetinghouse bustled with Sunday activity. After the village drummer summoned the congregation to service, the minister delivered his sermon, sometimes lasting for hours and punctuated with the congregation reciting psalms. Solemn affairs, these early church services were without music of any kind, as it was considered distracting and a step towards popery. By the eve of the American Revolution, however, such fears diminished and a church choir was organized to sing the psalms. Apparently, there was more good intention than talent in the formation of a choir. The church quickly found it necessary to take measures to "improve unity and the forwarding of psalmody among the group" in 1774.[6]

Following religious services the villagers often lingered outside of the meetinghouse exchanging conversation with neighbors on topics ranging from local gossip and church matters to colonial politics. Because Sunday service was one of the only means of regular, acceptable social contact among the townspeople, courtships and marriages oftentimes found their beginnings in a courteous hello among the younger members of the local congregation.

Artist's rendering of the New Haven's meetinghouse provides a view of how West Haven's meetinghouse may have appeared by the mid-1700s.

yaleinsight.library.yale.edu

During the week the meetinghouse was used by the parish vestry. Elected annually these men were responsible for the appointment or dismissal of the minister, regulated the parish budget, oversaw and levied the ministerial tax and supervised both the schoolmaster and the education of the village children.

Since public speaking was the most prevalent and accessible form of literature in the New England village, the West Haven meetinghouse often provided a podium for lectures on religious, historical and political subjects. Guest speakers delivered lectures by invitation. There were also a number of West Haveners who invited themselves to the podium to address the villagers on all matters of local concern.[7]

As West Haven grew in numbers so did its meetinghouse. By 1730 the original structure was added to and seating became "dignified," with the men seated in the center pews according to their status, women along the side aisles and children, servants and slaves located in the balconies.[8]

Within 15 years further expansion and improvements to the meetinghouse were needed. With additional pews added in the galleries, the meetinghouse was shingled, painted and sash windows installed to offer some relief to the congregation from the summer heat or the smoke-filled, stuffy air of winter's only heating devices, a small stove and foot warmers filled with hot embers.[9]

Repairs and improvements to the meetinghouse were frequent, but they were always utilitarian, even when a steeple and bell were added in 1774. Aside from enhancing the stateliness of the building the bell was meant to replace the traditional drummer in calling the parishioners to service, militia musters or in giving notice that someone had died within the parish.[10]

Constructing a meeting house was a major accomplishment for such a small community. Without a minister, however, West Haven's achievement was a hollow victory.

www.college.columbia.edu

The Rev. Mr. Samuel Johnson (1696 - 1772)
founded the first Episcopal mission in West
Haven, then went on to an illustrious career
that included serving as first president of King's
College, known today as Columbia University..

For the first two years of its existence the West Haven parish relied on visiting clergy to conduct its Sunday services. For both the minister and parishioners such visits provided each with an opportunity to sample the other prior to any formal negotiations being undertaken concerning a permanent settlement.

One young minister stood out above the others. In 1719 Samuel Johnson, a 23-year-old tutor at Yale College, so impressed West Haven's vestry with his preaching abilities that he was offered the position as their first permanent minister. In addition to an annual salary of £80, Johnson received a house lot and firewood, ostensibly allowing him to tend to his ministry full time.

As it turned out, Samuel Johnson did far more than that. Accepting the West Haven post provided the young clergyman with the opportunity to continue his association with his Yale colleagues and especially David Browne. Browne was a West Haven resident, who possessed a brilliant mind and served as an effective sounding board for Johnson's religious wanderings. Together the two men were about to change Connecticut history.[11]

Outwardly complacent in his role as West Haven's spiritual leader, Johnson gave no hint of the stormy doubts raging within him. In fact, he was so highly regarded by his peers that he earned an appointment to the body of ministers upon which the Colony depended for the propagation of the Congregational faith.[12]

It was that very faith he now questioned. Since his ordination Johnson could not sufficiently justify the validity of his Presbyterian calling. "Alas, I have ever since had growing suspicions that it is not right and that I am an usurper in the house of God," he confided to his diary. "... sometimes I must confess [it] fills my mind with a great deal of perplexity and I know not what to do, my case is very unhappy," he wrote.[13]

For three years Johnson was a man divided. As minister to the West Haven congregation he felt an obligation to its people to continue on as their spiritual leader. But his growing doubts led him to seek solace among his Yale colleagues, who were also raising troubling questions about the validity of Presbyterianism. By 1722 what began as a discussion group among these six Presbyterian ministers became the advance guard of New England's Episcopal movement in which Samuel Johnson was to play a critical role.

Concerned with the well-being of their parish, West Haven's vestry demanded that Mr. Johnson explain his affiliations with the Yale group, which had now come under suspicion by the New Haven elders. In answering, Johnson and his five colleagues, David Browne among them, jolted the spiritual community by declaring themselves for Episcopacy on Thursday, September 13, 1722.[14]

Come Sunday morning the West Haven congregation was in an uproar. Shocked by their minister's declaration, the infant parish was thrust into a religious schism. The loss of its minister was devastating enough. But as the Sunday services unfolded it became clear that up to 15 percent of the congregation was willing to follow Johnson into establishing an Episcopal Church in West Haven.[15]

Amid the turmoil wrought upon the parish by its own minister, West Haven neither expected nor asked for New Haven's help. Bitterness over the parish boundaries continued to rankle relationships, and some New Haveners no doubt adopted a "told-you-so" attitude towards their West Haven brethren. Now strained relationships grew even more tenuous. The creation of an Episcopal ministry in the village was akin to a direct assault on Congregationalism itself.

With the Reverend Mr. Johnson's resignation in September of 1722, West Haven became a "widowed" parish, and it continued as such until the summer of 1724.[16] During those two years the parish vestry concerned itself with devising a means to prevent a repetition of the Johnson episode. In addition to the standard contract, future ministers would be required to return their salary if they changed their religious affiliation. That clause was considered penalty enough to dissuade future clergy from ever questioning their allegiance to the saints.[17]

It was thus implied that those terms proved agreeable to the Reverend Mr. Jonathan Arnold when he accepted the West Haven ministry in July of 1724. Five months later, Arnold voiced his displeasure over his £80 salary. Eager to keep their new minister happy, the vestry doubled local taxes in order to provide Arnold with a £20 raise.[18]

For nearly a decade, the Reverend Mr. Arnold provided the West

Haven parish with a period of relative calm between Congregationalists and Episcopalians in the small village. Arnold was even visited by Johnson on a quarterly basis whenever the latter conducted services in West Haven. The two clergymen could even be seen strolling about the green discussing religious affairs between the two churches. On the surface, all seemed well.[19]

As a result of those seemingly causal conversations, however, Johnson decided to suggest a bold move to his Puritan counterpart. After patiently sounding out Arnold for nearly a decade, Johnson suggested that Arnold and his entire West Haven congregation convert to Anglicanism. In a letter to the Bishop of London dated December 1733, Johnson revealed:

> There are two or three very worthy young ministers in this
> colony who, I have reason to believe, will declare them-
> selves for us and two of them, especially, have hopes that
> most of their congregation will conform with them. One
> of them is Mr. Arnold, who succeeded me at West Haven,
> near the college, where I preach once a quarter.[20]

Once again, West Haven's parish vestry grew suspicious of their minister. In a meeting held in February 1734, its members voted to approach Arnold and ask if he had come to doubt his Presbyterian ordination. His answer shocked the committee. He would continue as their minister, he proposed, on condition that he now be a spokesman for the Church of England.[21]

Angered by his audacity, the vestry demanded Arnold's immediate resignation. He reluctantly agreed, but he refused to refund his salary as called for in his contract. He also succeeded in taking a handful of additional parishioners along with him, and he vowed to one day return.[22]

For the second time in a decade, the West Haven parish was in crisis. Not only had it become home to the Anglican Church in Connecticut, but its own first two Presbyterian ministers had led the way to its organization. Unwillingly, the village was earning an unenviable reputation as the weakest link in Connecticut's Standing Order.

With its authority as a church government in shambles and its resources depleted, the congregation turned to the Connecticut General Assembly for help in 1734. Appointing a committee to look into West Haven's affairs, the Assembly determined that the parish lacked the adequate funds needed to attract a new Presbyterian minister. To avoid any further embarrassment, the Deputies pledged £200 in additional funds to help settle an orthodox minister.[23]

The added funding did little to help quell the turmoil. The Reverend Mr. Arnold was about to make good on his promise to return. Only this time he was an itinerant Anglican missionary willing to drive a stake into the very heart of Puritan New Haven.

While in England to receive Episcopal orders, Arnold secured a deed to land located directly opposite the New Haven Green. Armed with this land title and his new-found religious zeal, he intended to use the site to build Connecticut's first Anglican Church. [24]

Not lacking courage, but perhaps short on common sense, Arnold drove a team of oxen across the West Bridge into New Haven proper in the fall of 1738. As a show of his rights to the land's ownership, he began tilling the plot in defiance of New Haven officials. If Arnold was looking for a confrontation, it came quickly. A mob of Yale students and townspeople began taunting the minister then assaulted him outright with a volley of rocks, insults and personal threats.[25]

Not easily discouraged, the Reverend Arnold now turned his attentions to his former congregation in West Haven. Securing a donation of land directly south of the Congregational meeting house from Samuel Brown, John Smith, Thomas Stevens and John Humphreville, all of whom were members of his new congregation, Arnold set about to build an Episcopal Church in the very shadows of his former parish.[26]

By 1740 the Reverend Arnold no doubt took great pleasure in

officiating at the ground-breaking ceremonies for what would become Christ Church. Unfortunately, he never saw his efforts completed. His lack of discretion among his ex-parishioners generated such open hostility towards himself and the Anglican cause, that he was transferred to St. Andrews on Long Island, where he became a vocal opponent of revivalism.[27]

With Arnold gone, the responsibilities of the Anglican mission fell upon a new rector, the Reverend Theophilus Morris. Under his direction the small congregation completed the church in 1742 and celebrated the event with a "raising" ceremony. In the church budget of 1740 an account was given of money spent for molasses, mutton and rum for the occasion. Also in the budget were a number of references to West Haveners of both denominations who received payment for services rendered during the construction of Christ Church. When it came to earning a day's wages, practicality, it seems, outweighed religious differences.[28]

As pleased as West Haven Anglicans may have been with the opening of Christ Church in 1742, their complacency was soon tempered by Morris' departure. According to the Reverend Samuel Johnson, Morris was a well-meaning but contentious Englishman ill-suited for a country parish, "so that I very much doubt whether he will be happy in them or they in him," Johnson confided to a friend.

His words were prophetic, and Morris was soon gone. But his replacement in 1743 suffered under even greater prejudices. An Irish immigrant educated in Dublin, the Reverend James Lyons encountered immediate opposition to his appointment at West Haven from Congregationalists and Anglicans alike.

As devout Calvinists West Haveners had bitter memories of the 1688 Papal Plot to return England to the Church of Rome and the French-supported Irish revolt that precipitated 10 years of bloody warfare in Europe and the colonies.[29]

Lyons did not help matters much. His heavy Irish accent and

haughty demeanor struck a jingoistic chord among West Haveners that predetermined the failure of his ministry. By 1746, only three years after his original settlement, Lyons was forced to request a transfer. In his resignation letter, he sadly noted that the community's prejudice toward him had led to a serious deterioration of West Haven's Anglican mission.[30]

Without a settled rector, West Haven Anglicans relied upon the services of the Reverend Richard Mansfield, the son of New Haven's deacon, Richard Mansfield, who lived in Derby and divided his time among his home town, West Haven and Waterbury. Occasionally, the Reverend Samuel Johnson visited his old parish to preach, and he was surprised to find that it had grown over the years, despite its difficulties in locating a permanent minister.[31] One reason was Mansfield himself. Born and bred in New Haven, he understood the needs of his congregation and its members, in turn, held him in high esteem. When the Reverend Mr. Mansfield was tending to his other parishes, Christ Church continued its weekly services and encouraged lay readers to provide the sermons.

By 1752 New Haven finally allowed an Anglican church to be built in town with the erection of Trinity Church on the New Haven Green. When the Reverend Ebenezar Punderson assumed its pulpit, however, New Haven regretted its decision almost immediately.

Although a New Haven native, Punderson was abrupt in manner and a staunch defender of Anglican rights, which often led him to confront Yale officials in protecting the religious privileges of Yale's Anglican students. In 1757 Punderson became embroiled in a controversy concerning a dissenter that so aroused the community, it threatened the very future of Trinity Church itself.

Punderson's frequent absences also did little to make the town's heart grow fonder of the clergyman. By 1763 Punderson's acerbic nature had alienated even his own congregation, which was on the verge of expiring, noted the Reverend Dr. Johnson in a letter to London. To save Trinity Church, Johnson arranged for Punderson's transfer to New York in order that "some politer person take his place."[32]

That person was Solomon Palmer, Yale graduate and Branford native, who led New Haven's Anglican mission until 1767. The high cost of living, coupled with a large family and a small salary, eventually forced Palmer's resignation.[34]

In his place came another Yale graduate and Guilford native, the Reverend Bela Hubbard. In Hubbard the Anglican Church had finally found its anchor. Renowned for his discretion and benevolence, Hubbard would labor quietly through severe financial hardships to steer his church on a moderate course through the trials of the Revolution. Within five years of his appointment, Hubbard happily reported that his West Haven parish numbered 220 members. Over his 45-year tenure Hubbard did more to promote and preserve Episcopacy in the New Haven area than any other cleric, including the Reverend Dr. Samuel Johnson.[35]

II

Across the West Haven Green, the health of the First Society remained on life support following the loss of its first two ministers and a number of leading families to Episcopacy. Little could be done to either prevent or reverse a traumatic turn of events in a community of "living saints" gone astray. The Church of England was the king's religion, and to challenge Episcopacy—even in the inhospitable soil of Puritan New England—was equivalent to high treason. That risked the wrath of royal retribution, including the possible revocation of the colony's cherished charter, which would jeopardize the very foundations of the Puritan state itself.

But there was more at play here than just politics and patriotism. The Puritan ethos was also in question, and it occurred much earlier than is generally believed. In the face of growing secularism and declining authority among second-generation Puritans, "half-way" measures towards religious reform failed to embrace even its own offspring in perpetuating their holy experiment uncontested. among second-generation Puritans, "half-way" measures towards religious reform failed to embrace even its offspring.

> "They were no longer participants in a great adventure, no longer residents of a 'city upon a hill,' no longer members of that special revolutionary elite who were destined to bend the course of history according to God's own word. They were only themselves, living alone in a remote corner of the world, and this seemed a modest end for a crusade which had begun with such high expectations."[34]

Reality has a way of disrupting the best of plans. Increasingly, the "half-way" saints sought alternatives to Puritanism's reliance upon desperate piety and fate. The Anglican concept of perfectibility, devoid of the Puritans' need for a conversion experience or self-effacing recognition of one's own sense of worthlessness, proved to be a breath of fresh air. In many respects it was the freedom of choice and conscience that led to the religious schism of West Haven. Two founding principles of an emerging American society were already in place, if not yet fully developed.

Neither principle eased the anguish of West Haven's remaining Puritan community. By 1735 four ministers refused the parish, leading the local vestry to once again plead for the Assembly's help. A commission reviewed West Haven's circumstances and determined its problems again stemmed from a lack of money. Colonial contributions to parish funds raised the ministerial salary to £120 a year, with a settlement fee of £250. But even this sum failed to keep a minister, as the Reverend Mr. Noah Derrick initially accepted the West Haven post in March 1737, only to leave six months later, citing financial hardship.[35]

Finally, in October 1738, the 22-year-old Reverend Timothy Allen accepted the West Haven post, but not before driving a hard bargain in the process. His salary was increased to £140 a year with a £350 settlement fee, a house lot and firewood, along with 50 acres of pasture land.[37] Considering the typical West Haven farm was worth no more than £100, Allen had done quite well for himself in a community desperate for spiritual guidance and a Puritan anchor. [36]

In West Haven, at least, that anchor had sunk too deep into the mire of the Calvinist past. When events called for a dynamic response to throw open the doors of Congregationalism to all who wished to fully participate in the church, as was even then happening with the New Light movement in eastern Connecticut, local church leaders responded with diatribes on how the visible saints had lost their way.

With Calvinist thought in a state of near *rigor mortis* in West Haven, Christ Church offered sanctuary from the unrelenting message that people were unrepentant sinners destined to a life of depravity.

> In short, these villagers knew they were very far from a bad lot; and when they pondered on this fact they must have discovered increasing difficulty in reconciling Sunday dogma and weekday experience. Although they repeated the familiar creed, the sanction for that creed was gone; it was the voice of dogma that spoke, and not the voice of reason and experience.[37]

Experience, in fact, exposed a wide gulf between the theory and practice of Congregationalism in West Haven. Under the threat of a competing doctrine that challenged the very foundation of the Puritan experiment, church authorities initially failed to protect their own vested interests, then provided only superficial fixes instead of addressing their root cause. It was a hard-wrought lesson West Haveners would never forget. The affairs of church and state were already showing signs of parting ways and paving a path to even more fateful decisions to be made between king and country in the not-too-distant future.

CHAPTER FIVE

Growing Pains

H istory has the advantage of knowing what happens next. Far removed from the influences that shaped the course of everyday events, it sees trends, formulates theories and creates or ends epochs as it sees fit to make some sense of the past. In its effort to promote understanding, however, there are trade-offs.

From our own life experiences we know an era is not easily captured or fully understood. Events have a tendency to flow into each other to become interwoven into our daily routines to define our lives. Pulling them apart is difficult, if not futile. Even if we could neatly catalogue every event, the sum would likely still only provide a myopic reading of our times. Considered individually, all but a few of us would appear to lack dimension. And the very stuff that makes us worth knowing as individuals would be lost to history forever.

In many ways, colonial West Haveners suffered that very fate. Some of their names may be inscribed in stone, but all of them seem to lack any real sense of dimension or humanity. We fail to connect with them as real people who were born, who lived and loved, fought and died and left only their words and deeds behind them for us to gain a measure of their world. Against the backdrop of such epoch-defining events as the founding of a nation, everyday lives have been lost in the shadows of more sweeping events. But strung together, the quiet, unrelenting challenges that faced the average colonial family every day are what actually shaped their actions as well as the future course of their society. Equally important are the hardscrabble aspects of colonial life that help put things into a human perspective we can all understand as universally shared experiences.[1]

One of these was the pursuit of wealth. For colonial West Haven that usually meant acquiring land. No other incident proved how important property ownership was to the colonials than the nagging boundary disputes between West Haven and Milford that soured neighborly relations and nearly ended in a shooting war.

Erupting in 1719, and chronically flaring up over the next 40 years, the controversy's beginnings can be traced to New Haven's third land division in 1680 and Milford's 1687 division of adjacent properties, which distributed contested lands along the towns' shared borders north of the Oyster River.[2]

Through the years residents of both towns continually argued over who owned what, and neither town could show definitive proof as to what constituted its legal boundaries. It did not help matters that Milford reserved a portion of the disputed property for its huge flock of town-owned sheep, which competed with West Haven livestock for grazing land. The disputes became so frequent and troublesome that they prompted West Haven's John Benham to ask New Haven officials to settle the matter once and for all in 1719.

A committee approached Milford with hopes of a quick settlement. But Milford's remaining lands were now in the hands of a corporation of private individuals, or proprietors, who were not about to surrender property to New Haven, especially when it came to prized farmlands located north of the Oyster River. So the dispute continued to fester until 1757, when the farmers, themselves, weighed the possibility of settling the issue by force.[3]

Anxious to keep the peace, officials in both towns resumed negotiations. Ten years later they finally agreed to lay out a permanent boundary between the two towns that would be clearly marked by monuments every 80 rods.[4]

Considering that land was the basic building block of wealth in an agricultural economy, it was no surprise that its ownership was cause for tense relations among neighbors. How far one progressed up the social ladder was directly related to land ownership and what it provided, not only in essentials for living but in raising cash crops as well. A noticeable decline in productive farmland by 1700 only served to heighten pressures on a growing population vying for a limited amount of property.[5] In the land of plenty, colonists were simply running out of room along shoreline communities. Eventually, sons and daughters were forced to abandon their ancestral homes in search of available property and better prospects elsewhere. In the short term, the scarcity of good farmland made for some very sour neighborly relations. In the long run, westward migration into New York, Pennsylvania, Ohio and beyond was inevitable.[6]

II

Another constant issue in West Haven was the threat of disease, especially epidemics of scarlet fever, yellow fever and smallpox. While the first two diseases periodically ravaged the area, smallpox was the most feared of all and it occasionally paid an unwanted visit to the village with the first documented case occurring in 1732. A hundred years earlier, smallpox decimated Native tribes. Now the disease wrought havoc on English settlers as well. By May of 1732 smallpox was prevalent enough throughout the colony for the Connecticut General Assembly to order all those suspected of having the pox to hoist a white flag in front of their homes as fair warning of what lay inside. It additionally ordered all dogs appearing to have symptoms of the disease to be destroyed, either by their owner or anyone else who did so lawfully.[7]

Such precautions did little good for the Daniel Sperry, Jr. family. By December of 1732, a white flag fluttered solemnly outside their home, and Sperry was forced to ask for the town's assistance. It came in the form of £25 to help defray the family's medical expenses in battling the dreaded disease.[8]

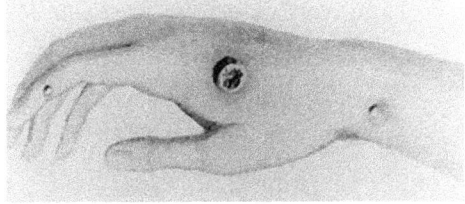

View of a typical site for smallpox vaccination with an initial eruption of the pox. This procedure was normally performed by rubbing smallpox postulate from a mild case of the disease into a small scratch. The resulting infection was usually less severe, left fewer facial scars, and provided immunity in the future.

While inoculation against smallpox was first administered in the colonies as early as 1722, it was no minor procedure. Usually reserved for the upper classes because of its associated cost, the process called for making a scratch in the arm or hand, then applying a small amount of pus taken from an active smallpox sore. The inoculated were then confined in isolation for up to three weeks, suffering from a variety of symptoms ranging from aches and fever to the telltale pox marks themselves.

Beyond inoculation, treatment for smallpox was rudimentary and doctors trained in the inoculation procedure were in scarce supply. Occasionally, the New Haven Town Records made mention of a resident practicing medicine, but the profession was not fully established for many years after the town's settlement. It was not until after the American Revolution that New Haven physicians founded the town's first medical society.[9]

Yale College did graduate over 200 students who went on to practice medicine in the 18th century. Most medical treatment, however, remained of the homemade variety, consisting largely of a hodgepodge of medicinal plants, herbs, isolation and self-care. Because of poor sanitation, diseases such as malaria, fevers, the flu, pneumonia, rickets and tuberculosis killed thousands of colonials each year. Bleeding patients and overprescribing enemas hastened the death of thousands more, including George Washington. He contracted a streptococcal throat infection in

1799 and was "bled" of 35 percent of his blood supply, which certainly contributed to his death.

Doctors and bleeding aside, very little could be done for smallpox victims. Because of their highly contagious nature, pox victims and their families were forced into quarantine with bed rest and warm, damp wraps offering the only form of relief. Death occurred in about 25 percent of victims, and all sufferers bore disfiguring scars for life.

As the medical crisis worsened in New Haven, Joseph Tuttle, Sr., who no doubt had survived a bout of smallpox and was now immune, provided care for the afflicted and received a small salary for his services. As the disease spread beyond Tuttle's ability to provide individual attention, New Haven's selectmen ordered the immediate construction of a pest house at Oyster Point in 1753. Since little could be done to prevent its spread, smallpox claimed enough sufferers to require the pest house to be eventually enlarged and a plot of land to be set aside as a graveyard for its victims.[10]

The advent of the War for Empire, better known in America as the French and Indian War (1755 - 1763), renewed fears of a smallpox epidemic in the region. Troops who may have carried the disease continually passed through the area exposing the local population to the heightened risk of infection. While town records made no specific mention of a smallpox outbreak at the time, New Haven officials ordered the repair of the old pest house at Oyster Point, and they had a separate well dug nearby since it was thought that the disease was transmitted by water.

Subsequent medical research later confirmed the water theory. What the colonials did not clearly understand, however, was that the highly contagious virus could also be transmitted just as easily by air and on victims' clothing. Despite New Haven's continuing efforts to fight the disease, and its increased concerns over public health issues in general, smallpox continued to claim lives well after the colonial period and beyond the advent of widespread inoculation in 1792.[11]

III

S till another major public concern was education. An important part of the Puritan ethic, education helped to perpetuate the concept of learning as a basic requirement in a society that placed so high a value on reasoned religion. When West Haven earned parish status in 1715, it was implied that the opening of a school would soon follow.[12]

Constant religious upheaval and the lack of funds in the village prevented the opening of West Haven's first public school until 1729. Located a few yards north of the Congregational meetinghouse on the village Green, the first school was no more than a large log cabin, complete with thatched roof, fireplace, dirt floor and benches for the students. Instead of expensive glass for window panes, larded paper was used in order to cut down on both costs and daydreaming among the scholars.[13]

Directly managed by the First Ecclesiastical Society, the school's operation was the responsibility of a special church committee. Appointed annually, the school committee consulted with the minister in the selection of a teacher, recommended books and made sure that teachers adhered to the doctrines of Congregationalism regardless of the fact that some children were Anglicans or from other dissenter groups. Attendance for all children was mandantory.[14]

In theory, formal education only polished skills supposedly already acquired at home. Increasingly, that family responsibility was shunted onto the local schoolmaster, whose duties came to include primary instruction.[15] The transfer of such a basic responsibility as literacy and religious training, however, did not imply the imminent breakdown of the Puritan family. Instead, it signaled the growing importance of public institutions in seeing that the doctrines of Puritanism and citizenship were preserved universally in what was, after all, a religious state.

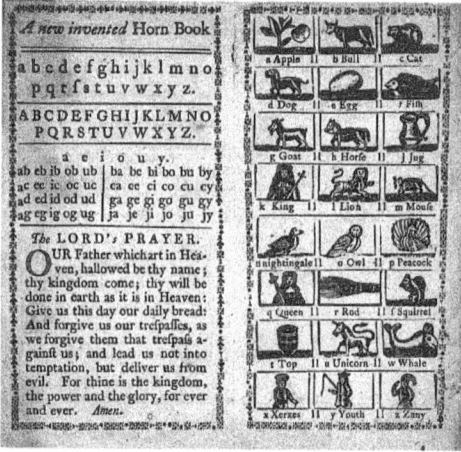

First published in Boston in the late 17th century,
The New England Primer *became a teaching standard throughout the colonies. In addition to the alphabet and grammar it contained the Lord's Prayer and Puritan world views. The now famous "Now I lay me down to sleep..." prayer originated in the* Primer.

Aware of the family's declining role in education, the common school offered a practical solution. Not only would the young be instructed by someone deemed competent for the purpose, but parish officials could more effectively regulate what was taught and see to it that the principles of Congregationalism played an integral part in the educational process.

Money for the school was derived from three sources. The Connecticut General Assembly initiated a plan in 1713 whereby parishes received 40s. per £1000 of valued real estate. Since that sum fell short of covering expenses, West Haven taxed its residents in goods and services if they were short on cash. By 1746, for example, parents were ordered to provide the school with one half load of wood, or its monetary equivalent, for each child attending. Families additionally absorbed an occasional tax increase (averaging about 2d. on the pound) to provide for salaries, repairs and school improvements.[16]

Fortunately for struggling communities like West Haven, additional school funds were eventually provided through Connecticut's sale of land in its Western Reserve in Ohio. Monies raised from these sales provided funds, which towns could use for founding common schools throughout the state.[17]

Sanctioned and financed by colonial law, the school's curriculum was utilitarian in purpose. Training was provided in reading, writing and casting sums, as these were the basic requirements of a society that placed heavy demands upon the individual, both in civil responsibilities and religious conduct. Instruction was also provided in the practical arts, such as making soap and candles, sewing and embroidery. During Saturday sessions religious

calisto.slv.vic.gov.au

Above is a reproduction of the famed Hornbook, consisting of a sheet containing the letters of the alphabet, mounted on wood, bone, or leather and protected by a thin sheet of transparent horn or mica.

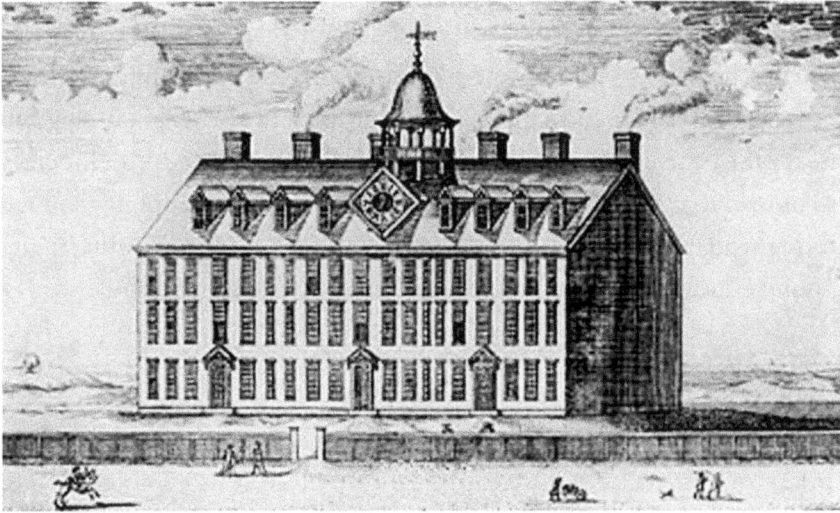

Courtesy Yale Alumni Magazine

The original Yale College (above), stood at the corner of present-day Church and Chapel streets from 1717 - 1782. It included a dormitory, classrooms and a library.

matters prevailed with Bible readings and Puritan theology providing the central themes. Local young men interested in higher education as the next generation of leaders for the ministry attended Hopkins School, then moved on to Yale College. It was expected that these students had already mastered the basics so instruction focused on English, Latin and Greek. Numerous citations in the New Haven Town Records, however, tell a different story of preparedness. Schools struggled from the start for lack of serious students and, on occasion, from no students at all. The quality of teaching was also spotty, even after the founding of the Hopkins School in 1660. Indeed, Ezekiel Cheever, who was New Haven's first schoolmaster hired to teach Latin, found that a number of his students were unable to even read or write.[18]

Following its union with the Connecticut Colony in 1665, New Haven was obliged by law to support a public school for the education of all children, regardless of their state of preparedness, in the rudiments of reading, writing and mathematics.[19]

While primary education did not assume any standardized form until the 19th century, the creation of a public school system in Connecticut as early as the 1660s still reaped rewards far in excess of its costs. Rich or poor, all children were provided with the opportunity to learn how to read, write and cipher. Although part of the original religious mission of the colony, education provided the seedbed for democracy to blossom. Eventually, the survival of a self-governed republic required thoughtful citizens and intelligent, literate leadership. Connecticut's public education system would provide an abundance of both.

CHAPTER SIX

Testing the Limits of Authority

U ntil 1740 West Haveners grappled with a series of issues resulting from their growing diversification. Their struggle for an independent parish, the Anglican movement and the lingering village boundary dispute can all be explained as manifestations of explosive growth. To deal with these issues West Haveners may well have challenged the established authority in order to simply get things done. But their solutions always fell within the acceptable framework of the predominant social order.

While tarnished by social and religious upheaval in West Haven and elsewhere in the colony, Connecticut's traditional authority nonetheless remained intact. That, however, proved to be only temporary. The village had early conceded to diversity and opposition as precedents now firmly established in its sense of evolving community. The fact that these precedents shadowed the growth of the community itself was understandable. They precipitated the village battle to establish its own church, then were used against the First Society to found Christ Church. Once successful, these same precedents to challenge tradition and Puritan restraint remained a viable means for dissidents to further confront the colonial *status quo*. Only this time, they would tug at the very fibers of the colony's social order.[1]

Not surprisingly, the issues centered on economics and religion. Since financial insecurity had long been a part of West Haven's history, no one was surprised to see it as a continuing threat to the community's sense of cohesiveness. What took everyone by surprise, however, was the intensity of a religious revival that swept across Connecticut's religious and political landscape. It came with such fury, it set a course for eventual revolution first in ideas and then in colonial government.

Predictably, it started out of hardship. With the outbreak of King George's War *(1739 - 1748)*, Connecticut was hard pressed financially. For years, the colony's credit suffered from the lack of a sound fiscal plan. To cope with the crisis, the General Assembly adopted deficit spending to finance the colony's business. To do so, it issued bills of credit to pay its expenses.[2] But the marketplace was soon flooded with paper money that depreciated substantially, while its silver base increased proportionately.[3]

View of front and reverse of a Connecticut five Shilling note of 1770.

www.coins.nd.edu

Realizing its inflationary habits, the Assembly reissued paper currency as New Tenor bills in hopes that they would withstand devaluation. But cheap currency prevailed and the colony sank deeper into debt. Since the demands of war outweighed its costs, Connecticut continued to issue cheap money. That only added to spiralling inflation and the hardships of small communities like West Haven. To gain some idea as to how much prices increased over a 14-year period, the local minister's salary rose an average of £36 a year, from £160 to £650 in 1756 — a 30-percent annual increase.[4]

The Anglican mission suffered far less from the monetary crisis, although its minister probably did not think so. His salary was fixed

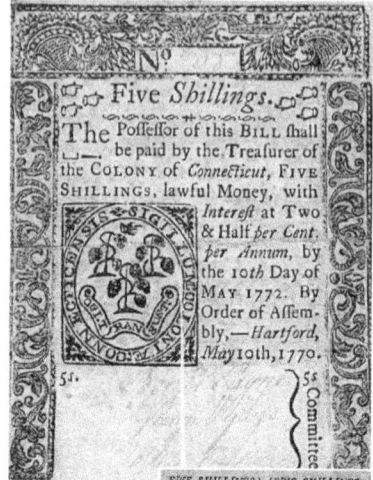

at £60 per annum and that was shared with the New Haven mission. Considering it was the Reverend Arnold, money was not so much at issue as were his principles. In fact, he led his small congregation to take full advantage of cheap colonial money by undertaking the construction of two Anglican churches at the peak of the fiscal crisis. According to the church records, he paid cash for at least one of them.[5]

While Anglicans benefited from cheap money, Congregationalists became increasingly distrusting of easy credit and enormous debt. They placed little confidence in the hope that they would be able to pay next year what they borrowed this year. As a result, the parish vestry demanded that tax collections, which had not yet fallen into arrears, be stepped up. Furthermore, the need for money without credit forced West Haven's First Society to sell off some of its property. In line with this belt-tightening decision, 50 acres of church land were auctioned off for £450. 7s. 6d. in 1742. Despite these measures church debts continued to increase, as the ministry and the school were constantly pressed for more cash.[6]

Realizing its inability to overcome the colony-wide tendency towards easy money, credit and interest, West Haven Congregationalists re-evaluated the church's financial position and voted to now take advantage of cheap money itself. Their solution was to establish a bank in hopes of stabilizing, or at least offsetting, rising costs. Parishioners enthusiastically supported the bank idea and collected £1,500 in donations even before the General Assembly donated an additional £1,000 to the project.[7]

It was doomed from the start. Cautious in its investments, the First Society Bank was closely regulated. Strong stipulations prohibited the use of the bank's principal to pay any outstanding debts, and the interest gained was used solely for the purpose of defraying the costs of operating the parish. To insure its proper organization and operation, a committee was elected annually to oversee the bank's affairs. The first such banking committee consisted of three well-known churchmen: Deliverance Painter, Joseph Thompson and Josiah Platt. They made for better Puritans than bankers.[8]

Despite its cautionary approach to investments, and perhaps because of it, the bank represented more than just a reasonable risk in a volatile economy. Not only was paper currency a depreciating medium of exchange, but it allowed those with criminal leanings to ply their skills in forgery and counterfeiting, much to the chagrin of the West Haven bank. In the end, the bank lost more than it gained through poor investments and theft. In 1747, Samuel Weed of Derby was lent £131 with the provision that he would pay back the loan at a seven percent interest rate. He was happy to do so, but with forged bills. While Weed was eventually imprisoned on charges of forgery, West Haven was still short £131. Embittered by their experience, the bank's officials approached the General Assembly with outstretched hands in hopes of receiving restitution.[9]

While West Haveners were eventually reimbursed for their losses, the Weed affair was not without its consequences. Embarrassed by its losses, the bank's future investments became so few in number, and so conservative in nature, that by 1760, its total earnings amounted to a mere £9.4s.7d. What portended to be a cash cow at its founding turned into more of a financial albatross for the parish.[10] Reputations had also been tarnished, not least among them being the colonial authorities themselves. In their search for a scapegoat, West Haveners were quick to lay blame at the General Assembly's doorstep. Had it not been so lax in allowing the colony to slip deeper into debt, critics argued, there would have been no need for a bank in the first place. And once established, policing for counterfeiters or offering any other type of financial safeguards proved nonexistent.

Eventually the currency debate faded as an issue in the 1760s as a wartime economy allowed West Haveners to eventually prosper. While their finances stabilized to a point that they could pay their

Congregational minister regularly,[11] their dwindling faith in civil authority festered. Increasingly Connecticut people were turning inward, weighing the claims of traditional authority against their own bitter experiences. In their attempts for some kind of personal reconciliation with their God, colonists were noticeably more insistent in raising doubts about their blind allegiance to a church-state that had failed them repeatedly in times of crisis.

II

To a great extent the introspective temperament among Connecticut people was firmly rooted in their religion. When West Haven opposed church authority in its earliest years, it was pursuing an instinctive desire for growth based upon ambition and self-improvement. Yet, these developments were undertaken at the risk of fostering deep feelings of personal guilt.

Puritan social organization prided itself on the belief that its authority was divinely sanctioned. The pursuit of wealth and self-improvement was encouraged so long as it benefited the spiritual well-being of the individual and community at large. These were principles firmly rooted in Calvinist thought. When West Haveners challenged these fundamental beliefs to suit their own earthly needs, they did so with mixed emotions sensing that their actions may well have been at odds with Divine will.

With tension mounting over the inner crisis between traditional authority and personal gain, West Haveners became extra-sensitive to their spiritual decline. They were not alone in their dilemma.

Most New Englanders grappled with the same ordeal of helplessness in the face of a visibly declining church authority and an overwhelming sense of moral and spiritual laxity. While people secretly loved wealth more than they did religion, they nonetheless cowered before an authority which they believed to be licensed by their forefathers and by God.

In combination with the financial strife of the colony, social anxieties sought a release valve through the very institution people were rebelling against — the church. The atmosphere was ripe for a revivalist movement bent on calming the unsettled spirits of a troubled generation.

Religious revivals were not new to New England. Cotton Mather's version of fire and brimstone enjoyed widespread appeal in the 17th century, and Puritanism, itself, was the result of a revival in reaction to moral decay in Europe. Most New England clergymen even expressed enthusiasm over the apparent success of early revival movements that were now spreading throughout the Southern and Middle Colonies. Impressed by its initial effects, local ministers lined up to extend an open invitation to the leading proponents of revivalism, George Whitefield, Gilbert Tennent, Jonathan Edwards and James Davenport. In doing so they unwittingly unleashed a force they eventually could not contain, and it changed the Established Church forever.[12]

Commanding an extraordinary influence over his listeners, Whitefield traveled throughout Connecticut in 1740, drawing huge crowds wherever he preached. The one-time merchant turned Anglican minister who now embraced the Puritan divines, Whitefield spoke of a revitalized spirit and scorned the Established Church's stodgy preaching as the work of "dead men." In the wake of his spellbinding oratory, Whitefield left a stirring call for repentance, reform and spiritual rebirth. Benjamin Franklin, a man not easily affected by the revivalist spirit and certainly close with his wallet, found himself "emptying my pockets wholly into the collector's dish, gold and all," he admitted after hearing Whitefield speak.[13]

Encouraged by Whitefield's example, others followed. Urging revitalized Christians to break away from their spiritually moribund churches, James Davenport went so far as to name ministers who met his revivalist criteria. Some local Congregational ministers soon

One of the most influential of the Revivalist preachers The Reverend George Whitefield (1714 - 1770) was so powerful a speaker that even the normally tight-fisted Benjamin Franklin found himself emptying his pockets after a Whitefield sermon. The above woodcut depicts one of Whitefield's open-air sermons, likely a scene in England. The print at right, produced in London for John Royall, depicted Whitefield's strabismus.

www.georgiahistory.com

adopted the revivalist style for themselves, leading their flocks in emotion-packed exposes of man's depravity before God. So vivid were these sermons that entire congregations reportedly cried out their sins, begging for mercy in near hysteria.[14]

As remarkable as this phenomenon was, the ultimate success of revivalism was a foregone conclusion. Not only did it fill the void for a rekindling of religious purpose, it also offered Puritans a sorely-needed spiritual release valve. Tensions long nurtured by traditional authority were allowed, and even encouraged, to surface. Once publicly aired,

magicwonder.wordpress.com

Born in East Windsor, Connecticut and educated at Yale, the Reverend Jonathan Edwards (1703 - 1758) is considered the first great American philosopher whose revivalist teachings led to the Great Awakening and gave rise to the New Light movement in Congregationalism. He was the grandfather of Aaron Burr. The above engraving is based on a portrait of Edwards at Princeton University.

whether through emotional outcries, trances or visions, the effects were generally the same. For those who had filled the ranks of wayward Puritans, the Awakening provided a genuine sense of relief and spiritual rebirth in the belief that they too could be saved. Converts were reluctant to return to an established order, which they felt was based on "head-knowledge, without that of the heart." More significantly, they fervently opposed its continued predominance over their lives. The tempers of the "Awakened" spirits thus revealed themselves as powerful adversaries of conventional society. The *status quo* was the work of those "who have never tasted grace... the plagues of the church and the unhappy occasion of the damnation of multitudes."[15]

In facing a near revolt within its established churches, conservative Congregationalists attempted to discredit the charges of the "converted." Those, they argued, were the babbling of emotional degenerates bent on destroying the sacred institutions of steady Christians. True or not, such charges did little to dampen the revived spirits of what amounted to a religious revolution in Connecticut.

With Puritans thrown into bitter discord their organized religious society quickly lapsed into a state of helpless factionalism between New and Old Lights.[16] As this internal conflict gathered momentum it became clear that the Old Lights were steadily losing ground. Once confident that their traditional institutions would weather the attacks of evangelical radicals, Old Lights now realized that the very foundations of their holy state were crumbling around them. Defections of unprecedented numbers of people to New Light churches only substantiated fears that their once unshakable faith in conservative religion and the civil authority it had sanctioned had let them down.

Upstanding Puritans were daily joining the ranks of the New Light movement. Even more distressing, many conservatives were retreating to their last hope of refuge, Episcopacy. Appalled by the deteriorating state of Congregationalism, many people found solace in the Church of England, where they could worship in peace without the distractions of evangelical rants that seemed to cater to the lower sort. Episcopacy, with its King and bishops, came to represent stability at a time of tremendous upheaval. Once vilified by the "saints," Episcopacy's well-defined structure now appeared to be more attractive to those desirous of reestablishing a sense of order in their lives.[17]

The Established Church, meanwhile, fought hard to win back lost ground. Troubled by the decline in their authority, the conservative clergy and Connecticut officials met at Hartford in 1741. Their agenda: seek out an official means to reverse a trend that they, themselves, had unwittingly promoted. Their purpose, they said, was to reverse the ill effects of the Great Awakening and halt its continued spread, "bringing peace, love, and charity back into the colony."[18]

To achieve that end the Established Order brought the full weight of colonial law to bear down against its enemies. Strict Congregationalists were keenly aware that traditional, independent churches were incapable of fending off spirited opposition by the dissenters alone. West Haven was an all-too-obvious case in point. In little more than 20 years since its founding, the parish was wracked by two clergymen defecting to Episcopacy and a third declaring himself a New Light. In each instance, the minister attempted to play the congregation against the church vestry. In all cases, the vestry proved inadequate in forestalling religious and social chaos within the community and, as it tuned out, in the colony.

Bitter experience taught hard lessons. To counteract future challenges to their authority, leaders of the Established Church created consociations of local Congregational churches. By banding independent parishes together, these consociations were now better prepared to fend off revivalist and dissenting threats by adopting a united opposition that was backed up by swift disciplinary actions against offenders "according to the letter of God's Laws."[19]

All churches were now required to appeal to their local consociation in matters that could not effectively be handled on the parish level. To insure that the consociations, themselves, were not misled, a General Association for Connecticut was also put into place. Composed of local representatives from each consociation, this body invoked ordinances that cascaded down to the regional and local levels in order to keep all member churches on the straight and narrow path to a Puritan God.[20]

Whatever their goals, the consociations proved their immediate worth in putting a quick end to the Great Awakening in Connecticut. In 1742 the General Assembly passed a flurry of laws prohibiting itinerant preaching, and private religious meetings were banned entirely. In one stroke of the legislative pen, revivalism suffered the loss of its primary method of expansion, the itinerant preacher. New Lights were forced underground with threats of heavy fines and even banishment from the colony.[21]

West Haven was noticeably affected amid these years of continued religious strife. While the majority of the First Society remained loyal to the conservative Old Light tenets of Congregationalism, significant losses were suffered to both the New Lights and the Anglicans. The Reverend Dr. Samuel Johnson noted that the West Haven Anglican mission had grown to 250 souls by 1749. It was not by coincidence. Most were reactionary saints so disillusioned by the changing temper of Congregationalism that they saw no recourse but to join Christ Church to escape the revivalists.

West Haven was not alone in this trend. Johnson wrote that when he first returned to the colony as an Anglican missionary, "there were but 80 adult Church people [in all of Connecticut]... and now there are above two thousand."[22] West Haven's Christ Church provided a ready harbor for an increasing number of one-time Puritans unwilling to live through still another religious battle, especially when the Great Awakening finally struck so close to home.

By all accounts West Haven's Timothy Allen (1716 - 1806) was a model Congregationalist clergyman and pillar of the conservative Puritan church. Young and persuasive, he was a 1736 graduate of Yale, who was so highly regarded by his peers that they asked the West Haven cleric to approach a New Haven colleague and persuade the minister to abandon his New Light leanings. Throughout 1742 Allen held several such meetings with his New Haven counterpart. Then events took an unexpected turn. The Reverend Mr. Allen, himself, became enamored with New Light theology, and he decided to share his revivalist views with his West Haven congregation.[23]

On one momentous Sunday morning, the Reverend Mr. Allen ascended the pulpit of the First Society of West Haven and told his congregation that "the word of God contained in the Old and New Testaments will no more convert a sinner than the reading of an almanac." [24]

Such a pronouncement today might raise an eyebrow as to where such a homily might lead. In 1742 it caused immediate outrage and charges of blasphemy. Instead of his envisioned role as leader of a West Haven religious revival, Allen found himself out of a job and standing before New Haven's Consociation on charges of "blatant irregularities and heresy."[25]

To West Haven's conservative First Society, the Bible was the primary means of obtaining God's grace. Its pages were scoured incessantly for advice on every facet of living from the mundane to the fine points of theology. With such a reasoned approach to religion traditional Puritans abhorred religious enthusiasm of the type now extolled by their own young minister. The parish was quick to silence the clergyman before he could cause any more damage, especially after his profane comments about the written Word.

Forcing the minister's resignation in the past had always provoked heated controversy and further division within the parish organization. With the creation of the consociation, however, Allen's dismissal in 1742 was both swift and efficient.[26]

The consociation proved equally adept in locating a new orthodox minister for the parish. Within a matter of weeks following Allen's dismissal, West Haven's First Society offered settlement to the Reverend Nathan Birdseye (1714 - 1818), a recent graduate of Yale known for his pious nature.

In the course of his 15-year tenure, Birdseye patiently worked to spiritually refurbish the parish. Under his leadership West Haven Congregationalists came to be accepted among the staunchest defenders of the conservative Established Church.[27]

Unfortunately, Birdseye eventually fell victim to his own conservatism. Where his leadership succeeded in reaffirming the traditional principles of Congregationalism, it also crippled the financial development of the parish. Bold investments were needed to put the church on a more solid financial footing. But Birdseye proved to be an inapt businessman. As a result of his conservatism, his influence over the First Society's bank led it to its near bankruptcy and eventually his own departure.

With no means of support beyond the irregular payment of his salary, Birdseye lived in near poverty. His caring for a family of 13 did not help the situation. When his brother bequeathed him a large estate in Stratford in 1757, the minister happily resigned his parish post and moved away from the struggles of always trying to make financial ends meet.[28]

Two years passed before the West Haven parish again found a new permanent minister. But the Birdseye resignation did have its positive effects. With the settlement of its new minister, Noah Williston (1734 - 1811), West Haven's First Society made sure his salary was paid on a regular basis, even if it meant instituting pew rentals and reviving the bank as sources of income. In 1760, the struggling parish voted to use the money obtained through pew rentals to increase the bank's principal and broaden its investment policies.[29] The Reverend Mr. Williston was apparently quite content with the arrangements. He remained in West Haven's pulpit for the next 52 years until his death in 1811.

The New Lights, meanwhile, continued to press for their own religious rights. While colonial authorities proved unyielding in their suppression of all separatist movements, New Light adherents grew in such numbers and influence throughout the colony that they could no longer be ignored. By 1759 the New Lights won recognition from the town and permanent separation from the more conservative New Haven Congregational Church. Political separation was not far behind. New Light thinkers from the eastern part of the colony eventually became the primary propagators of the Sons of Liberty who were intent on ridding Connecticut of not only the obnoxious Stamp Tax but the unresponsive Old Light leadership entirely.[30]

After a century of settlement the parish of West Haven was still struggling to survive. Only now, it was religious diversity and the power of opposing ideas that threatened its sense of community. New Light, Old Light and Anglicans alike never again regarded their religious leadership in quite the same revered light. The Great Awakening challenged the strict theology of Connecticut's Established Order and left it badly shaken. There were too many unanswered questions, too many learned men searching for new answers to revitalize the human spirit and too many honest citizens demanding the right to worship as they saw fit without fear of suffering either political or religious retribution from their neighbors.

Having finally witnessed the sanctity of unresponsive religious institutions first buckle, then struggle to reform at the will of the people, West Haveners now looked around them with a more critical eye towards imperial politics and what it held for them in the future.

CHAPTER SEVEN

On the Eve of Revolution

It was cause for celebration when New Haven first learned of King George III's coronation in 1760. Militia companies paraded through the streets, speeches were given and a 21 cannon salute on the Green noisily proclaimed New Haveners' loyalty to king, colony and the British empire.[1]

The colonies had good reason to celebrate. After years of setbacks and living under the constant threat of attack during the French and Indian War, the "wonderful year of 1759" finally secured English supremacy in North America. One sweeping military victory after another reduced French opposition in North America to but a memory. Ticonderoga fell first, then Niagara and finally the fortress city of Quebec surrendered. New France was no more.[2]

The struggle for British hegemony in North America now turned inward. Blundering and obstinacy on both sides of the Atlantic would eventually turn that effort to dust. In 1760, however, the dissolution of the British empire was the furthest thing from the minds of even the most radical colonial thinkers.

Times were good. The war's increasing demand for supplies and services had spurred a slumping colonial economy, and New Haven's commerce was brisk with trade among her sister towns, colonies and the West Indies. Yale College was flourishing and the town was far more cosmopolitan following the war than it was at its start. The war increased contact among colonials beyond their traditional boundaries and led to the advancement of a North American perspective of empire. Flush with victory the Americans believed that they were as much responsible for winning the war as were British regulars.[3]

London viewed the situation differently. The cost of victory over France was staggering. Contrary to what the colonists believed, Britain severely taxed its treasury and standing army in the French and Indian War. It had been a conflict of logistics rather than military brilliance, and it cost the empire dearly. With Great Britain's debt soaring to over £75,000,000, Parliament felt justified in raising money in the colonies for maintaining its newly-acquired territory and unchallenged supremacy in North America. In the case of Connecticut, for instance, Britain's reimbursement policy proved so generous that for every pound actually paid by the people of Connecticut in taxes during the course of the war, the Mother Country made a gift to the colony of an equal amount.[3]

It was only a matter of coincidence, however, that the major theater of operations happened to be in America. If the stakes were higher in some other part of the world, priority would have been assigned accordingly. When the British engaged the French in North America, they did so out of self-interest, and not out of parental affection or emotional ties to the colonies.[4] True, the colonies benefited from victory over France. But the wartime economy that fueled colonial prosperity was now waning. When it came to the question of increased taxation to cover the costs of maintaining garrisons of professional British troops at strategic points in North America, the colonies resisted. The idea of a permanent army in America was unwelcome under any circumstances. When an unpopular idea required money out of colonial pockets to support, it turned downright repulsive.[5]

Connecticut was well prepared to oppose increased taxation. Its citizens resented the idea of paying the Crown for services which they believed were unneeded. They also had a history of challenging established authority, especially when it came to protecting their own interests. During the Great Awakening they fought amongst themselves over their right to religious self-determination. Now that battle turned political and a clash with king and Parliament seemed inevitable. As they viewed it, their clearly defined rights as Englishmen were at stake.

Since obtaining its charter in 1662, Connecticut paid little attention to royal rule. Contrary to British policy, the colony often passed laws objectionable to the Mother Country, including capital punishment in murder and robbery trials. Town meetings elected local officials and colonial affairs were left to a few ruling families who held office for decades, so long as they attended to the interests of the majority.

Enjoying virtual home rule Connecticut and New Haven were content to leave well enough alone. Their allegiance to the king was never in question. In their view, it was more than just a tax issue. Parliament was to blame for meddling in the internal affairs of the colonies and grasping for power it did not deserve.

By 1764 New Haveners got their chance to prove the courage of their convictions. Amid a increasingly severe recession in the colonies that saw the number of foreclosures increase dramatically, Parliament passed the Sugar Act. Unwilling and unable to pay increased taxes on European luxury items, most of which they were forced to import through Boston or New York anyway, New Haveners led the colonies in resisting the law. In a town meeting residents voted to encourage home production, "so that the use of superfluous goods from abroad be lessened."[5]

New Haven's boycott spread rapidly. Within the year other colonial towns adopted the measure and praised New Haveners, "for setting so laudable an example... those who visit New Haven will think themselves better entertained with a good glass of beer or cider, offered them upon such principles, than they could be, with the best punch or Madeira." In reality, the boycott got its start among Yale students.[8]

While principles seemed more palatable — and certainly less costly — than taxation in New Haven, Parliament had only just begun its assessment of the colonies' fair share in the cost of maintaining its North American empire.

Britain realized that the Sugar Act provided only a small fraction of what was needed to maintain professional troops in its North American outposts. While there was some debate concerning methodology, there was never any doubt that further taxes were justified for the colonies. After an initial debate and compromise, a stamp tax was adopted by Parliament in 1765.[9]

The Granger Collection, New York

The ill-fated stamp tax adopted for the colonies by the British Parliament in 1765 as a means to defray the costs of defense caused widespread protest in America.

Although not nearly as demanding as the stamp bill then in force in Britain, the famous Stamp Act gave rise to the beginnings of organized opposition to English rule in North America. The tax also had a high nuisance value, since every sheet and document subject to the duty was either printed on specially stamped paper or affixed with a stamp. In either case the special paper and the stamp were obtainable only through the office of the official stamp distributor.

For West Haveners the Stamp Act was not merely a question of increased taxes and personal inconvenience. It was an issue ideally suited to precipitate a more fundamental debate involving the future of religious and political power in the village.

Until 1740 West Haven Congregationalists had been quick to express their loyalty to Connecticut's ruling order. It had been the conservative element of the General Assembly that had lent a sympathetic ear to West Haven's initial fight for parish status in 1715. Once established, the parish found continued support from the General Assembly in the troubled times accompanying the Anglican movement, in being repeatedly bailed out of insolvency and in dealing with the debilitating effects of the Great Awakening. Naturally, West Haven Congregationalists were grateful for the help they had received. Underlying their sense of loyalty and gratitude was a more practical rationale. They sensed the necessity of continuing their conservative political affiliations in order to preserve their own sense of self-identity.

The Great Awakening dramatically altered the long-standing relationship between church and colony in Connecticut. Civil authorities underestimated the early effects of revivalism. When they finally did take action to stem its challenge to traditional authority in the colony, much of the damage could not be undone. Radicals and conservatives alike considered Connecticut's leadership ineffective for opposite reasons. For the New Lights the Standing Order was out of step with the revived spirit of the times.

In the eyes of Old Light Congregationalists, the colonial government failed to protect the conservative interests that had helped Connecticut flourish in its first hundred years. To prevent religious anarchy, parish autonomy gave way to consociations of local churches and an alternative to the guiding hand of the General Assembly. Church and state were becoming increasingly stratified in the minds of Connecticut residents.

Quick to recognize an opportunity, New Lights wasted little time in exploiting West Haven's waning allegiance to old-line colonial authority. With the Stamp Act as their pivotal issue, the radicals soon won over the support of West Haveners, both Anglican and Congregationalist. As unlikely an alliance as it seemed the New Lights shrewdly pitted religious interests of the village's two predominant churches against one another to benefit their own agenda. West Haven Congregationalists feared the repercussions of opposing a political realignment of the colony, while the Anglicans had been promised a seat in the Upper House.[10]

West Haven's clergymen were soon using their pulpits to denounce the lethargy of Connecticut officials in allowing themselves to drift so far from public sentiment concerning the Stamp Act. In leveling their attacks, the ministers made the very name of the Stamp Act synonymous with those of sin, Satan and unrighteousness.[11] Owing to these condemnations West Haveners were naturally aroused to the sense of pending danger that this tax could somehow lead to a tightening of Parliamentary authority over a nearly autonomous colony. Needless to say, Connecticut's conservative officials, and especially their neighbor and Connecticut's Stamp Distributor, Jared Ingersoll, were fast becoming the objects of their collective scorn for participating in such a scheme. Connecticut's political landscape was in the process of being radicalized overnight.

On the evening of September 10, 1765, West Haven's Sons of Liberty, led by Lamberton Smith, Jr., made their opposition to the Stamp Act and Mr. Ingersoll well known throughout Connecticut:

> West Side was visited by a horrible monster, or male giant, twelve feet high, whose terrible head was internally illuminated. He was mounted on a generous horse, groaning under the enormous weight. This giant seemed to threaten destruction to every person, or thing around him which raised the resentment of a number of stout fellows, who constantly pelted him with stones till he fled. The assailants pursued and soon took him captive and triumphantly drove him about a mile in the town, attended with the discordant noise of drums, fiddles and taunting huzzas. The people then directed their course toward a hill called Mt. Misery. There the giant was accused, fairly tried and condemned by a special jury and impartial judge as an unjust intruder, a patron of ignorance, a foe of English freedom, etc., and was sentenced to be burnt.
>
> The sentence was accordingly executed, amidst the

joyful acclamations of near three hundred Libertines, men, women and children. It should be mentioned that through the whole of this rare show, no unlawful disorder happened as was the case in the last truly deplorable and truly detestable riot in Boston.[12]

Only seven days separated this demonstration from New Haven's spirited debate of the Stamp Act at a town meeting on September 17, 1765. In a unanimous decision, the townspeople instructed their representatives in the General Assembly, "to use their utmost endeavors" to obtain a repeal of the Act. In addition, a demand was read aloud calling for Ingersoll to resign his "Stamp Office immediately." Furious, he "arose and declared in the strongest terms that he would not resign till he discovered how the General Assembly were inclined in that respect."[13]

Ingersoll never got the chance to hear the Assembly's position. On his way to Hartford, he was stopped by a large mob near Wethersfield and, with threats of violence, he was forced to resign as Connecticut's stamp distributor. He was then escorted to Hartford by the mob, where he again made public his resignation before the Assembly, no doubt under duress.[14]

Connecticut's reactions to the Stamp Act illustrated the general attitude of all the colonies. They seemed perfectly prepared to resist the law by force if necessary. So ardent were the resulting protests from around the colonies that Parliament faced the dilemma of enforcing a law that hurt trade and would most likely risk an unwanted civil war.[15]

That prospect would benefit no one. With protests mounting both in the colonies and at home among London merchants suffering from the American boycott, Parliament reluctantly acknowledged colonial opposition to internal taxation when it repealed the Stamp Act in 1766. But it was not about to relinquish its right to levy taxes in the colonies altogether. The very day the Stamp Act's repeal gained the King's signature, the Declaratory Act was also signed into law, pronouncing that Parliament "had, hath, and of right ought to have full power and authority to make laws and statutes of sufficient force and validity to bind the colonies and the people of America in all cases whatsoever."[16]

The Americans were not really listening to Parliamentarian rhetoric. All they heard was of the Stamp Act's repeal and it was cause for spontaneous celebration throughout the colonies and New Haven. Small arms were fired throughout the day, cannon roared the glad tidings and the militia paraded on the green. By nightfall, fireworks burst above New Haven's skyline, while huge bonfires silhouetted those who danced in the streets. New Haveners had joined hands with fellow colonists to win a major victory, but in reality they had only earned a brief reprieve.

Within a year of the Stamp Act's repeal, there was little reason to celebrate. When the Townshend Acts passed into law in 1767, they represented a renewed taxing effort which again stirred deep colonial resentments. This time, the imperial tax was on selected imported goods, including English tea.[17]

The colonists again decided to resist the new taxes. Prompted by a letter from Boston's selectmen, which was read at a New Haven town meeting on February 8, 1768, it was voted in the affirmative to again support a general boycott of British and West Indian goods.[18]

Nonimportation agreements, however, proved difficult to enforce, especially in a coastal community. New Haveners' sentiment was not nearly as united against the Townshend duties as it had been in opposing the Stamp Act. With the chance to make a tidy profit, smugglers did a brisk business along the Connecticut shoreline, and many a Connecticut family continued to secretly enjoy their spot of tea.[19]

Despite such violations imports decreased substantially in New Haven and elsewhere throughout the colonies. British merchants were annoyed by the boycott as their profits again began to suffer. King George III struck a conciliatory tone. By 1770 he supported the repeal of the Townshend duties, except the one on tea. This, he insisted, must be maintained as a mark of Parliament's supremacy over colonial resistance to law and order. Instead, it would eventually lead to revolution.

Notable Names Database

Popular at home, George III refused to relinquish the Crown's right to tax the colonies as a matter of royal prerogative.

When West Haveners expressed their opposition to the conservative response of Connecticut's leaders during the Stamp Act crisis, they — and many similar communities — were setting the stage for a change in government. The New Lights surfaced as the true voice of Connecticut's people, as their fierce opposition to the Stamp Act made the conservatives appear negligent. By the spring of 1766, the New Light victory in Connecticut was complete. In the colonial elections of that year, they narrowly defeated Governor Fitch and the conservative old guard to take control over Connecticut's future government.[20]

With Connecticut's leadership now in the hands of New Lights, West Haveners found their resulting condition a precarious one. While they justified their stance during the Stamp Act crisis as unavoidable in protecting their rights as British citizens, they had, by necessity, cut against the grain of their own conservative leanings. Some began to wonder whether the cause of their liberties had been carried too far. Was liberty worth the destruction of civil authority and the de-sanctification of government, as they had known it for over a century? Should they align themselves with a new political order, which, by its very nature, placed West Haven's Old Light church in jeopardy?

If West Haveners grappled with such questions in 1766, developments within their own community soon helped to dispel any doubts about whether they had chosen the right course of action.

Long distraught by the political and religious turmoil in the colony, West Haven Anglicans now felt betrayed by the New Lights. Their support of the new political order in the colony had done little for the cause of Episcopacy. Congregationalists, and radicals at that, were still in full control of the colonial government, and they exhibited no signs that they would ever share their political power with conservative churchmen.

So the Anglicans resorted to a more radical solution. They realized that order could be restored to the colonies and their own status immediately upgraded by "Demolishing the pernicious charter governments, reducing them to one form, in immediate dependence on the King."[21]

In the face of a growing political crisis, many Anglicans believed that Connecticut should surrender its charter to the irrefutable authority of the king. After all, as British citizens they owed ultimate allegiance to the Crown. Why not settle the issue once and for all by revoking Connecticut's dubious charter and establish a royal colony? That solution would also conveniently improve their own current status as dissenters.

If West Haven Congregationalists shared the desire to restore some sense of political order to a colony now seemingly spinning out of control, this "plot" to Anglicanize them was a call to arms. John Adams of Massachusetts summed it up best for Puritan New England:

If any gentlemen supposed this controversy to be nothing to the present purpose, he is grossly mistaken. It
(the plan to Episcopalianize the colonies, especially New
England) spread a universal alarm against the authority
of Parliament. It excited a general and just apprehension
that bishops and dioceses and churches and priests and
tithes were to be imposed on us by archbishops who could
appoint bishops in America without an act of Parliament;
and if Parliament could tax us, they could establish the
Church of England and prohibit all other churches as
conventicles and schism.[22]

West Haven Congregationalists fully shared Adams' views, which
were no doubt reinforced week after week from the First Church pulpit.
The Puritans may have regretted the loss of some of their traditional
values, but they were not about to see them destroyed altogether. The
Anglican call for royal intervention threatened to do just that, and the
West Haven Old Lights saw no choice but to cast their support with the
less drastic rationale of the New Light government. Self-preservation
was a powerful motivator in casting the mold for revolution.

When Parliament withdrew all but the 3d. per pound tax on tea
in 1770, New Haveners had little to complain about. With the boycott
on English goods suspended and trade resumed, New Haveners were
among the most prosperous people in Connecticut.

Well might a writer in a local paper "contemplate New Haveners great increase within those few years past, by the many and
elegant buildings erected."[23] But their dandruff was up, and every
Parliamentary action affecting the colonies was interpreted by the
radical spin doctors of the colonial press as yet another affront to
American liberty.

Affairs in Boston went from bad to worse. In March 1770 British

*Perpetrated by the Sons of Liberty, the Boston Tea Party led Parliament to pass the ill-conceived
Coercise Acts, which further fused colonial resistance against Parliament's heavy handedness.*

regulars and a Boston mob clashed in what was immediately coined
"a massacre." Hardly that, the incident proved that tensions ran high
enough between the British army and American civilians to result in
violent outbursts and the death of average citizens. Bostonians' goad-
ing of the army continued unabated and the relationship between the
civil and military authority eroded to the point of open hostility.

Even after the Tea Act of 1773 reduced the price paid for tea,
New Haveners expressed fears that the creation of the East India
Company's monopoly on tea cleared the path for other monopolies
that would cast the colonists into a subservient role.[24] In opposing the
Tea Act and others like it, New Haveners knew very well that their
actions would be viewed by London as a direct challenge to Parliament's supremacy over the colonies. While they could well afford
the price of tea, they felt that their rights and liberties as Englishmen could not. Resolved in their decision to resist, New Haveners
pensively awaited further developments while Britain stumbled in

search of an effective policy.

As the first tea chests broke apart in Boston's Tea Party in December 1773 so too was the uneasy calm between colonies and empire thrown overboard into stormy waters. Once again the political epicenter was Boston. Property destruction, and tea at that, goaded the British government into stern acts of reprisal.

Within four months following the Boston Tea Party, the British Parliament passed the Restraining Acts (better known as the Coercive Acts) to teach the Boston "hoodlums" a lesson.[25] With Boston's port now closed, its town meetings restricted and Massachusetts' government severely altered, open rebellion in the Bay Colony now seemed inevitable.

In West Haven, where people recoiled from the Anglican call for a royal colony, the Coercive Acts hammered home the realization that the British Parliament could rework Connecticut's charter just as quickly as it had done in Massachusetts. Outraged by Parliament's treatment of their Boston neighbors, New Haveners voted at a town meeting held on May 23, 1774:

> That we will to the utmost of our abilities assert and defend the liberties and immunities of British America and that we will cooperate with our sister towns in this and the other colonies in any constitutional measures that may be thought most conducive to the preservation of our invaluable rights and privileges. For the maintenance of public peace and support of general Union, which at this time is so absolutely requisite to be preserved throughout this continent. That it is the opinion of this town that a subscription be set afoot for the relief of inhabitants of the town of Boston that are now suffering in the common cause of American freedom and that... Silas Kimberly, Samuel Candee, Simeon Bristol, Issac Beecher Jr., Timothy Ball, and

Samuel Beecher be a committee to receive in subscrip-
tions and transmit what may be collected to the selectmen of the town of Boston....[26]

Such proclamations were the result of a curious blend of emotions and self-interest. New Haveners were obviously sympathetic to Boston's plight. More importantly, they realized Boston's cause could easily be their own. They also knew that the Coercive Acts and subsequent repressions placed on Boston constituted an affront to the colonies and demanded a concerted response if Parliamentarian policy was to be answered forcefully. In past crises, combined opposition proved its worth. So New Haveners did not hesitate to again join the growing number of towns in opposing Great Britain's colonial policies in calling for an intercolonial convention equal to the Stamp Act Congress of a decade ago. It seemed to offer the last best hope for a peaceful settlement to an imperial quarrel that was swirling rapidly out of control.[26]

Many American communities shared New Haven's sentiment for a colonial conference. After three months of exchanging views among committees of correspondence, the First Continental Congress convened in Philadelphia on September 5, 1775. The issues facing the delegates were monumental. Most colonists did not favor complete independence. But the question of their rights and liberties within the imperial framework was a delicate one. In their mind, civil authority was meant to serve as the public's agent and not simply its disciplinarian. They conceded Parliament's authority to regulate external commerce and the king's royal prerogatives so long as both remained consistent with colonial rights and, more importantly, America's interpretation of them. If legislation was thought to be destructive, such as the Declaratory and Coercive acts, it was roundly denounced. And if not redressed, colonial protests would be backed up by non-importation, non-exportation and non-consumption associations across the colonies.

Within a month of first convening, the delegates moved well beyond drafting a simple list of colonial grievances. Disavowing Parliament's recent enactments as illegal, they denied Parliament's authority to legislate over the colonies at all. Instead, the Congress addressed King George III directly in hopes of seeking a royal redress. To demonstrate their united resolve, the delegates also adopted the nonimportation, non-exportation and non-consumption association to fight economic fire with fire of their own. If the king failed to act by May, they resolved to meet again. By anyone's measure, the First Continental Congress charted a radical course that begged for a strong Parliamentary response.[27]

Radical or not, most New Haveners considered the Congressional resolves as their only means to combat Parliament's increasing coercion of the colonies. In adopting their own economic sanctions, they hoped that hard-pressed London merchants would pressure Parliament to repeal the onerous acts. Despite the fact that some 300 merchant ships were eventually backed up at London's wharves "with brooms tied to their masts, thereby advertising them for sale by merchants whose business had been destroyed,"[28] Parliament refused to back down.

So did the colonials. New Haveners wasted little time in adopting non-importation of all British goods. And if size alone is any indication of West Haven's resolve, of the 51 members of the town's Committee of Inspection created to police the ban, West Haven was well represented by Daniel Benham, Stephen Smith, Jonathan Smith, John Benham, Issac Beecher, Jr., Stephen Ball, Lamberton Painter and Lamberton Smith, Jr.[29]

While some New Haveners worried that such radical actions pushed them closer to the abyss, others seemed to welcome the coming confrontation. At the request of 70 members of his train band, Hezekiah Sabin, Jr. petitioned the Connecticut legislature to have his military company commissioned as the Second Company of the Governor's Foot Guard. The petition was quickly granted.[30] Connecticut was preparing for war against the world's most powerful military machine. And they did not have long to wait.

A 1775 illustration of the Battle of Lexington and "the shot heard round the world" by Amos Doolittle (engraver) and Ralph Earl (artist) was meant to depict the bravery of the Massachusetts minutemen against British regulars.

When word reached England of the colonies' non-importation actions, Parliament responded with the passage of yet another coercive bill, the New England Restraining Act. In forbidding access to the fisheries of Newfoundland and Nova Scotia, it was meant to make an example of the rebellious New Englanders. Timing destined the measure to be anticlimactic. Early on April 19, 1775, the Massachusetts militia squared off against British regulars on the Concord and Lexington greens. Before the day was over, 73 British soldiers lay dead while 95 colonials had been killed or wounded. The paper war of Parliament and Congress was now replaced by steel and shot. The American Revolution had begun.

CHAPTER EIGHT

Crisis of Allegiance

April 21, 1775 was a Friday. Only two days before, New Haveners observed a day of fasting and prayer in hopes that King George III would intercede to resolve the escalating colonial crisis with Parliament.

Sometime that Friday afternoon, Israel Bissell approached West Haven. A post rider, Bissell had traveled from his native Lexington, Massachusetts, pausing only to exchange mounts as he made his way into Connecticut at a breakneck pace. His news of the battles of Concord and Lexington stunned New Haven.[1]

By nightfall a large crowd assembled at the Middle Brick Meetinghouse in what constituted an extralegal town meeting. Everyone wanted to know how New Haven would respond to the pleas for help from neighboring Massachusetts. Roger Sherman, a local merchant and hard-line radical, was elected

Roger Sherman (1721 - 1793) sat for his portrait by Ralph Earle in 1777. Already a wealthy merchant, he would go on to a distinguished career in business and government.

Courtesy of Yale University Art Gallery

93

moderator by a single vote over the former Stamp Tax collector and arch-conservative, Ralph Ingersoll. The meeting was tense. [2]

As arguments unfolded, those who urged an armed response to British aggression were sorely disappointed. When push came to shove, most New Haveners were reluctant to take up arms against Britain without first fully weighing the consequences. They felt there was little to be gained from insurrection, as the revenue dispute, which led up to these distressing events, neither implied or necessitated war. New Haveners, in fact, had always been careful to prevent civil disorders in their protests in order to keep the main issue — their genuine indignation over British colonial policy — in the forefront of the dispute. They feared the loss of the colony's charter, and war against the world's most powerful military force seemed to be pure folly.[3]

This was, after all, a constitutional issue over taxes. Despite their rhetoric, the townspeople felt their grievances could be better addressed in Whitehall than on American battlefields. But the British home government fumbled badly in handling the crisis. Sending an army to Boston unaccompanied by a constructive policy elevated a constitutional issue into a moral one. New Haveners could not help but think that British regulars were now silencing colonial critics with muskets and brute force instead of reasoned debate and enlightened answers. With their pleas for reconciliation ignored, New

New Haven resident Benedict Arnold entered the Revolution a fierce patriot only to become a traitor to the cause later in the war.

Haveners were left to wonder
if Britain intended to rework
colonial government entirely
through the force of arms.

Weighing the alternatives
of submission to civil war, New
Haveners, as of April 21, 1775,
chose the former, "until the
consequences of the latter were
less, far less tremendous than
the effects of oppression," reads
the official record. In the face of
a superpower, the townspeople
ordered their selectmen to look
after New Haven's own interests
first and leave military matters
in the hands of the colony.[4]

General David Wooster (1711 - 1777) was in command of Connecticut's provincial militia before his death in the Battle of Danbury in 1777.

Benedict Arnold would hear none of it. Arguably one of the
wealthiest men in Connecticut and a captain of the Foot Guard, Arnold wasted little time in charting a historic course for New Haven
and for himself. Assembling his militiamen on the New Haven Green,
he proposed they march to Massachusetts immediately. Sixty-three of
77 men agreed to ignore the outcome of the town meeting and go to
war. It was a mandate which led Arnold and his troops to the door of
Beers' Tavern on the morning of April 22, where the town's selectmen
and Committee of Safety were in emergency session. Harsh words
were exchanged between its members and Captain Arnold, while David Wooster, soon to become a major general himself, tried to reason
with the impetuous captain. "None but Almighty God shall prevent
my marching," Arnold insisted. Fearing violence, Arnold's men were
given the keys to the town's powder house. Supplying themselves with
munitions from its stores, Arnold and the Second Company of the

Governor's Foot Guard marched off to war, sealing New Haven's fate as a town now in open rebellion against the Crown.[5]

That fact did not sit easily with many townspeople, who were torn between their loyalties to home and empire. History is written by the victors. Those on the losing side of the equation are predictably portrayed as having been disloyal. When Arnold and his company marched off to Massachusetts on that Saturday morning in April 1775, the majority of his fellow townsmen thought they would be marching right back home again once the Second Continental Congress met in Philadelphia. Little thought was given to taking permanent sides in what was hoped to be a negotiable misunderstanding.

Initially, New Haveners' optimism for a peaceful settlement was the majority, if not the inconsistent, opinion of the Congress then meeting in Philadelphia. While delegates offered the olive branch in one hand, they carried a sabre in the other. In short order they sanctioned the Massachusetts insurrection, launched an expedition against Quebec and appointed Col. George Washington of Virginia as commander-in-chief of the Army of the United Colonies.[6] The necessity of finally choosing sides drew ever closer at hand.

The appearance of Washington, himself, in West Haven along with his senior staff on their way to Boston polarized opinions even further. Wanted or not, the united colonies were now at war, and Washington's presence only helped to harden arguments on either side of the issue. People lined the roads to catch a glimpse of the 43-year-old commander-in chief, shouting out words of encouragement as the tall Virginian rode by. Spending the night in New Haven, Washington's entourage was escorted out of town the following day by three military companies. One was made up of Yale students and the other two wore the spanking new uniforms of the Governor's Foot Guard, or what was left of it after Arnold marched off with the Second Company. A considerable number of other townspeople, however, stayed at home throughout the martial pomp and circumstance. As loyal English subjects, they wondered what the future would bring now that there was open talk of American independence.[7]

The Rev. Mr. Noah Williston was decidedly not amongst those questioning the future. As with most Congregational clergymen, Williston opposed the idea of an American Episcopate. And he no doubt believed now that war had come, it was part of a more duplicitous conspiracy to force Episcopacy upon the "visible saints."[8] Williston was not about to let that go unchallenged. And he was in a position to act upon his convictions. Wielding considerable influence throughout the

The earliest known portrait of George Washington in the uniform of the Virginia militia, was painted by Charles Wilson Peale in 1772. Washington traveled through West Haven on two separate occasions.

Courtesy of Washington and Lee University

parish, he soon followed the example of his close friend, the Reverend Mr. Benjamin Trumbull of North Haven, in using the West Haven meetinghouse as a recruiting station for the Continental Army.[9]

That put West Haven Anglicans in a dangerous position. To take sides in 1775 would have been self-defeating. Not only were they fearful of increased discrimination against the likes of Williston should Connecticut declare its independence, but their religious affiliations with the king and Church of England would be severely altered, if not totally eradicated, by Congregational zealots under the guise of patriotism.[7] So they quietly clung to their Loyalist views as much out of not knowing what else to do as in defiance of Congregational rule.

Their Congregational neighbors would not stand idly by. In a town meeting of December 11, 1775, New Haveners politely asked Loyalist sympathizers to leave town, while the "most obnoxious Tories" were already under lock and key in the county jail.[10]

Such ordinances prompted the Connecticut General Assembly to follow suit with an official colony-wide renunciation of British sympathizers. Obliging its overwhelmingly Congregationalist constituency, the Assembly acted with extraordinary speed in declaring Connecticut "a free and independent State," in June 1776. It also ordered "the confiscation of all property of any person who has or shall join the ministerial army or have aided the present ministerial measures."[11]

Armed with the weight of civil authority and fueled by their own sense of religious zealotry, some West Haven radicals quickly lashed out at their Anglican neighbors. Lamberton Smith, Jr., for example, demanded the removal of two "treasonous" individuals from the village, "whose conduct has evinced that they are dangerous to the said town of New Haven," he charged. There were no doubt dozens of other villagers who came under the increasing suspicion of the Patriots, especially if they also happened to be communicants of Christ Church. In fact, the ferreting out of suspected Loyalists took place so swiftly as to deny them any chance whatever of mounting an organized opposition. They had no recourse but to acquiesce with the radicals or leave.[12]

As the war intensified, so did Patriotic pressure to conform to the new State of Connecticut. By 1777 West Haven Congregationalists were running roughshod over Anglicans unwilling to cooperate. Loyalty oaths were required of voters and public officials and those who refused faced the threat of suspension from office, disenfranchisement, confiscation of their property, imprisonment and even banishment. Such pecuniary measures had their desired effect. During the course of the war approximately five percent of the total male membership of West Haven's Christ Church relocated to Canada rather than surrender their principles to the rebels. Among them were Thaddeus, John, Richard and Nehemiah Clark; and Joseph and Elijah Prindle.

Throughout Connecticut as a whole, more than 2,000 Loyalists finally abandoned their homes due to their allegiance to the Crown.[13]

Intimidated by local authorities, ostracized by society and feeling neglected by the British home government, West Haven Anglicans faced a difficult decision. While some eventually deserted their country rather than their loyalties to Church and king, the overwhelming majority of Loyalists simply stayed put, grit their teeth and bore the insults of their neighbors.[14] In fact, by 1778 many Anglicans were scrutinizing British policies as vehemently as were Congregationalists. As the war dragged on, some even felt it was being deliberately prolonged to serve the interests of British war profiteers rather than restoring law and order in America. They only had to look to New York to see the failure of Great Britain's promise to restore civil rule once territory had been reoccupied and the Patriots subdued.[15]

Changing attitudes of Anglicans was one thing. Changing the fundamental underpinnings of their religion was quite another. That came when West Haven Anglicans were eventually relieved of the burden of religious objections to American independence. In 1778, Christ Church excluded prayers to the king and Church of England. This was no small gesture of conciliation since Anglican liturgy had always been regarded as a mask for Loyalist plots and associations. To further placate the rebels, services at Christ Church were curtailed for a time. The Reverend Bela Hubbard knew better than to provoke criticism and possibly violence by quoting from the Book of Common Prayer. When Christ Church finally reopened, Reverend Hubbard prudently omitted all references to the royal family.[16]

Already wary of British good faith, Anglican suspicions of total abandonment received bitter final affirmation when West Haven became the target of a series of free booting expeditions led by Loyalist and British raiders. These raids answered only the purpose of plunderers, robbers and marauders, who cared less about the religious persuasion of their victims. Perhaps more so than any other factor, indiscriminate violence did much to forward Anglican disaffection for the mother country.

While enemy invasions allowed some West Haveners to openly align themselves with the British, and on at least one occasion even to help direct troops through the village, most Anglican muskets were poised alongside their Congregationalist neighbors against a common invader.[17]

Amid the indiscriminate plundering and murder by British and mercenary troops, parish animosities were muted in a communal effort to defend each other's property. Property rights were held so sacrosanct that they equalled, if not transcended, loyalty to a particular government. Consequently, it was difficult to maintain animosity towards Anglicans who proved ready to take up arms in defense of their neighbor's property. Among those Anglicans who came to the defense of the town during the 1779 invasion, for instance, were Juduthan Thompson, who was killed; Pomp, a black, who was also killed; Samuel Benham, Thomas Smith, Thomas Painter, James Reynolds, Benjamin Smith, Warham Smith, Samuel Humphreville and David Tolles. These men comprised a surprising 40 percent of West Haveners known to have participated in the July 5, 1779 battle.[18]

As the war dragged on, the British floundered through a dizzying number of military and political blunders to further harden the hearts and minds of Americans against their cause. The Patriots, meanwhile, were using every available opportunity "... to bring over the disaffected to espouse their cause," one observer wrote. "They hang the turbulent, imprison the dangerous, fine the wealthy.... And by such means as these, they have strengthened their cause amazingly. Whereas on the part of the King, nothing has ever been done of this kind."[19]

CHAPTER NINE

Dire Sense of Expectancy

There is a sense of supreme irony to New Haven's rather embarrassing entry into the American Revolution. It came at the hands of no less than Benedict Arnold. Little did that impetuous captain of the Second Company of the Governor's Foot Guard — or anyone else in 1775 — foresee his impertinent actions on that April morning ever becoming the centerpiece of New Haven's commemoration of the war. If only once a year, Benedict Arnold is still the hero of Powderhouse Day. The event has been staged annually on the New Haven Green since 1906 not far from the actual event and closer still to where the native-son-turned-traitor was burned in effigy in 1781. That event followed Arnold's aborted attack on New Haven itself and his successfully overseeing the destruction of New London.[1]

New Haven has good reason to remember Arnold and the American Revolution. Historians have been quick to point out that in spite of Arnold, the town supplied more than its share of heroes to the winning of independence. Roger Sherman, signer of the Declaration of Independence, Articles of Confederation and United States Constitution; General David Wooster, the hero-martyr of the Danbury raid; Nathan Hale, who, by virtue of attending Yale College, was adopted by New Haven following his death as an amateur spy; and David Humpherys, a man of such considerable talents and accomplishment and who was so close to the commander-in-chief that he was known as "the belov'd of Washington."[2]

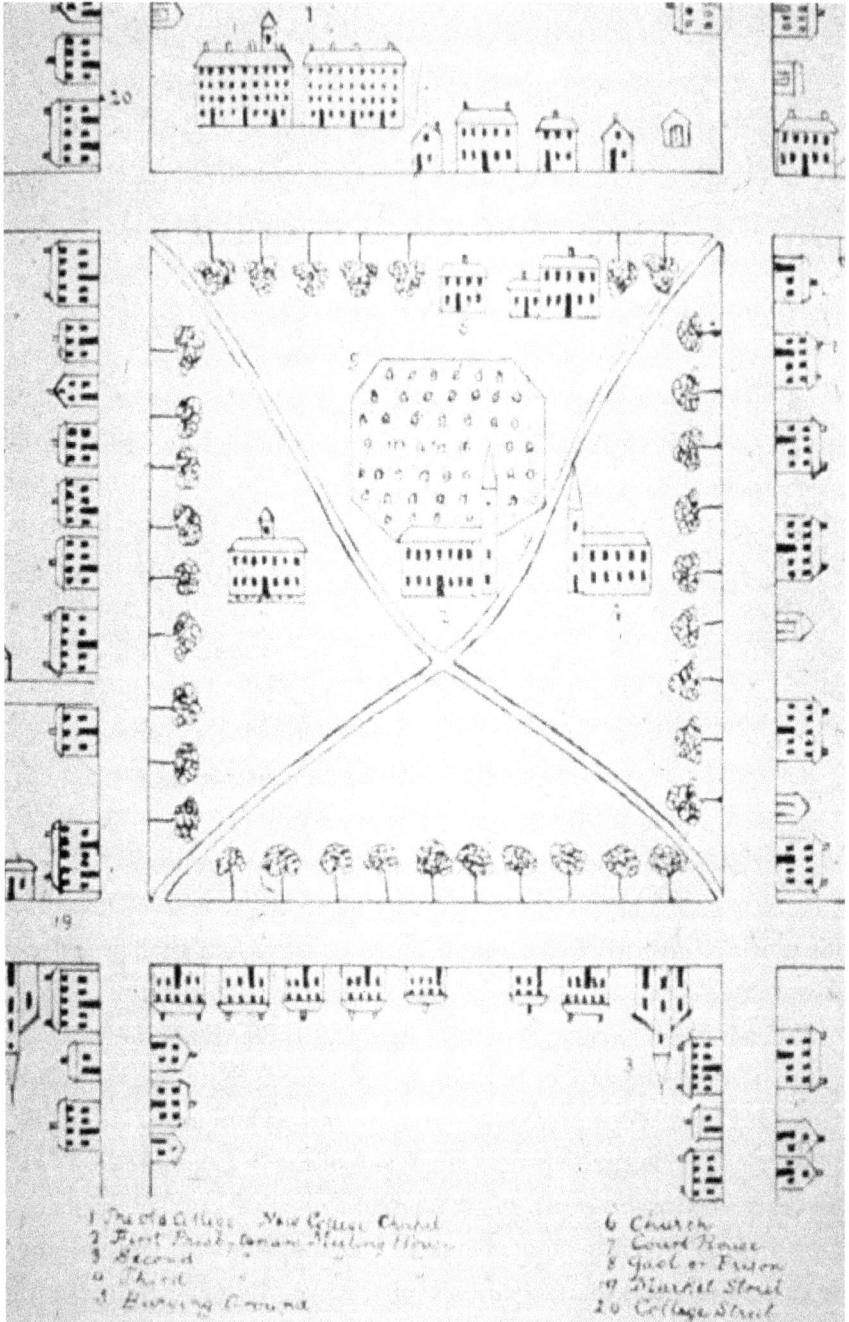

View of central New Haven, 1775, after Ezra Stiles's map.

As if these men were not enough to convince the skeptical at heart of New Haven's patriotic fervor, its historians have traditionally played their trump card — the British invasion of the town on July 5, 1779 — as the singular event that forged New Haveners into becoming "more determined than ever to win their independence and make it possible for their descendants to celebrate the Fourth of July in peace if not in quiet."[3]

No wonder the Revolution remains a paradox. Characterized as a "Glorious Cause," we appear to shrink in comparison to our Revolutionary forbearers. After more than two centuries, most of us have difficulty even remembering let alone caring about the historical purpose of the Revolution.[4]

What we do remember are mere glimpses of the past — the Founding Fathers, Paul Revere's ride, Redcoats lining up like so many ducks in a gallery for the sharpshooting Americans or being hunted down by fictitious heroes in the error-prone but highly acclaimed motion picture *The Patriot* (2000). How one-dimensional the Revolution has become in our mind's eye. In the sanitized process of history and Hollywood, we agree on only one major point. The American Revolution was a remarkable event the likes of which has never been repeated.[5]

Now look again at that canvas with a more discerning eye. You will likely see that it is far from complete. In our preoccupation with the broad strokes of the Revolution, we have overlooked one of its most important details, the impact of war on the individuals who fought it on both sides. We have stressed the exceptional at the expense of the ordinary. In so doing we have missed the richest vein of all, that of human experience.[6]

What was it like to live through the American Revolution as a common citizen or solider? To have your world, as British General John Burgoyne so aptly put it after losing the Battle of Saratoga to General Horatio Gates in 1777, "turned upside down"? Was it really so glorious to face adversity, deprivation, fear, poverty and death for the better part of a decade? Despite the high-handed rhetoric, our Revolutionary forbearers were motivated by the same fears and hopes that motivate us. Their will to survive, to win, to profit, settle old scores, to love and hate — and above all else to follow what they felt was the right thing to do — all were intricately interwoven into the fabric of the Revolutionary experience.

Only after the crisis passed did events and personalities begin to take on mythical proportions defined by the victors. As the daily prosecution of the war faded from collective memory, its more remarkable incidents and characters were propped up to fill the void, leaving behind an extraordinary, if incomplete, story of a people at war in America's sixth largest town, New Haven.[7]

I

At the start of the Revolution, New Haven was an impressive sight. It encompassed the present cities of West Haven, East Haven, North Haven, Hamden, Bethany and Amity. Around its already famed nine squares were 300 homes and some of the most impressive examples of colonial architecture in America. With over 8,000 residents, 108 vessels registered to its port and 10 percent of its population employed at sea, New Haven easily qualified as Connecticut's leading urban center, its largest seaport and home to America's largest college, which, as early as 1765, was eyed suspiciously by British General Thomas Gage as that "seminary of Democracy."[8]

The reputation seemed well deserved. Throughout the decade prior to the Revolution and continuing on through the war, New Haven officials had their hands full in controlling "a Bold & Irreverant Behaviour towards Superiors and a Contempt of Government" among all strata of society.[9] Ministers constantly complained that church attendance was low and parishioners were becoming abusive. At Yale it became a tradition for graduating seniors to descend upon the President's home and pelt it with missiles of every description in the middle of the night. Considering the rather tenuous relationship between then President Thomas Clap and the student body, Yale's scholars no doubt relished the opportunity to collectively express their opinion against Clap's arbitrary rule with a few well aimed rocks under cover of darkness.[10]

But civil disobedience ran deeper than skipping Sunday services and schoolboy pranks. When all else failed, violence increasingly became an acceptable way of getting your point across in New Haven. Jared Ingersoll's home was attacked by a mob during the Stamp Act crisis. Not satisfied with pelting his house with rocks, the mob threatened to tear it down entirely if Ingersoll did not resign as stamp collector. In West Haven, 300 men, women and children burned Ingersoll in effigy and pelted this "horrible monster" with stones amid drumbeats and huzzas. It was all in a night's fun, and officials grew increasingly nervous.[11]

Other instances of public protest called for even more dramatic action. When Benedict Arnold heard that one of his employees was talking about reporting him to British authorities for not using stamps, he led a mob against the poor devil and summarily whipped him at the public pillar. When Arnold was subsequently arrested and found guilty of "cruel, shocking, and dangerous" behavior, fellow townspeople burned effigies of the two grand jurymen in broad daylight and grew so unruly that New Haven officials released Arnold for fear that an all-out riot might ensue. Levritt Hubbard voiced the worried concern of many New Haveners when he complained, "all that don't run [with] a giddy and distracted mob are looked upon as Eminies to their Country and Betrayers of its Liberties." Arnold boldly retorted that anyone interested in trade would treat such an "infamous informer" in exactly the same fashion.[12]

Unfortunately for New Haven's more law abiding citizens Arnold proved right. Nathan Smith learned the hard way in 1769. Accused of smuggling against New Haven's non-importation agreements, Smith was charged, investigated and cleared. His fellow merchants were not satisfied with that judgement. So they took the law into their own hands, tied Smith down, and applied a new coat of tar and feathers on the merchant.[13]

Levelling such serious charges against neighbors could just as easily backfire. When Adonijah Thomas accused Timothy Jones, Jr., of smuggling rum into Connecticut, Thomas' reward was "as much tar, feathers, and infamy" as could be heaped upon him with an additional warning "that whosoever attempts to do the like ... may expect to receive a Reward adequate to their crimes." Apparently, New Haven's mercantile overruns included plenty of pine tar and goose down.[14]

The outbreak of the Revolution only escalated the lawlessness and violence in town. Six months following Arnold's bold demand for the powder house keys on the New Haven Green, Issac Sears and a band of renegade patriots, including 16 New Haveners, paraded the kidnapped Reverend Samuel Seabury, a prominent Anglican minister, through the streets of New Haven amid jeers and catcalls. The minister's pro-British stance earned him a stint in a Connecticut jail thanks to the extralegal doings of Sears.

The Reverend Samuel Seabury (1729 - 1796) was a physician, cleric, and devout Loyalist who spent six weeks in a Connecticut prison before being released. He later served as the chaplain to the King's American Regiment during the war and played a major role in American Episcopacy.

Not content with simply abducting the minister, the patriots also kidnapped two other prominent Tories and left the New York editorial offices of ultra-Loyalist James Rivington in shambles. They broke up his presses and commandeered his type, apparently, says Sears' biographer, to even up an old score under a patriotic guise. It appears that *Rivington's*

Gazeteer found a favorite whipping boy in Sears during the Stamp Act crisis of 1765, and continually referred to him as "the laughing stock of the whole town," repeatedly drawing attention to the patriot's large ears. Now 10 year later, there was no doubt who had the last laugh. Personal vendettas die hard.[15]

So does a bad reputation, and the Sears raid brought unwanted attention to New Haven's ongoing predicament with lawlessness. It was bad enough that the town seemed powerless to prevent its citizens from repeatedly taking the law into their own hands. Making matters worse, New Haveners were now involved in the destruction of property and kidnapping citizens from another sovereign colony. Many more staid New Haveners feared such brash behavior would lead to a British reprisal. Only a few weeks earlier, Falmouth, Maine, was bombarded to rubble for a lesser offense.[16]

Fears of a British attack turned to a crisis after the fall of New York to British troops in the summer of 1776. For the next seven years, the threat of invasion gave rise to what President Ezra Stiles of Yale called "a Dire Sense of Expectancy," a nagging, persistent fear that no matter what steps were taken to prevent it, New Haven was preordained for destruction.[17] Inevitably, that sense of doom altered the course of how New Haveners fought and faced the unalterable fact that they occupied a front row seat in the war for Long Island Sound.[18] Some residents simply opted to surrender their homes and livelihoods to move inland or off to British jurisdiction.[19] Others, such as Ezra Stiles, never really moved into town to begin with, having located his family and belongings in Durham until the end of the war.[20] Richard Woodhall, Oliver Burr and their small congregation of Sandemanians tried to ignore the problem altogether by charting a pro-British but non-belligerent course in their weekly religious services. Initially they all signed an oath of allegiance to Connecticut. When pressed on the issue, however, they recanted, claiming they had done so, "out of fear of man and not of God." Constantly harassed — as much out of New Haven's long-standing disdain for dissenters as for their loyalties to the Crown — the Sandemanians finally sailed off to Long Island in 1777.[20]

Abraham Blakeslee was not nearly so patient. A captain in Connecticut's Second Regiment, Blakeslee made no bones about the fact that he welcomed a British invasion of New Haven as early as 1775. And should that ever happen, he promised, he would "come down with his company and fight against the people, on the side of the king's Troops...." That rash statement earned Blakeslee a court-martial, and he eventually got what he wanted when he left town to join the King's American Regiment.[21] Blakeslee's decision was not unique. At least 27 other New Haveners are known to have joined the British army during the Revolution.[22]

Still more New Haveners decided to play both sides of the fence. Samuel Mix, for instance, was actively supplying the British on Long Island in 1778. Two years later he joined the Continental Army.[23] Samuel Butler worked in reverse. Having fought with the Continental troops in 1779, he joined evacuating Loyalists for St. John, New Brunswick at the end of the war.[24] Eldad Camp also served in the Connecticut Line for over two years before deserting in 1779 and moving to St. John with his family.[25] Most intriguing of all was Samuel Thomas. Already pledged to serve in Connecticut's Sixth Regiment for the duration of the war, he also fought with the Loyalist's Queen's Rangers, at least on paper. For Thomas' sake it was fortunate that the two opposing military units never engaged each other. Eventually, he, too, fled to New Brunswick.[26]

The litany of dual service and divided loyalties might well continue. Suffice it to say that during the course of the war, a good number of New Haveners fought on both sides of the struggle.[27] Even this does not begin to describe the full extent of New Haveners' peculiar ambiguity towards the Revolution. While the record shows that New Haven provided nearly one thousand men to the cause of independence and lost over 200 in the course of the war, not everyone was quite so anxious to serve his new country. In 1777 nearly 70 men were charged with dereliction of duty in New Haven, while close to 600 others did nothing at all to defend the town during its July 1779 invasion. Most were too busy getting their families and property out of harm's way to ever think about defending the town.[28]

There was also a good number of prominent townspeople who were, if not true Loyalists, at least sympathetic to the king's cause. John Miles, a wealthy merchant and vestryman at Trinity Episcopal Church in New Haven, was called before the committee of inspection in 1777 on suspicion of his Loyalist leanings. This, however, did little to affect his public trust, as he continued to hold several town offices, including a seat on the town committee to consider the Articles of Confederation and, ironically, the very same committee of inspection that subjected him to interrogation the previous year.[29]

John Whiting, brother-in-law of the ill-fated stamp collector, Jared Ingersoll, was also a well-known Tory, as was Ingersoll himself. Yet, Whiting served on the committee to review the Articles of Confederation, continued as a judge of probate and was even asked to plead New Haven's case for additional defenses in 1781.[30]

Other notable New Haveners who were sometimes under suspicion, but more often in public office, included Joshua Chandler, who was a selectman placed under house arrest and finally left with the British invaders in 1779, Edward Carrington, Thomas Howell and Isaac Hubbard, to name a few. Why these men and others like them escaped retribution may well have something to do with what they all held in common: prominence, wealth, education, connections and, most importantly, the political savvy to keep their private thoughts to themselves, at least most of the time.[31]

Here, in fact, were some of the very same men, in the same offices, worrying about the same "growing disorders, violences and breaches of the Law" that so concerned the town a decade before the Revolution. Only now the stakes were higher and the outcome less predictable. Officially these men were among the leaders of Revolutionary New Haven. Privately many of them feared the war's outcome. Publicly they could do little more than hope their pleas and mandates would steer the town safely through the whirlwind of events in which they found themselves nearly helpless to control.[32]

In many respects the New Haven area came dangerously close to anarchy. Distrustful of authority and its ability to meet their needs, residents were quick to devise their own means of surviving the war on a daily basis. Oftentimes it would take the form of a blacklist against suspected neighbors. Yale students subjected their disaffected classmates to dunking, shunning and incessant harassment. Merchants suspected of price gouging were regularly boycotted and occasionally roughed up. Ezra Stiles resorted to the arbitrary dismissal of Yale students who were loyal to the Crown. Even the local civil and religious leaders partook in questionable practices of denying the uncommitted the right to fully partake in church services or to obtain their fair share of rationed commodities until they pledged their allegiance to the State of Connecticut, at least on paper.[33]

II

War forces difficult decisions that under any other circumstances would never be considered. In the face of staggering inflation, shortages and high unemployment, many New Haveners turned to the sea as privateers and smugglers. In the case of privateers, it seemed the golden opportunity of the war, a practice not merely sanctioned but encouraged by the State as a means of prosecuting the war and, if your luck held out, growing rich while doing it.[34] Many of New Haven's first citizens pooled their resources to outfit blockade runners and privateers, which captured and towed into New Haven harbor no fewer than 38 ships during the course of the Revolution. The ships were condemned as prizes and sold at auction with the State keeping half the revenue and the remainder divided among the crew and privateer's owners.[35]

Reproduction of a typical 18th-century longboat, which could vary in length and accommodate up to 30 passengers, including oarsmen. Vessels such as these were commonly employed by partisan raiders in both Connecticut and New York.

But the spoils of war were not solely the domain of the rich. Whaleboats on either side of the Sound inflicted the most damage during the Revolution. Fishermen by day and raiders by night, patriots and Loyalists alike made frequent incursions against one another. If you had the intestinal fortitude, a trusty musket and a strong back, the enemy and their possessions were within easy grasp.

One such celebrated raid took place on Sag Harbor in May 1777. Originating out of New Haven, over 300 men under the command of Return J. Meigs were ferried across the Sound in darkness to conduct what remains one of the most successful attacks of the Revolution. After returning to New Haven the next day, private Elnathan Jennings proudly boasted that the Connecticut troops killed six of the enemy, burned 12 ships, and captured 90 prisoners without the loss of a single man. While the prisoners were paraded through town on their way to prison, caution played the better part of valor for Jennings, who changed his name in fear of reprisal for taking part in the raid.[36]

Such fears were not unwarranted. In 1780, seven Loyalists from Long Island rowed across the Sound to Oyster Point on the West Haven – New Haven line and made their way to Bethany and the home of

Ebenezer Dayton, New Haven's most successful privateer. They bound and gagged Dayton's wife and children and stole, according to Dayton, at least £430 in gold and silver, destroying everything else they could not carry. Dayton staged a counter raid, brought the seven men back to Connecticut, where they were imprisoned but then escaped to Canada.[37]

While privateers were used effectively for military, para-military and espionage missions, including Nathan Hale's ill-fated efforts, the vast majority of sorties were staged for the expressed purpose of revenge, kidnapping hostages as bargaining chips in prisoner exchanges or for pure profit.[38]

During the Americans' helter-skelter evacuation of Long Island in the summer of 1776, New Haven helped to transport thousands of troops and refugees to safety. Inevitably there were abuses and a share of horror stories involving New Haveners. The public records are checkered with all too many references of men, women and entire families being subjected to ill treatment, robbery and murder by those who were supposedly there to help them. Caleb Brewster and John Grinnel admitted to 23 such robberies, while the young Loyalist Prudence Punderson complained bitterly in 1779 that the incidence of "Horrid stealing" was so great even the house she lived in would have been taken "were not the strength of sampson wanting." Frustrated and angered that her family and many others like them were being victimized by marauding bands on both sides, she dejectedly described her situation as "the shattered remains of prosperity."[39]

Desperate times and the prospect of personal gain led many New Haveners to dabble in illicit trade. Some townsmen, like Benjamin Prescott, were unlucky enough to be caught and convicted of smuggling. Sentenced to 15 months at Newgate Prison in Granby, he petitioned the State for leniency, offering to pay the costs of his prosecution, jailing and promised to leave Connecticut immediately. With the prison already bursting at the seams, his offer was accepted and he was given 10 days to leave.[40]

Captain Jesse Levenworth was more fortunate. A 1740 graduate of Yale College, Levenworth was an otherwise respectable New Haven citizen who had become deeply involved in smuggling during the war. Upon his apprehension he produced a special permit from the Continental Congress exempting him from prosecution, most likely due to his services as an American spy.[41]

Most luckless of all was Captain Soloman Phipps of West Haven. Phipps was bound for port with a suspicious cargo. Whether he actually intended to avoid the harbor patrol or not is unknown, but a warning shot was fired from Black Rock Fort for him to heave to. Unfortunately, the gunner's aim proved too low and the shot tore away Phipps's jaw.[42]

Phipps was one of the unlucky few. During the course of the war countless citizens of every stripe were involved in smuggling and privateering. But investigations into illicit trade never went far before the name of a friend or even the investigators themselves were brought into question. Even Governor Trumbull was suspected of having an occasional hand in the illicit business.[43]

Eventually the participants themselves grew sick of it. West Haven's Thomas Painter had been ripe for adventure at the beginning of the war and eagerly participated in a number of raiding expeditions. By 1780 he could not bring himself to go on another. "After recollecting how I had seen the Boats go from the Privateer to which I belonged, on board of Neutral Vessels, and plunder them under false colors," Painter said, "I came to the conclusion that Privateering was nothing better than Highway Robbery...."[44]

Painter's fellow townsmen apparently agreed with him. Sickened by the near endless horror tales of murder and plunder in Long Island Sound, New Haveners reacted in the only way they knew worked — through the swift administration of vigilante justice. Their target was no less than New Haven's most celebrated privateer, Ebenezer Dayton. A refugee from Coram, Long Island, Dayton came to New Haven in 1776 and soon proved adept at the business of profiteering.

Within six months he brought 17 prizes into New Haven harbor. One of the most feared and notorious guerillas of the Revolution, Dayton plundered, terrorized, kidnapped and murdered seemingly anyone who got in his way. But it was his rumored double dealings with the British that finally proved his undoing in 1782.[45]

At an unauthorized town meeting held in early December of that year, New Haveners vowed to destroy all vessels believed to be involved in the illicit trade. Dayton's name came up immediately as someone who frequently "prostituted his commission" for personal gain. The townspeople took a vote and decided "that Capt. Dayton's Boat [be taken] into the public market place of this town, in open light, and there destroy her by fire; and if any prosecution should arrive thereupon, we agree to be at equal expense."[46]

Soon after the war Dayton resurfaced on Long Island as a travelling merchant, though his ethics remained true to form. While visiting East Hampton, he contracted the measles and refused to stay in quarantine. Instead, he walked into a crowded church, whereupon the panicked congregation threw him out and threatened his life. He quickly left town, but was met by several young men who beat him severely, tied him to a rail then dunked him. Dayton sued the boys' parents and his lawyer, Aaron Burr, won damages of $1,000 for the miscreant. Tragically, several of the townspeople contracted measles from the church episode and died from what has ever since been called the Dayton Measles.[47]

As Dayton's boat burned that cold December morning in 1782, New Haveners stood around its smouldering ashes, their private thoughts known only to themselves. One thing was certain. They were sick of the plundering, destruction and senseless killing. The enemy had come to their shores on at least six occasions, resulting in millions of dollars in damages, lost property and many lives. The war had taught them a hard-wrought lesson. "We have met the enemy and they are us."[48]

CHAPTER TEN

The War Comes Home

By 1779 the American Revolution had been fought to a stalemate. With the major Southern campaigns yet to unfold and a prolonged chess match quality to the Northern theatre, Sir Henry Clinton pondered his fate as commander of British forces in America and did not like what he saw. The war had become a British quagmire and the ruination of military careers. Clinton was not about to become another victim. He demanded more troops or he would resign.[1]

The Home Government rejected that threat completely. Lord George Germain, Secretary of State for the American Colonies, promised more troops and more. He devised the sketch of a plan that he artfully forced Clinton to execute. For Germain, who earned notoriety then disgrace as a military officer who ultimately ignored the orders of his superior during the Seven Years War, victory in America hinged on one overriding strategy: draw Washington's army into a decisive battle for America. With Washington defeated, Germain was convinced that the majority of colonists would see their folly and end their insurrection. And it would all begin with a series of assaults on Chesapeake Bay, up the Hudson River, and along the Connecticut coastline.[2]

Since the beginning of the war, Connecticut privateers proved themselves to be more than just an annoyance. Their constant raids along Long Island and success in ferrying provisions and capturing merchant supply ships bound for New York seriously hindered the British war machine. A series of lightening strikes against Portsmouth and

General Sir Henry Clinton (1730 - 1795)
served as the commander-in-chief of British
forces from 1778 -1782.

Courtesy Museum of Ventura County

Norfolk, Virginia, Connecticut's coastal ports and rebel works at Stony Creek and Verplank's Point would reap multiple rewards, Germain argued. It would put an end to the privateers and snuff out foreign trade, regain control of Loyalist-leaning western Connecticut and possibly even draw Washington's forces into the open field of battle.[3]

Clinton cared little for London's meddling, but he followed orders. After putting his own touches to the strategy with the help of Sir George Collier, senior British naval commander in America and Major General William Tryon, former royal governor of New York, Clinton dispatched General Edward Matthew with 2,500 troops to destroy Portsmouth and Norfolk, Virginia, in late April 1779.

Clinton himself directed the next leg of the strategy. Leading a force of approximately 8,000 troops up the Hudson, he captured Stony Creek and Verplanck's Point in June 1779. That placed the all-important West Point in jeopardy, forcing Washington back into New York to defend the highlands, just as Clinton expected. His trap was nearly set and only awaited the success of the Connecticut campaigns to fully bait the Continental Army.[4]

To execute the Connecticut attacks, Clinton tapped Major General William Tryon, a man he personally despised but begrudgingly recognized as a confidant of Lord Germain. A member of the famed First Guards ,Tryon, like Germain, was convinced that the Americans had been led astray by a few radicals. Once taught a hard lesson, the people of Connecticut and elsewhere would quickly return to their senses and their king.[5]

As devised by Clinton, Tryon and Collier, their plan called for rapid-fire raids against New London, New Haven, Milford, Fairfield and Norwalk. In each they would stay only long enough to deliver a powerful message, courtesy of the British army: submit or suffer the consequences.[6]

Armed with fresh intelligence from coastal surveys conducted by Captain Patrick Ferguson, which predicted light resistance and a warm reception, Tryon targeted New Haven as his first stop.[7]

Sir George Collier (1738 - 1795) served as British senior naval commander in support of Gen. William Tryon's failed campaign to draw Washington into Connecticut in the summer of 1779.

II

The shrill piping of a boatswain's whistle pierced the still morning air off Huntington Bay on July 3, 1779. All hands snapped to attention as Commodore Sir George Collier boarded his flagship, the 20-gun frigate *Camilla*. Collier wasted little time before issuing orders to get under way with the tides.[8]

Amid the bustle of sailors and soldiers preparing to get under sail, American spies surveyed the fleet from ashore and sent word to General Washington that the British were planning to invade Connecticut. Including Collier's flagship there were 48 ships of sail and troop transports in the armada. The 16-gun *Scorpion*, the two-masted schooner *Halifax*, the frigates *Greyhound*, *Virginia* and the row galley

Photo courtesy Freebase

Replica of the Rose, *a 20-gun frigate similar to Collier's flagship* Camilla *used in the 1779 raids along the Connecticut coast.*

Hussar were easy to identify. Less obvious were the 5,000 sailors, marines and troops crowded above and below decks in the sweltering summertime heat.[9]

Among those men were some of the most elite troops in the British army. They included the 54th Regiment of Foot, the 7th Royal and 23rd Welch Fusilers, detachments of Jägers from Landgraf and the famed British Third Guards, a company of the Royal Artillery and the King's American Regiment, commanded by Yale graduate Colonel Edmund Fanning, made up entirely of Loyalist troops. For these men, the anticipation of a short voyage did little to offset their near intolerable circumstances. The British navy was not known for its accommodations. Amid the heavy armaments and horse flesh, men jostled for breathing space. Clad in their traditional wool uniforms, the troops hoped for favorable winds and a quick voyage. They got neither. Progress was agonizingly slow as the fleet inched eastward on its way towards New Haven harbor in the dead winds of summer.[10]

Against the advancing British, West Haven was woefully ill-prepared. Normally proud of their seacoast, the war soured local residents on their precarious geography. Forming the western bank of Connecticut's second largest seaport, West Haven's miles of exposed

Built in 1776, and since reconstructed, Black Rock Fort is located on the eastern bank of New Haven harbor. During the British invasion of 1779, the fort was heavily bombarded by the Scorpion *and* Camilla *and its 19 defenders either escaped or were captured by the British under Major General William Tryon. When the British departed New Haven the following day, they torched the barracks.*

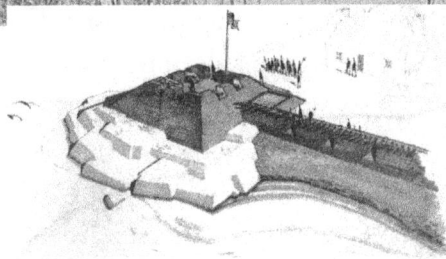

coastline became an immediate liability and the cause of much consternation during the war. It was sobering enough to realize Britain's obvious control of Long Island Sound. Worse still was the enigma of protecting the indefensible. There were simply too many vulnerable shore points to guard against local smugglers let alone a formidable invasion force.[11]

In response to West Haven's pleas for help over the years the state government offered little in the way of assistance or preparations. Connecticut was hard pressed to meet its quota of men, money and material. The Trumbull administration could offer no more than its empathy.

Meager compensation came in the way of Black Rock Fort. Built in 1776 on the eastern shore of New Haven, the fort had little success in discouraging smugglers and even less in warding off invaders. While capable of offering some measure of protection by day, it could do very little about nighttime raids against outlying regions such as West Haven.[12]

To compensate, mobile defenses were adopted for the outlying parishes. West Haveners constructed their share of small groundworks at a variety of strategic locations, including West Bridge, Oyster Point and Morris Cove. Each site was capable of receiving small carriage guns, which could be drawn up to any of the positions as circumstances warranted. Time and again, the batteries failed in their intended purpose. As West Haven's Thomas Painter noted, quasi-military raids were so commonplace, the limited number of cannon

James Hillhouse (1754 - 1832) at the time of the invasion, went on to an illustrious career as a successful businessman and politician, serving as both a Congressman and Senator.

rarely proved to be in the right place at the right time. One such occasion served to illustrate the obvious. Without the benefit of the shore battery, Painter was nearly killed when he found himself alone in repelling a band of Long Island Loyalists intent on setting the town's warehouse district on fire in the dead of night.[13]

To assist in the defense of New Haven harbor, whale boats were eventually employed off coastal waters. Their purpose was to stem the chronic attacks from across the Sound and put an end to the everyday trafficking of smugglers. But in many cases, even the patrollers made good on their opportunity to earn a few extra shillings by trading with the enemy. Realizing such temptations, the State promised half of all bounty to its captors. Even then such measures proved ineffective. On

any given night poachers could be found bartering contraband over a cup of ale at Clark's Tavern in West Haven near Oyster River.[14]

While such activities were widespread, they posed no real physical threat to the townspeople. Much more disturbing was the occasional presence of a British fleet offshore. If enemy vessels were sighted, coast watchers alerted the village by means of a small field gun located at Morris Cove.

Prior to 1779, passing British ships did just that. The roar of the alarm gun was so frequent it became a nuisance. In some instances the curious even gathered along the shoreline to witness the spectacle of 100 ships under full sail, as in the case of a passing British fleet on its way to the destruction of Newport, Rhode Island, in 1778.

Residents also attended the infrequent exchange of prisoners in hopes that a kinsman might be among those released.[15] With such a ubiquitous British presence in the Sound, West Haveners watched uneasily as the war sailed them by. It was never far from their thoughts that one day might be their turn. Unbeknownst to them, recent shifts in British war policy were about to make those fears a reality.[16]

www.birthofamerica.com

III

July 4, 1779 was a Sunday. Because the three-year-old holiday fell on the Sabbath, the parish of West Haven celebrated the event with day-long church services. Led by their minister, the Reverend Mr. Noah Williston, the Congregationalists offered up prayers in the name of the Continental Congress and the cause of its struggling army

As major-general of provincial forces, William Tryon's "total war" strategy against civilians earned the enmity of General Clinton, who refused Tryon any future significant commands.

Artist's depiction of British fleet disembarking troops via longboats. In the early morning hours of July 5, 1779, a similar scene greeted West Haven residents as some 2,700 troops landed at West Haven and East Haven.

encamped in neighboring New York. No record remains of how Christ Church commemorated the holiday. Odds are high that its communicants held services at their homes as they had most Sundays since the start of the war.

But this particular July Sunday would be different. Most of the town looked forward to Monday and New Haven's first public parade in celebration of Independence Day. Come Sunday night, the New Haven meeting house was bursting with residents anxious to hear the line of march and activities planned for the following morning. The Governor's Foot Guard would step off the parade and Colonel Hezekiah Sabin and Captain James Hillhouse would serve as grand marshals. It would certainly be a day to remember, if for reasons never imagined on that sultry summer night.[17]

Some West Haveners were unable to attend the public meeting. As they patrolled the deserted shoreline, they took solace in what little breeze

Top view depicts Savin Rock as it appeared at the time of the British invasion. Above is the same area as it looked in the 19th century as a resort destination, while at right is a present-day aerial view of the same area.

Courtesy Google Earth

there was on a sweltering July night. As they looked out over the placid Sound, they gave little thought to reports of a British fleet on the move. Like so many times before, they thought, the ships would pass them by.

At least one observer grew anxious over the easterly course of the British that weekend. From his encampment in New York, General David Wooster got word of the British plans and penned an ominous note to his friends in New Haven warning of a pending attack. He pleaded that the town be evacuated and its defenses be put in a state of high alert. Tragically, General Wooster's warning went unheeded.[18]

Among those standing watch along West Haven's shoreline that July 4th night was 20-year-old Thomas Painter, then a member of Lieutenant Aziel Kimberly's artillery company. Stationed at the shore front home of Josiah Platt, Painter grew concerned on hearing that a British fleet was sighted off Stratford and was continuing in an easterly direction close to shore. Persuading a few friends to accompany him, Painter extended his patrol to Clark's Point, where the small group could better view the southwesterly approach to West Haven. For two hours they waited in the early morning darkness. Shortly before 2 a.m., a dark cloud of canvas slowly sailed into view. Then another and another, until it seemed the whole Sound was full of sails. The British fleet was making its way east ever so slowly close to shore. Running along the coastline to keep pace, Painter watched anxiously as the ships maneuvered and dropped anchor off Old Field shore not far from Savin Rock.[19]

The British were deliberate in their actions. Not only were they familiar with Long Island Sound, but they possessed detailed information on landing sites, maps and defenses courtesy of local sympathizers. Originally, Major General William Tryon considered beginning his attack at dawn against East Haven's Black Rock Fort, then proceed through New Haven and on to West Haven. But Tryon revised his plans following a visit from West Haven's Prindle brothers, Stephen and Joseph, who assured the general that defenses were weak on both sides of the harbor. The two young men were Loyalists and members of Christ Church. Armed with new intelligence that verified what Ferguson supplied earlier, Tryon opted to launch a coordinated attack on both sides of the harbor simultaneously.[20]

While the British made ready for landing, young Painter first fired the alarm gun then ran door to door to alert residents of the impending attack. "But they were extremely incredulous, and not disposed to believe there was much danger," Painter later said.[21]

As dawn broke over Long Island Sound, Painter's warnings needed

The Reverend Ezra Stiles drew the above map to document the course of New Haven's invasion. Stiles was president of Yale College, who watched the invasion unfold from the steeple of the college chapel.

no explanation. Word spread quickly of what lay off shore. Many residents hastily packed what they could carry and made off to safety. Others frantically buried their valuables, hid them in chimneys and wells or simply abandoned them altogether. A few grabbed their muskets and hurried towards the Old Field shore.

Monday morning brought brilliant sunshine and the promise of a stifling hot summer's day. From aboard the *Camilla*, the roar of a solitary signal cannon echoed its own promise that the Revolutionary War was about to visit West Haven firsthand. It was 4:00 a.m.·[22]

"Instantly a string of boats was seen dropping astern of every transport ship full of soldiers and pulled directly for the shore," Painter recalled. Even from nearly five miles away, the Reverend Ezra Stiles, armed with his spyglass in the Yale Chapel tower, could see dozens of boats pulling towards West Haven's Old Field.[23]

From Painter's vantage point, the sight sent chills down the 20-year-old's back. But he stayed put. As the British drew closer to shore, Painter and a few other brazen villagers leveled their muskets and fired into the crowded boats. They did not wait to survey the damage. Hopelessly outnumbered, the defenders ran for their lives amid heavy return fire. Within minutes the royal marines secured a beach head at Old Field and the remaining troops came ashore unmolested.[24]

The above artist's depiction illustrates a typical whaleboat with six seamen and approximately 10 troops aboard. Testimony to the skill of British seamen, the transports ferried 1,500 men, horses, and four canon to the West Haven shore in approximately two hours.

Within two hours time, 1,500 troops were lined up on the West Haven shore front. Under the command of Brigadier General George Garth of the British Guards, the three divisions included detachments of the Third Guards, the Royal Fusileers, the 54th Regiment of Foot, a detachment of Jägers, the King's American Regiment, composed of Loyalist troops, and four field pieces from the Royal Artillery. [25]

On the village green the steeple bell rang out incessantly. Only a few dozen men answered the call. Some had either already joined the defenders, others fled and still more were unwilling to leave their homes unprotected. With so few troops at hand, Lieutenant Aziel Kimberly realized the foolhardiness of opposing the invaders outright. Instead, he deployed his men along the hillsides of what is now Savin Avenue to take advantage of the woods and elevated position in hopes of harassing the advance guard. They did not have long to wait to test their mettle.

By 6:00 a.m., the British were on the march. Guided by three New Haveners-turned-invaders, the troops proceeded up Savin Avenue in three divisions. Fully aware of the colonial preference for ambush, skirmishers and light infantry flankers from the Guards were deployed alongside the main force in hopes of flushing the rebels out into the open. Already stifling hot and humid, the troopers had difficulty keeping their formations tight. Wide gaps appeared between divisions and an occasional shot rang out, felling a trooper. When the advance guard trudged up the hillsides to investigate, the defenders had already moved on in what proved to be a deadly cat-and-mouse game all the way to the West Haven Green.[26]

What the British early discovered in that short march of a mile was the opportunity for plunder. Despite strict orders against the practice and harsh punishments awaiting offenders, rank-and-file troopers had grown accustomed to taking whatever they wanted — by force if necessary. In their search for hidden valuables, whatever they could not easily carry off they often destroyed. In letters home throughout the war British officers shared their despair over their troops' boorish and savage behavior. Their march through West Haven proved no exception. Troops pillaged the Thomas and Kimberly homes, with one solider reportedly thrusting his bayonet through the Kimberly family bible. Another wretched a gold ring from the finger of a local housewife. Furious, she ran after the culprit and encountered Adjutant William Campbell of the Third Guards. After listening to her complaint, the Scotsman told the woman if she could identify the thief he would have the man arrested. With the troops massing on the Green and hundreds of soldiers breaking ranks in search of rebels, valuables and mischief, Campbell had his hands full to keep order.[27]

Oblivious to the commotion, General Garth was pleased with his army's progress. He was two hours ahead of General Tryon's landing at East Haven. Time enough, he thought, to rest his troops and impose upon the Gideon Kimberly family to prepare breakfast for his staff.[28]

As the general and his officers took leave of the hot July sun, most of the troopers sought refuge from the heat on the Green. Others amused themselves by harassing the locals. As one such band of soldiers approached the parsonage of the First Congregational Church, they spied the Reverend Mr. Noah Williston, arms full of church documents, running out the back door. Local Tories reportedly egged the soldiers on. Threats were issued for the clergyman to stop, but he ran all the harder. With troopers in hot pursuit, Williston attempted to scale a stone wall only to catch his foot, breaking his leg. Surrounding the fallen minister, the soldiers taunted the clergyman with bayonets and threats of hanging. Hearing the commotion, Adjutant Campbell witnessed what was happening and quickly put an end to his troops' malicious taunting. "We make war on soldiers, not civilians," he reportedly said, then ordered the men to assist the minister back to the parsonage. Campbell then summoned the regimental surgeon to set the clergyman's leg.[29]

Following his brush with death, Williston, at the time a widowed father of four, is said to spent the rest of the day singing praises to the

Lord as the happiest day of his life. Ironically, his eldest son, Payson, was just then marching to meet the British at Milford Hill at the very same time of his father's fortuitous rescue by the Adjutant.[30]

A career solider who had worked himself up through the ranks, Campbell was a seasoned veteran of war. He first arrived in America in August 1776 as sergeant major of a detachment of Third Guards. He had seen extensive action at the Battles of Long Island, Harlem, White Plains, Brandywine, Germantown, Valley Forge and Monmouth Courthouse, among many others engagements. His unit had been so actively engaged in the war that its officers' corps was nearly depleted by 1777. That provided the sergeant major with the opportunity to become acting Adjutant of the 2nd Battalion in August of 1777. As Adjutant, he served as the principal aide to the commanding officer and was in charge of administration, organization and troop discipline. In time of battle, he was also responsible for commanding the flanking guards in the field.[31]

Likely in this late thirties, Campbell was a Highlander thought to have been a native of the Fort William, Scotland area. Married with children of his own, Campbell's act of mercy towards the Reverend Mr. Williston may have earned him a unique place in American history, but it came instinctively. Campbell's own immediate family, for example,

Portrait of Col. Thomas Dowdeswell of the British Guards, painted by Joseph Blackburn in 1777, depicts the style of uniform likely worn by Adjutant William Campbell. Notice the cockaded hat, gaitered trousers and shortened field jacket adopted for fighting in heavily wooded North America.

www.military-historians.org

Photo courtesy Brian Page

Located at the junction of Davenport, Congress and Columbus avenues, Defenders Monument, by James E. Kelly, was erected in 1911 in recognition of Captain Bradley's artillery company and its defense of the West Bridge.

had been subjected to one of the most barbaric episodes of British military abuse following the Battle of Culloden in 1746. After their surrender, hundreds of unarmed clansmen and civilians were senselessly slaughtered by the British. Memories of that tragedy were seared into the hearts and minds of all Highlander families, especially those of the first generation. "For William, therefore, to attack civilians would have been an abhorrence above all others and, in respecting civilians, he would have been very consciously honouring the family and community from which he sprang and whose values he cherished."[32]

Equally important in explaining Campbell's actions on that July 5 morning was his military breeding. He was an officer in the most elite unit of the British army. As the king's personal bodyguards, the Foot Guards represented not only the best and brightest but also the most disciplined of his majesty's troops.[33]

Campbell also had years of practical experience in dealing with civilians. Lacking an official police department, London officials often called on the Foot Guards to handle the city's all-too-frequent mobs, and Campbell undoubtedly took part in many of those assignments. Finally, the Guards were famous for their legendary tolerance — even earning an official commendation from King George III who cited their admirable restraint in quelling the infamous Wilkes Riots of 1768. By virtue of his training and his heritage, Campbell's actions on behalf of an unarmed civilian simply came naturally.[34]

IV

By 10:00 a.m. the roar of distant cannon fire signaled the beginning of General Tryon's assault on Black Rock Fort. As the two armies planned to rendezvous in New Haven by noon, Garth ordered his troops to fall in and resume their line of march.[35]

As the British advance guard moved north towards Allingtown, Aziel Kimberly's militia unit, now supported by a contingent of Yale students and a detachment of the Governor's Foot Guard, lay in ambush along the left flank. A volley was fired and the British left flank fell back. Stirred on by their momentary success, the militiamen chased the stunned troopers the length of several fields until they met up with the main invading army. "It was now our turn to run," related one combatant, "and run we did, for our lives."[36]

Some defenders were not so fortunate. While many were wounded by gunfire, they were then bayoneted or clubbed to death by the irate troops. At the intersection of the Old Post Road and Milford Hill

Col. Aaron Burr was visiting relatives in New Haven at the time of the British invasion and helped in its defense.

New Haven Register, March 22, 1981

Unknown artist's rendering of General Tryon's troops confronting American defenders near the Amos Morris House in East Haven. The battle was brief but brutal, as the Morris home, seen here in the upper left, was burned to the ground by the British.

Colonel Sabin, Captain James Hillhouse and Col. Aaron Burr (who would later become Vice President of the United States) deployed 150 colonials in a defensive position behind trees and a stone wall along the crest of the 142-foot hill. Another contingent of militia under Captain Bradley was busily peppering the British from the east bank of the West River, where they played their two cannon with deadly effect on the open marshland in front of them. Still more militiamen were frantically tearing up the West River bridge itself to prevent a British crossing.[37]

Outmanned and poorly trained by British standards, the defenders were considered no match for the seasoned troops bearing down on their position. An hour of intense fighting and heavy casualties proved otherwise. Under the direction of the veteran Col. Burr, the defenders on the left flank succeeded in stalling an army ten times their number. And what remained of the West Bridge was just too well defended by

Bradley's cannon. After several unsuccessful British sallies and a cannonade of their own, General Garth abandoned his original plans for an alternative route. The troops would proceed up Forest Road to the Derby Pike and Thompson Bridge adding 3.5 miles to a march that already had cost them dearly.[38]

The outcome of the Battle of Allingtown was never in doubt. Eventually outflanked the defenders were forced to retreat, some running off into the woods towards what is now Orange and others up present-day Forest Road, where snipers continued to harass the British advance.

One such local defender was John Johnson, a 25-year-old West Havener whose family lived nearby.[39] According to the family's oral tradition, Johnson was among the 150 or so defenders facing the British advance guard as the troops left the West Haven Green. By the time Johnson and his comrades reached Milford Hill, Johnson had fallen behind, apparently from heat exhaustion. Close on his heels was a British flanking unit composed of the Third Guards. A fire fight soon erupted, and Johnson hunkered down behind a clump of bushes.

Seeing the flankers bogged down by the rebels, a mounted Brit-

Erected in 1891 in the vicinity of Campbell's death, the Adjutant William Campbell Memorial carries a simple inscription from Matthew 5:1-12 1: "Blessed Are The Merciful." Located on Prudden Street in West Haven the site is now owned and maintained by The West Haven Historical Society.

Photos by Peter J. Malia

133

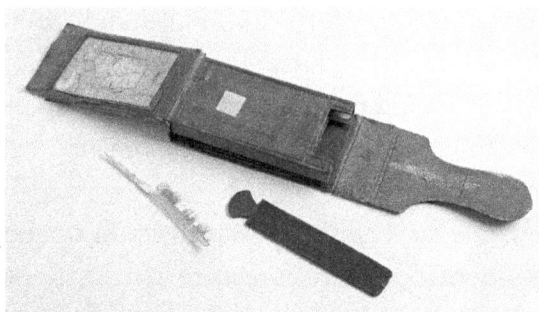

Remaining as testament to the Foot Guards' attention to personal appearance, Adjutant William Campbell's dressing case – complete with mirror, a combination comb/pick, Emory board, tooth powder and scissors – was first stolen then sold by Campbell's orderly to John Townshend of New Haven following the Adjutant's death. The Townshend family later donated the case to the New Haven Museum.

ish officer galloped up Milford Hill to rally his men and gain a better view of the colonial defenses across the West River, some three-quarters of a mile away. As the horseman approached, Johnson's friends alledgedly began to shout, "Watch out, John, he'll take you." Whereupon the panicked Johnson raised his musket and fired along with his friends. The officer slumped to the ground and the panic-stricken Johnson bolted into the woods.[40]

The wounded officer was carried to the nearest homestead by his aide. Though suffering a mortal chest wound, the dying British officer purportedly endeared himself to the local family, asking if they would send his plume, sash and watch to his wife. When he died soon after, his face was covered with kerchief bearing his initials. His body was later wrapped in a blanket, loaded in a sheep cart and was buried in a shallow grave not far from where he had first fallen. What few personal effects he had were stolen by his aide, and some were then sold to a local man, John Townshend. The dead solider's uniform was also taken by a Milford militiaman, who was said to have worn the Guardsman's tunic on subsequent celebrations of Independence Day. The dead officer's name was William Campbell — the very same Adjutant Campbell who saved the life of the village minister only a few hours earlier. To the end of his own life, John Johnson is said to have often wondered if it was his shot that actually fell Campbell. In telling the story to his family and friends, he would always end by saying, "and I fear it must have been I who killed him."[41]

For his act of kindness in a time of war, Campbell would later be honored by West Haveners, who named their main thoroughfare after the fallen British Adjutant in 1874, and dedicated a monument to his memory in 1891. Some of his personal effects are in the possession of The New Haven Museum. He remains the only known British invader so honored in American history.[42]

Yet another rebel sniper at Milford Hill was 51-year-old Reverend Mr. Naphthali Daggett, former president of Yale College and

professor of divinity. Cheered on by his students as he past West Bridge, the professor ended up on Milford Hill, fired to no effect, and soon found himself surrounded by enraged British troops.

"What did you fire upon us for?," demanded one of his captors. "Because it is the exercise of war," Daggett answered. Infuriated, the trooper attempted to bayonet the minister, but Daggett deflected his thrust, only to be slashed across the forehead by a second solider. "But what is a thousand times worse than all that has been related is the blows and bruises they gave me with the heavy barrels of their guns in the bowels by which I was knocked down once or more and almost deprived of life," Daggett later testified. Fortunately for Daggett, one of his for-

The Reverend Mister Naphthali Daggett (1727-1780) was a graduate of Yale and its sixth president. Daggett left a compelling deposition of his ill treatment at the hands of the British that appeared in the September 4, 1779 Pennsylvania Packet, *among other papers.*

mer students, Lt. Col. Fanning, interceded on his behalf. His life spared, Daggett was paraded into New Haven at the head of the British army, barefoot, bleeding and humiliated.[42]

The militia under Hillhouse and Burr, meanwhile, continued its harassing fire on the British march to Westville. A British sortie sent to destroy a local powder mill ended in disaster for the invaders when they met up with a superior colonial force. A few soldiers were killed outright and several others were taken prisoner.[43]

Still more sharp fighting awaited the British at Ditch Corner, near where Whalley, Goffe and Dixwell avenues now intersect. From as far off as Bethany, Amity, Cheshire and Guilford, the militia grew stronger by the hour. Sporadic firing stalemated the contest until the British finally rushed forward in a bayonet charge that scattered the defenders.[44]

Fighting in East Haven proved more methodical and damaging. General William Tryon's troops made quick work of the defenders at Black Rock Fort, then busied themselves looking for livestock and valuables to steal, burning six homes along the way. In order to secure their safe evacuation, the troops were ordered to capture Neck Bridge over the Mill River. But resistance proved stiff, and the British soon lost both their advantage and the bridge. Seemingly insignificant at the time, the Neck Bridge would soon play an important role in the fate of New Haven.[45]

It was nearly 12:45 p.m. when General Garth's troops finally trudged onto the New Haven Green. Their eight-mile detour from West Haven had been marred by blistering heat and the incessant sniping of the rebel forces. No one knew the exact extent of their losses on their march from West Haven, but they were significant enough to leave General George Garth in a foul mood, believing the town "merits the flames."[46]

Waiting to consult with Tryon, Garth had the general's proclamation read aloud to New Haveners on the Green:

The War Comes Home

The ungenerous and wanton insurrection against the sovereignty of Great Britain, into which this colony has been deluded by the artifices of designing men, for private purposes, might well justify in you every fear which conscious guilt could form, respecting the intentions of the present armament. Your town, your property, yourselves, lie within the grasp of the power whose forbearance you have ungenerously construed into fear; but whose lenity has persisted in its mild and noble efforts, even though branded with the most unworthy imputation.

The existence of a single habitation on your defenceless coast ought to be a subject of constant reproof to your ingratitude. Can the strength of your whole province cope with the force which might at any time be poured through every district in your country? You are conscious it cannot. Why, then, will you persist in a ruinous and ill-judged resistance? We hoped that you would recover from the frenzy which has distracted this unhappy country; and we believe the day to be near come when the greater part of this continent will begin to blush at their delusion. You who lie so much in our power afford that most striking monument of our mercy, and therefore ought to set the first example of returning to our allegiance.

Reflect on what gratitude requires of you; if that is insufficient to move you, attend to your own interest: we offer you a refuge against the distress which, you universally acknowledge, broods with increasing and intolerable weight over all your country.

Leaving you to consult with each other upon this invitation, we do now declare that whosoever shall be found, and remain in peace, at his usual place of residence, shall be shielded from any insult, either to his person or his property, excepting such as bear offices, either civil or military, under your present usurped government, of whom it will be further required, that they shall give proofs of their penitence and voluntary submission; and they shall then partake of the like immunity.

Those whose folly and obstinacy may slight this favorable warning must take notice that they are not to expect a continuance of that lenity which their inveteracy would now render unblamable.

The formalities over, Garth's soldiers now swarmed the central part of town in search of food, drink and valuables. Their discovery of New Haven's ample supply of West Indian rum, conveniently left out in open sight to placate the troops in hopes that they would spare the town, only made matters worse. Barrels of rum were rolled into the streets and what was not drunk outright was loaded into carts to be taken as booty.[47] Fortified by too much rum and fueled by the summer's intense heat, troopers smashed their way into stores and homes. One old man was murdered in his sitting room for making a derisive comment to the intruders and another was shot down in his doorway. A deranged man unable to answer his interrogators had his tongue cut out with a bayonet. Women were assaulted and at least two were raped. As the afternoon wore on into evening, military regimen gave way to drunken reverie. Sailors from the fleet now attempted to reach shore and partake in the looting, but an increasingly worried Garth ordered them back. All the while contingents of the Connecticut militia streamed in towards New Haven hoping to cut off Garth's escape route.[48]

Initially, Garth considered naval reinforcements to capture the Neck Bridge from the rebels. The British fleet "lay anchored the whole length of the bay," wrote Captain Thompson of the local militia, "with springs on their cables and guns run out on both sides ready to belch forth fire and destruction as soon as the expected order should be given to fire on the town."[49]

That order never came. Garth informed Tryon that his troops were exhausted and a fair share of them were now thoroughly drunk. With his back to the sea and his advantage gone, Garth abandoned his plans to burn the town. Instead, he was forced to use his ploy of sparing New Haven as a bargaining chip to ensure his troops' safe departure.[50]

The terms were plain enough: Garth would spare New Haven on condition that his troops would be allowed to depart unmolested. Heated debate among the colonial militia led to a be-

Copy of William Tryon's address read at New Haven on July 5, 1779.

grudging acceptance of British terms. Silently, the militia initially stood by as the invaders began their evacuation in the early hours of July 6, four Loyalist families and 22 local prisoners among them.[51]

It proved to be a ridiculous affair. Soldiers reportedly staggered drunkenly in their lines to the waiting transports. Others, unable even to walk, were brought to the wharf piled atop one another in carts and wheelbarrows. Some were even left behind.[52]

Throughout the day, the transports ferried soldiers back to their ships, some laden down with stolen items, while others struggled with six field pieces and a number of cattle. With the bulk of his army now out of harm's way, Tryon ordered the 54th Regiment to destroy six stores and seven moored vessels suspected of being privateers. Amid the flames and thick smoke of the burning wharf, the British rear guard moved to Black Rock Fort under the protective fire of the *Hussar*. Intermittent skirmishing between the invaders and a growing number of militia broke out in the early afternoon. The Americans did what they could, but the British held the high ground. By 4:00 p.m. the last of the British troops finally retreated, but not before torching the fort's barracks and the fleet firing a cannonade into its works as one final act of defiance.[53]

As the British fleet sailed off to Long Island before staging even more devastating raids against Fairfield and Norwalk, their strategy had already failed them. Although they commandeered New Haven for a few terror-stricken hours, they paid a high price for their brief occupation of a town they intended to destroy but eventually could not. British casualties were also unexpectedly high with 44 killed or missing in action and an equal number wounded. Patriot losses totaled 27 killed or captured and 17 wounded.[54]

More importantly, the British failed to lure Washington's army into Connecticut and the decisive showdown they so much desired. Ten days after the attack, Continental troops recaptured Stony Point, and Washington regained lost ground in the strategic Hudson River Valley. About the only thing Tryon's invasion accomplished was to ruin that officer's career and create new enemies among those who had been previously uncommitted.[55]

By July 7 even the staunchest supporters of the king felt betrayed. Whether they had been timid Whigs or vocal Loyalists, both suffered indiscriminate and extensive property damage, especially in West Haven. One day of war had done wonders for the cause of American independence.[56] Even those New Haveners who had refused to oppose the British were favorably influenced by the demeanor of their Patriot neighbors. Many Tories feared that the depredations of the British would bear heavily on their subsequent treatment by the town.[57] Yet, no vendetta followed.

Instead, New Haveners adopted a lenient policy towards dissenters, allowing them to escape punishment on the condition that they abide by the law in the future.[58] If New Haveners were quick to treat political dissenters with moderation, they did so out of a desire to keep them as productive citizens. Britain's ill-advised policy of indiscriminate violence only made their task of reorganizing a once divided society that much easier.

V

Although the invasion of 1779 was the largest and wrought the heaviest financial damages on West Haven (state examiners estimated damages at £24,890, or nearly $5.4 million in 2009 currency),[59] it was by no means the most murderous. Especially as the war's major battles moved to the southern colonies, Long Island Loyalist marauders continued to stage raids on the village in order to keep the threat of invasion fresh in the villagers' minds.

One such attack took place on February 2, 1781. While the marauders limited their activities to the immediate shore front, they battled off the few coast watchers on duty, set fire to Deacon Platt's home, and ransacked several other residences before manning their whale boats to engage the skeleton crew of Black Rock Fort. In this latter skirmish, they were not nearly as successful as they had been in West Haven. Neighboring militia units flocked to the fort and the would-be invaders were quickly repelled.[60]

A more deadly incursion seized the village on August 20, 1781. Again under cover of night, five enemy ships anchored off Old Field shore. Within minutes, several companies of British troops were landed and sporadic gunfire shattered the night.[61]

The outcome was predictable, as the dozen or so defenders were soon overpowered. Throughout the small hours of the morning, the British stormed through West Haven, abducting cattle, horses and hostages.

By dawn, the troops quit the village, taking with them 17 prisoners and leaving behind three dead and a number of West Haven homes ransacked. Adding to the tragedy, many of the prisoners were later downed off Stratford Point when their ship sunk in a storm.[62]

Only two weeks separated the August attack from Benedict Arnold's return to New Haven. Now a British general at the head of a combined force of 1,732 British regulars, German mercenaries and Loyalists, Arnold intended to deliver a crippling blow to the state's economy by destroying Connecticut's two largest ports.

His initial attack on New London on September 4th proved devastating. By the time Arnold's troops departed with the midday tide on the 6th, New London was in flames. At Fort Griswold Arnold's troops earned a lasting reputation for infamy. During a pitched battle, a stray ball cut the fort's lanyard, lowering the American colors. Believing the defenders were surrendering, the invaders rushed forward only to be mowed down by the Americans. Infuriated, the British forces stormed the fort again, this time breaking through its defenses. A massacre ensued. Of the 140 Americans within the fort, 88 were killed outright and 35 more were seriously wounded. Arnold's losses were also extraordinarily high, with one in four either killed or wounded in what proved to be one of the most vicious battles of the war.[63]

But Arnold was not yet finished. As his flotilla made its way back towards New York, he gave orders to anchor off West Haven intending to deliver a similarly destructive blow to his hometown. By that time word had already spread of New London's destruction. Responding to a general alarm issued the previous night, over 2,000 militiamen lined West Haven's coast ready to defend the village.[64]

If nothing else, Arnold's depleted forces proved persistent. After several unsuccessful attempts to land, the invaders abandoned their plans and Arnold would never again set foot on Connecticut soil. Within six months, he moved his family to England, a traitor to a lost cause.

As the details of what happened in New London trickled back

to West Haven, the villagers felt all the more reason to boast of their run-in with Arnold. Only word of Washington's victory over Lord Cornwallis at Yorktown in October seemed to quiet their bravado. With Washington now moving his army northward to besiege New York, the war was drawing to a close.

Arnold's attack on West Haven proved to be the last major British assault on Connecticut. While peace negotiations dragged on for more than a year and a half, the war in the north was virtually over. West Haveners set about the task of rebuilding their village and tattered economy.

Like all of Connecticut, the war brought spiraling inflation, higher taxes and a dramatic decrease in the value of homes and property throughout the New Haven area.[65] In combination with widespread damages from four major invasions, West Haveners faced financial ruin. Once again they had no alternative but to approach the General Assembly for relief.

On the 13th of March 1782, a state committee met at West Haven to examine the extent of damages and interview claimants under oath. While the investigation resulted in a tax abatement of £30. 5s. 2d., together with a cash refund of £365 (approximately $80,000 in 2009 dollars), it did little to improve a distressed local economy.[66] Relief finally came from within the town itself.

Even while the state committee rounded the village of West Haven making note of its losses, New Haveners busily circulated a petition asking town officials to invite wealthy Tory families from New York City to settle in town. How many took the town up on the offer is unknown. Some unquestionably did and prospered as a result. More significantly was the offer of amnesty. It signaled New Haven's willingness to put the war behind it in the interest of future growth. Progressive, perhaps, but it was Yankee practicality that extended the welcome mat to one-time enemies. So long as they had not taken up arms against the American cause, all were welcomed to a New Haven and the promise of a new nation.

CHAPTER ELEVEN

From Saints to Citizens

On the morning of April 25, 1783, cannon fire echoed across the harbor from the New Haven Green. First one, then another and another loud report followed in rapid succession until 13 rounds boomed out across Long Island Sound on this early spring morning.

Throughout the war cannon signalled danger and a call to arms. Not this time. In a salute to the 13 states, the cannonade on this April morning roared in celebration. Only the evening before, New Haveners learned of the preliminary Peace of Paris, which would be signed formally in September, ending the American Revolution. The instruments of war now trumpeted the coming of peace and hopefully a return to prosperity.[1]

For seven years both had alluded West Haveners. By virtue of their proximity to Connecticut's second largest seaport, and offering an all-too-convenient beachhead for frequent invasion, West Haveners suffered more than their fair share on the front lines of the war. The loss of life and property staggered an already struggling village that was still doggedly pursuing independence from New Haven. Throughout the Revolution — and perhaps hastened by New Haven's inability to afford the village much in the way of real protection — some West Haveners joined other surrounding communities in agitating for their own township. Unlike its initial efforts to establish a separate parish in 1715, West Haven's request for town privileges was now favorably received by New Haven in 1785, which had itself been incorporated as one of five Connecticut municipalities only the previous year.[2]

West Haven was not alone in its bid for town status. As early as 1781 it joined a number of surrounding settlements seeking independence from New Haven, including Amity, Woodbridge, North Haven, East Haven and Hamden.

Facing a virtual flood of requests for independent status, the state legislature agreed to create the towns of East Haven, Hamden, Woodbridge, Amity and North Haven in 1785. West Haven's plea for self governance came at the end of the year, and it quickly fell victim to a combination of bad timing and loud protests from neighboring Milford.[3]

Never amenable to its own dismemberment, Milford had historically fought separatist efforts at every turn. By the 1720s a large tract of land some four miles from the Milford meetinghouse attracted settlers because of its fertile farmlands. Known as Byram Farms, North Milford and later Orange, these roughly 208 acres lay adjacent to West Haven and were a near constant source of bickering between the two settlements of Milford and New Haven over their legal boundaries.[4]

In an agrarian economy, productive farmland was highly valued as a source of produce and revenue. Livelihoods were at stake and residents of both villages proved on more than one occasion to be all too ready to come to blows over their respective property rights. Still, the residents of North Milford longed for their own parish apart from Milford proper, much like West Haveners did from New Haven, and for much the same reasons — they simply wanted to better accommodate their own needs and reduce the burden of traveling to and from Milford proper every Sunday morning.[5]

By 1750, the residents in North Milford finally won approval from the town for a seasonal school to avoid the eight-mile round trip in winter, but no such consideration was granted adult churchgoers, a decision likely based on the desire to avoid the sour experience of neighboring West Haven's early financial struggles.[6]

When talk of a separate West Haven again surfaced as early as 1781, North Milford was part of the proposal, hence Milford's immediate opposition to the idea. Not unlike New Haven's efforts to prevent the formation of the West Haven parish in 1715, Milford argued that the proposed new town would deprive it of productive land and residents, thus weakening the Milford politically and economically. The Connecticut General Assembly agreed. What would have been one of Connecticut's earliest incorporated towns in 1785 became the state's last, when the independent town of West Haven was finally created in 1921.[7]

Bad timing also played a role in West Haven's defeat for town status. Having already lost a substantial part of its tax-paying population to the newly incorporated towns, New Haven was not overly anxious to champion West Haven's cause for independence at the expense of its own welfare. At the very next meeting of the New Haven board of aldermen, for example, concerns over the town's finances became apparent. With far fewer residents New Haven's tax base had eroded to such low levels that the city collectors were being called in for a full accounting. Under such circumstances New Haveners had more urgent matters to address than dealing with their neighbors's concerns on the opposite banks of the West River. Not least among them was plunging headlong into the task of rebuilding their new city into a major seaport that would, they believed, benefit not only the village of West Haven but the entire state.[8]

To placate its outlying regions New Haven devised a peculiar governmental arrangement whereby West Haven fell within the jurisdiction of the township of New Haven, much as it always had. Meanwhile, the city proper, which roughly equated to modern-day New Haven, became something of a free trade zone within its own township. The mayor, aldermen, selectmen and a host of other officials thus coexisted with the traditional New England town meeting style of government in a complex, oftentimes redundant, system of a city government within a town until 1855.[9]

II

History's broad brush paints Connecticut as the land of steady habits. Even through the Revolution, there was a remarkably staid quality about the place and its people.[7]
Politically Connecticut fared far better than its neighbors in maintaining a sense of overall stability. Its colonial leadership weathered the Revolution almost to a man. From colony to state, Connecticut's transition lacked the high drama of its neighbors north and south. There were no royal charters to rewrite or occupying forces and royal governors to contend with. Once elected, Governor Jonathan Trumbull and associates remained steadfastly in place throughout the Revolution, the only colonial governor to have made that transition successfully.[10]

In many respects, Connecticut faced its political revolution in the 1760s, when the New Light radicals wrenched control of the colony from the conservative Old Light Congregationalists. Consequently, the war for independence in Connecticut was as much about preserving existing liberties as it was about obtaining new ones.[11]

Socially the war also loosened Connecticut's Puritan starched collar. It remained a church state in which Congregationalism continued as the established religion until 1818. But religious dissenters were now at least tolerated if still not openly accepted. Just how far Connecticut had come in allowing for dissenters was evidenced by Samuel Seabury's ordination as the first American bishop of the Anglican community in 1784. Nine years earlier he had been paraded through the streets of New Haven as a traitor before being thrown into prison.[12]

The Revolution had likewise done much to break down other

barriers in provincial Connecticut. War necessitated the exchange of men and ideas on an unprecedented scale. Inevitably it also helped to create a vision of democracy which, from Connecticut's perspective at least, conveniently embraced the Puritan ethos. Its gospel of good works had long determined an individual's worth in Connecticut. Now those same principles of "being good meant doing good" became the catalyst for building a new nation. In postwar New Haven, civic consciousness rose to heights that would have made even the town's original founders flushed with pride. And once again, the dream of molding New Haven into a commercial mecca seemed close at hand. It was an opportunity that New Haven's civic visionaries, men such as Roger Sherman, Ezra Stiles, James Hillhouse and West Haven's own Thomas Painter, seized with gusto.[13]

Within a year of the war's end, New Haven rivaled New London as the state's busiest seaport. Merchant traders, including Painter, vied for routes to the West Indies, the American coastal trade, across the Atlantic and even sailed to the Orient. Behind the three dozen or so ships registered to the Port of New Haven in 1785, there were dozens more who invested in these ventures in hopes of growing rich through international trade. Hundreds more New Haveners served aboard those ships or populated the ever-increasing ranks of shipwrights, tradesmen, dray men, farmers and the countless others needed to fuel the engines of New Haven's burgeoning commercial enterprises. In the two decades following the Revolution, New Haven was a city on the make in what would be its golden years as a seaport.[14]

Between 1784 and 1798, 57 merchant houses sprung up in New Haven carrying a huge selection of stock from around the world. Lumber, molasses, produce, tobacco and sugarcane choked the city's wharves and lined its streets. There were so many trade goods in the city, they required the passage of a municipal ordinance to kept the busy streets near the wharf clear for passage.

Amid the buzz of returning prosperity came improvements that dramatically altered the New Haven skyline, landscape and the attitudes of its people. Old roads were improved, new ones built and a number of streets were formally named by the new city government. A new long wharf jutted out nearly a half mile into Long Island Sound to accommodate the growing number of larger ships. The formation of a fire department, a legal association, medical society, board of health and one of the nation's first chambers of commerce soon followed to service the 3,500 residents and their more than 400 homes now located within the city's historic nine squares.[15]

Amid New Haven's resurgence, West Haven could not help but benefit by association. With ready markets for their produce and jobs to be had, West Haveners' call for independence dropped to a whisper in the frenzied race to accumulate wealth directly after the war.

But even more pressing issues loomed on the horizon to cloud any local calls for autonomy. By the mid-1780s the national government created under the Articles of Confederation was in disarray. War veterans demanding back pay marched on Philadelphia forcing the delegates to flee. Unauthorized to raise a national treasury, the Congress first stopped paying interest, then ceased payments altogether on the nation's war loans from France and Holland. Increasingly, states clashed over land, trade and money with no higher authority readily available to settle interstate disputes. Connecticut and New York nearly came to blows when the latter demanded the former to pay import taxes on products brought into the Empire State. Heavily involved in the coastal trade, New Haveners bitterly resented such strong-armed tactics employed by their bigger, more populous and successful neighbor to the south.[16]

They were not alone in their mounting grievances against the haphazard American confederacy. Across the new country, prosperity proved to be a fickle friend. While New Haven proper flourished, a good part of rural Connecticut and the country as a whole sunk deeper into debt. Merchandise was plentiful and credit

Courtesy of Yale University

The Reverend Ezra Stiles (1727 - 1792) served as president of Yale during the British invasion and was a noted scholar, patriot, and intrepid diarist.

was easy. But the monetary system itself was a labyrinth of currencies and promissory notes, hard money from Spain and England, treasury notes and soldiers' notes, which were based on interest-bearing certificates issued by the quartermaster general. And when notes came due, farmers throughout New England faced foreclosures or debtor's prison. There was a growing sense of resentment among the agrarian class that they were suffering under the constraints of economic bondage to the wealthy.[17]

The fact that only about 50 percent of the region's adult males were qualified to vote in 1784 did not help matters very much. Neither did the fact that about a third of New Haveners were former Loyalists with very conservative leanings, complained Yale President Ezra Stiles.[18]

The situation grew so desperate in Massachusetts that farmers led by Daniel Shays staged a rebellion that took the state militia months to quell and led more reflective men to call for a stronger, central government, including New Haven's leaders. Among the 13 independent states, there was growing uneasiness over the frequent arguments involving rights to waterways, land grants, taxes and state boundaries. Less than a decade old, the Confederation seemed destined to fall victim to squabbling sectionalism.[19]

Just how the Constitutional Convention came about and the

critically important role Roger Sherman played in shaping the U.S. Constitution are the subjects of voluminous literature. Needless to say, every state had cause to participate, if for very different reasons. Simply put, New Haveners wanted to preserve their bustling little seaport from the likes of New York and Boston, so they favored the protections that a strong central government could offer them. As merchants intent on collecting what was owed them, New Haven's leading citizens also favored the sound financial policies of hard money over paper currency, which would accompany the creation of a strong federal government.[20]

Then, too, there was the contentious issue of land. Based on its original charter, Connecticut laid claim to a vast portion of Pennsylvania known as the Wyoming Valley. Many Yankee settlers,

Artist's depiction of the Wyoming Valley Massacre that led to the deaths of more than 360 Connecticut settlers during the Revolution.

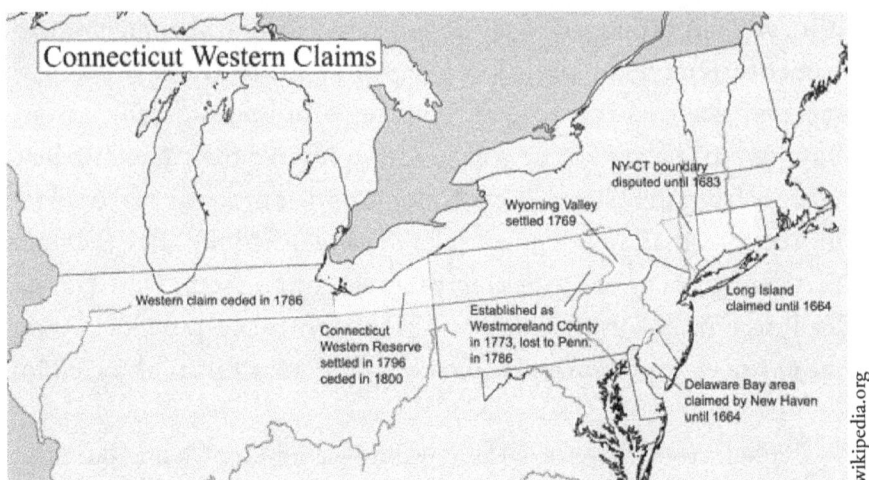

The above graphic portrays the extent of Connecticut's western land claims that reached West as far as Ohio and South to Delaware.

in fact, had moved there over the ensuing years, paid Connecticut taxes and were even represented in the Connecticut legislature. Pennsylvania vehemently protested Connecticut's apparent encroachment. A series of shooting wars broke out among the settlers through the years, culminating in what came to be known as the Wyoming Valley Massacre during the Revolution. Over 360 Connecticut men, women and children lost their lives to a combined force of British regulars, Pennsylvania Loyalists and Iroquois, who went on a rampage through the Valley in 1778 as much out of spite as loyalty to the Crown.[21]

Sporadic violence continued even after the war until Connecticut finally relinquished its claims to what it called Westmoreland County in exchange for three-and-a-half million acres of land known as the Western Reserve and located in present-day Ohio. To compensate those who suffered losses during the Revolution, Connecticut eventually carved out some 500,000 acres of the reserve located in present-day Erie and Hudson counties of Ohio. While several West

Haveners or their heirs were eligible for grants in what came to be called the Firelands, or Sufferers' Lands, more than 20 years passed before their claims were finally validated and the property secured for settlers. At the time there was the knotty problem of relocating Native Americans from the land. Some went willingly, but most were pushed out by force. By then many original victims who incurred losses in the Revolution were either dead or too old to relocate. Still more claimants simply sold their rights to land speculators at bargain-basement prices.

Speculators also purchased the remaining three million acres of the Western Reserve claimed by Connecticut. Forming The Connecticut Land Company, its 57 members funded the purchase through a series of personal bonds and mortgages held by the State and valued at $1.2 million in 1794. Interest from that transaction was placed into a special fund to support public education. As of 2005, the last time Connecticut reported on the fund, it stood at $9,197,637, and is widely regarded as one of the best investments ever made by the state.

Wise as that fund proved to be in the long run, many of New Haven's surrounding neighbors in the 1780s were more concerned by what a strong federal government and its promise of strict economic policies might portend. Unlike the City of New Haven and its mercantile free-market economy, these small towns and villages were agrarian communities that relied on easy credit and paper money. If either were put in jeopardy rural farmers and shoreline fisherman feared the worst.

But the dye was cast on passage of the Constitution. When state delegates were chosen to attend the ratifying convention in Hartford in January of 1788, New Haven sent two staunch Federalists. Most of the new towns created from the old New Haven voted against the Constitution, and some West Haveners likely did the same. Their protests were drowned out by a Federalist landslide.

In a vote of 128 to 40, Connecticut became the fifth state to ratify the U.S. Constitution.[22]

III

F ederalist domination of both state and local politics continued throughout the remainder of the 18th century. As New Haven grew larger and more urbane, disparities between town and country became more stark. Under the guiding hand of Federalist Mayor Roger Sherman, the mercantile class and City of New Haven prospered — but often at the expense of rural constituents.[23]

The growing social tendency towards materialism in all sectors of society especially worried the ministry. Across the country, gloomy reports portrayed a nation preoccupied by the pursuit of wealth and luxury. The old Puritan tenets of thrift and restraint were seemingly being cast aside by self-indulgence and greed. Ministers across Connecticut complained of growing moral laxity, drunkenness and a general preoccupation with materialism, especially in the seaport towns. Instead of John Winthrop's envisioned "City Upon a Hill," men like Noah Williston of West Haven, Ezra Stiles and Timothy Dwight of New Haven and Benjamin Trumbull of North Haven all detected the stench of Biblical money changers in their midst.[24]

Most West Haveners, however, had more secular reasons to be nonplused by the success of their parent town. With nearly half the male population unable to qualify as freeman and thus the vote, they increasingly felt under-represented by New Haven's peculiar arrangement of a protected city within a town. Taxes kept increasing, the seaport city kept growing and the parish of West Haven seemed to benefit only marginally by its association. The results were predictable. West Haveners were increasingly divided between the lure of commercializing their own shore front or remaining true to their agrarian and

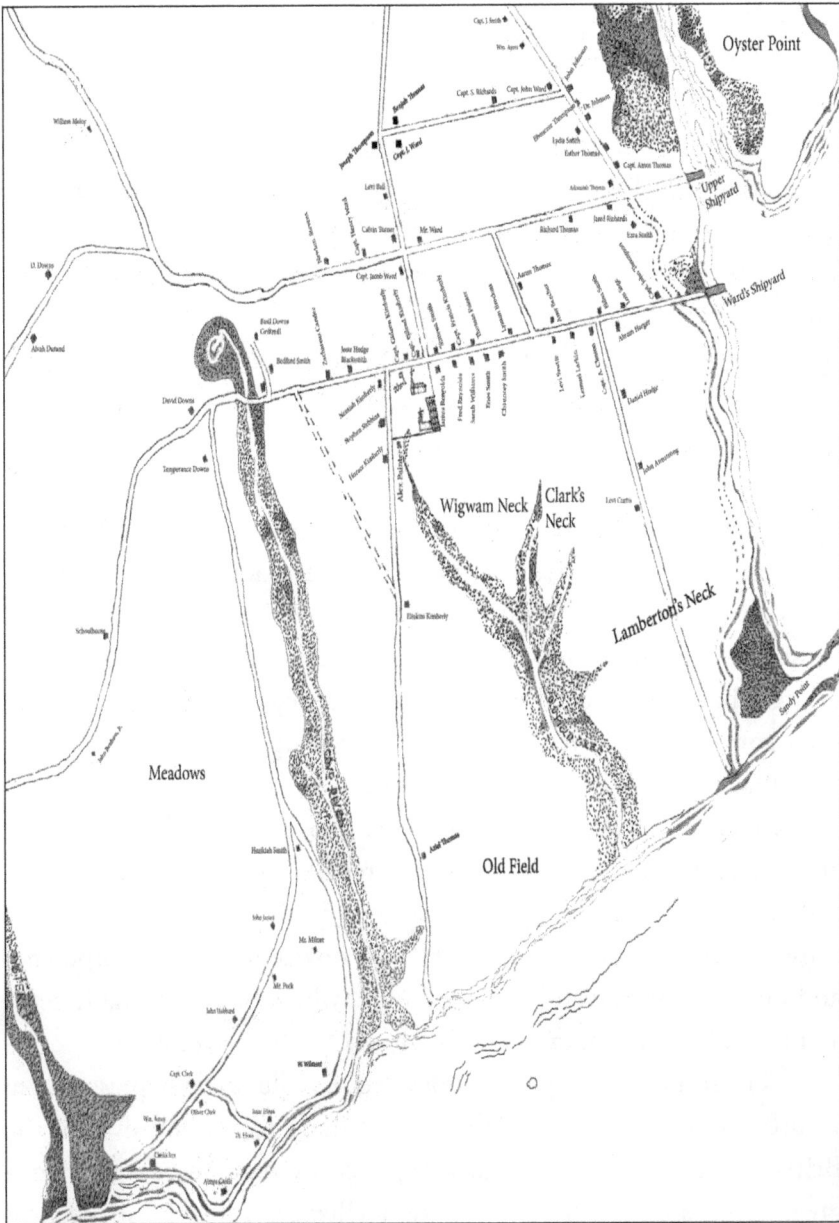

West Haven ca. 1800

Based on information contained
in Harry Ives Thompson Papers.
Not to scale.

Map by Peter J. Malia

155

Calvinist roots as a small Puritan village.

Concerns of under-representation grew stronger when Mayor Sherman used his considerable influence to stymie Connecticut's passage of the Bill of Rights in 1789 (it was not actually passed in the state until 1939). Sherman believed the amendments were unnecessary and did not want to establish a precedent whereby the U.S. Constitution would become lost amid a sea of amendments. Most Federalists agreed.[25]

The middle and lower classes in and around New Haven saw things differently. They worried that a growing aristocracy in New Haven was unwilling to acknowledge their hard-earned rights as equals under the law. In practice it seemed as if some people were more equal than others. Already denied town status in 1785 and again in 1787, ostensively based on protests lodged by neighboring Milford but conveniently masking New Haven's own concerns, West Haveners responded in their time-honored tradition of simply doing what they felt was best. And if not legally sanctioned to do so, a core group of activist citizens took it upon themselves to run the village as its own quasi-independent entity.

Chief among West Haven's primary boosters were Thomas Painter and the Reverend Mr. Williston. Painter had come a long way from his days as the teenaged militiaman who first spotted the British off West Haven's shoreline in 1779. He was now a prosperous shipowner and one of New Haven's emerging elite, who would eventually serve as a founding selectman of the Town of Orange in 1822.

Williston also had gone far beyond his role as the hapless victim whose life was spared by Adjutant William Campbell during the British invasion. He was highly regarded by the conservative Congregationalist establishment and was a village fixture who spent most days on horseback visiting church members. Married for the third time (his first two wives died), Williston was an early and ardent supporter of still another religious revival gaining momentum in the New Haven area in the early 1790s known as the Second Great Awakening. It was Williston's evangelism, in fact, that led to his most significant contribution to both West Haven and the nation.

It began in the form of a local library. Together with Thomas Painter, Williston raised donations from the Kimberly, Candee, Jones, Merwin and Smith families to underwrite the state's first lending library in West Haven in 1792 with the intention:

> "to subserve and advance the interests of religion and learning, and being fully persuaded that a choice collection of the best authors on geography, history, the belle letters, divinity and other branches of science may subserve those interests and being confident that we ourselves, our children and unborn generations, may receive much pleasure and literary improvement by frequent converse with such authors and be assisted in making progress in divine knowledge, we think it our indispensable duty to unite in purchasing such a collection and forming a library, to be under the direction of those we shall appoint to the Office of Librarian."[26]

The library became the talk of the town and led one young parishioner to make a small donation with a specific request that it be used to help preach the gospel among the destitute. Inspired by the young woman's generosity and fueled by the success of his own West Haven experiment, which his son, Payson, followed with equal success in Easthampton, Massachusetts, Williston approached the General Association of Congregational Churches with a bold suggestion: With donations solicited from the state's independent societies, the "saints" could underwrite the founding of libraries to spread the Gospel across the entire frontier. Within six years, Williston's original idea gave rise to the creation of the Connecticut Missionary Society, which pioneered the founding of grammar schools, lending libraries and literacy throughout the Northeast. Williston became so engrossed in the Missionary Society's work that he even volunteered as a missionary himself for two, six-month tours in Vermont.[27]

"He seemed intent on the salvation of every other human being, and willing that God should dispose of him, as He saw fit," Williston's grandson once wrote, and "His love and zeal for missions knew no bounds."[28.]

IV

Following the death of Roger Sherman in 1793, longtime town clerk, county judge and city alderman Samuel Bishop was elected mayor of New Haven. An anti-Federalist but unabashed civic booster, Bishop, at age 70, led New Haven through a whirlwind decade of municipal change that forever reshaped the city — and its satellite village of West Haven — physically, politically and intellectually.[29]

Public health proved to be the initial driver. Following a smallpox scare, the city authorized construction of an inoculation hospital run by two local physicians, who in turn founded New Haven's first medical society. When a scarlet fever epidemic swept through the region in 1795 - 1796, the city further enacted its first anti-pollution laws. The townspeople voted that slaughterhouses be moved away from waterways as potential sources of fouling creeks and streams. The shoreline was also to be kept clean of dead fish, clams, and oysters to curtail "the progress of any putrid or contagious disease." To enforce the new laws, public health officers were appointed to inspect homes and businesses to ensure that they were kept clean to prevent the spread of any infectious disease.[30]

Modern manufacturing also got its start in 1793, when a young

Eli Whitney patented his cotton gin and opened a factory near East Rock to mass produce his invention. Ever the enterprising Yankee, Whitney then added a production line using a concept first conceived by Jean Baptiste Vaquette de Gribeauval that incorporated interchangeable parts in manufacturing military muskets. While this first invention gave birth to King Cotton and indirectly led to the expansion of slavery by making cotton production

Eli Whitney (1765 - 1825)

hugely profitable in the Southern states, Whitney's tireless efforts to promote the use of interchangeable parts also helped to usher in America's industrial age.[31]

Public education also underwent a radical change in the 1790s as New Haven enacted state legislation to transfer the responsibility for public education from the Congregational Church into the hands of local public school boards. In West Haven the parish school continued with state funding until 1805. After some initial squabbling, a new public school was finally built on the Green in that year and stood until 1857 — its last eight years as a vacant building — when classes were merged into Union Avenue School in 1849.

The Yankee obsession with internal improvements that created a virtual spider web of new roads and bridges in and around town also flourished throughout the 1790s. One such project targeted the old Milford Turnpike (U.S. 1 or Boston Post Road) in 1797.

Details behind the improvements provide an extraordinary glimpse into Yankee practicality-in-action that involved both the city and its suburb. Weighing the costs of improvements, Thomas Painter, now one of the committee members overseeing the improvements, was asked to determine West Haven's fair share of the bill. That implied the village was allowed to exercise a certain amount of autonomy from New Haven proper so long as it also honored its fiscal commitments that attended its quasi-independent status.[32]

West Haven's sense of self-determination grew even stronger when Painter and company revived talks with their North Milford neighbors in yet another bid for town status in 1800. Once again, New Haven initially agreed, but Milford, fearing the loss of a substantial tax base and its premium farmlands, would hear none of it.[33]

As the new century began, bigger issues loomed on the horizon. War was now raging in Europe and threatening to involve America. The horrors of the French Revolution had given way to Napoleon and strained relations. The English navy began impressing American seamen, which outraged President Thomas Jefferson and eventually led to the passage of the Embargo Act of 1807, which all but ended New Haven's golden era as a major seaport.[35]

The decades ahead would be filled by war, a devastating depression, political infighting and an end to the special privileges so long enjoyed by the Congregationalist Standing Order. And West Haven's bid for independence would have to wait once again.

CHAPTER TWELVE

Dreams of Their Fathers

The American Revolution had a profound impact on West Haven. Patriotism transcended denominational lines to fuse a new religious and political order in the village at the expense of an old Puritan dream.

What seemed truly revolutionary about the Revolution was the community's transformation from Puritan village to American town. Like all of Connecticut most West Haveners entered the war to preserve and protect, not to expand, their rights and privileges as Englishmen. They emerged from that experience into a new age where those same rights and privileges now allowed them to entertain even more expansive visions, not as Puritans or Anglicans or Englishmen but as Americans.

How and why did this happen? Look closer at the history of this small village and you will discover that the Revolution — as remarkable as it was — merely served as a crucible that fired ideas and practices long in the making and the work of five generations in transition.

West Haven's earliest struggle to become its own parish was a case in point. To escape from under the shadows of New Haven, the visible saints first questioned authority, challenged tradition, and finally ignored it altogether in their pursuit of self-determination. It was a precedent that time and again reshaped their colonial experience. Successive generations of West Haveners repeatedly proved more than willing to challenge the Standing Order to get what they wanted. If those efforts earned them

The Thomas Painter House was located on Main Street prior to being dismantled and moved to Litchfield, CT in 1959.

a measure of self-rule through the years, they also elevated organized opposition to a precedent-setting level that presented unimaginable challenges to the visible saints. They did not have long to wait to see what they had wrought. Dissidents wasted little time in disrupting the infant parish. In founding Christ Church and declaring for Episcopacy, they drove a stake into the very heartland of Calvinist Connecticut. With religious and community interests polarized, the village saints were forced to stray from their time-honored practice of Puritan restraint. Their faith was severely tested. And if parishioners had once found it advantageous to challenge authority in creating the First Society, they soon discovered that their community of saints was hardly that and deeply divided.

In successive ministries at both village churches, the positive influences of Samuel Johnson, Noah Williston and Bela Hubbard were offset by the sour experiences of the Reverends Arnold, Allen and Punderson. Bitter and sometimes even violent reactions played out in a proverbial battleground in which Anglicans had little to lose and Puritans even less to gain. All the while, the very concept of Congregationalism was being pushed and pulled into a gradual transformation that New Haven's original founders would not have recognized.

But necessity bred invention, even in religion. New Englanders, as historian Daniel Boorstein so masterfully observed in his trilogy *The Americans*, were the paragons of ingenuity. The Anglican faith established a beachhead in the nascent community of West Haven precisely because its own minister exploited the weakest link of Congregationalism itself. That link was the fundamental belief in self-reliant, independent parishes. When it failed not once but twice in West Haven, Connecticut's leaders were too slow to react.[1]

At risk was the Puritan experiment itself. If Old Lights and New Lights eventually bickered over church membership and the effects of the Awakening, both agreed on one thing. As small a minority that Anglicans may have been, their persistent call for a bishop in America was growing louder. If that call was ever answered, the Puritans feared all would be lost. The British line of authority would extend beyond the economic and political spheres to embrace religion and threaten the very foundation of Connecticut's established church. Without question, Anglicanism in Connecticut was always perceived as an imperial issue and a sociopolitical flash point.[2]

And ground zero was the little village of West Haven. In their first two decades as a parish (1720 - 1740), West Haven Puritans struggled to attain the solidarity and respect they so much desired, but they failed. Religious schisms, financial insolvency and the absence of a permanent religious authority all took their toll in turning the village into the problem child of Connecticut's conservative order. No less remarkable, and likely regarded by the self-deprecating saints as a sign of their own failings, was the growth of Christ Church only steps away from the First Society. It must have rankled the saints to see their neighbors become Churchmen and practice a religion they considered to be an abomination.[3]

In a village that made little distinction between religion and politics, it was inevitable that the controversy would spill over into secular affairs. Public and private interests repeatedly collided with old-line Puritan traditions to short circuit the machinery of the established church. The reason why is not hard to fathom. Congregationalism's reliance on self-policing vestries proved a dismal failure. Independent parishes, especially those lacking strong leadership, were no match for the more universal forces of human nature and the charms of charismatic preachers. The vision of John Davenport's new haven was simply too confining for an increasingly diverse community. Salvation was important, but so was the here and now.

That dichotomy became very apparent early on in West Haven. Its small community of visible saints were not at all like-minded in their beliefs beyond sharing a desire for their own parish. In many respects, they simply wanted to avoid the inconvenience of traveling to New Haven every Sunday morning. But their simple desires tipped over a cauldron of blistering criticism to expose a raw nerve that had little to do with religion. Between the lines of sanctimonious banter opposing the creation of a West Haven parish were more earthly concerns, from lost tax revenue and diminished political power to lost prestige.[4]

If West Haveners won the initial round, they eventually lost what they had fought so hard to gain — solidarity. Unwittingly, their early challenge to the established church also exposed one of Congregationalism's deepest flaws — the inherent weakness of parochial authority. The emergence of Christ Church was only one by-product that grew out of this loophole. Another more injurious result came in the form of the Great Awakening.[5]

As revivalist preachers barnstormed the colony in the 1730s and early 1740s, they unleashed a torrent of pent-up religious emotions that occasionally bordered on mass hysteria. More West Haven Puritans defected to Christ Church. Those who remained with the First Society looked to the colony's old-line politicians for help, but it was too slow in coming. In the face of still another threat to the Puritan ideal, the Standing Order proved deficient once again. When such crises became politicized, as in the Stamp Act, West Haveners would strip the old guard of their sanctity and abandon them altogether.[6]

Only this time, West Haven's confrontational ideology was shared across the colony. With the rise of the New Lights, the winds of change were already showing signs that the New Haven Puritan was becoming the Connecticut Yankee.[7]

With conservatism gradually losing its iron grip on religion, it now lay exposed as the Achilles' heel of Connecticut's traditional leaders. It was the Stamp Act crisis that proved their final undoing.[8]

When Connecticut's old guard pledged to do the king's bidding and impose imperial taxes, many West Haveners, Puritan and Anglican alike, demanded a change in leadership. Initially, one's denomination had little to do with the widespread indignation over the Stamp tax. No one liked paying more taxes, especially when they had no say as to where or how those revenues would be spent. It was the handiwork of 18th-century spin doctors known as the Sons of Liberty who fanned the flames into a true crisis of allegiance and eventually one of armed conflict.[9]

In many respects West Haveners had already crossed the Rubicon on the issue of independence. All that was left was to act on it. But many Anglicans feared the popular civil protests of the 1760s, in which they also enthusiastically participated, had become too defiant of imperial authority by the 1770s. Where to draw that proverbial line between protest and treason became a personal, gut-wrenching decision. It was safe to assume that no matter how you felt about the growing imperial crisis, being Anglican in Connecticut was no easy course to follow. Many Anglicans harbored a sense of betrayal by the New Lights and increasingly felt threatened by the overt defiance of their neighbors. To some, the only recourse was to renew their pleas for an American Episcopate. Others complained that the New Light brand of Puritanism had gone too far and the only solution was to replace Connecticut's cherished charter with a royal governor.[10]

While such demands were more widely voiced in Connecticut than in London, perception fueled reality. Political differences had always been supercharged by religious antagonism between the saints and dissenters. The evolving crisis that resulted in the American Revolution was as much a struggle between religions as it was opposing political philosophies or the pursuit of personal liberties.[11]

When resistance finally turned to rebellion, some West Haveners used the war to strike out at Christ Churchmen and increase pressures on their neighbors to conform. While most residents went about their daily business, others seized the opportunity to even up old scores, chastise the unpopular or demand that their Anglican neighbors take an oath of allegiance. Many did and others simply left.

Of those Loyalists who remained, their numbers accounted for as many as a third of the town's population. As the war for independence wound to a conclusion, New Haven proved to be a remarkably forgiving and even opportunistic place. Conducting what amounted to an ad campaign, New Haveners formally invited one-time Loyalists from New York to town, especially if they had money in their pockets. How many actually took them up on the offer is unknown, but some did come and their presence not only helped to rejuvenate the local economy, it also restored a conservative tone to local politics.[12]

Throughout the remainder of the 18th century, New Haven residents seemed preoccupied with their new city and their own success. There were now more than 400 buildings within the city limits by 1784. New roads and bridges were built or improved and a new long wharf, complete with several new warehouses, jutted out into Long Island Sound for nearly a quarter mile. Two smaller wharves for shipbuilding appeared off Water Street in West Haven and later became known as Gessner and Mar. The little harbor was humming. Of the 30-some vessels owned by local residents, most were involved in the West Indies trade or plied coastal waters.[13] One such sloop was the *Nancy*, owned by West Haven's Thomas Painter. As town records indicated throughout these early days of the Confederation and New Haven's era of civic boosterism, Painter was one West Havener on the make.[14]

Painter's hometown, however, did not fare quite as well. The Revolution hit the small community hard in lost lives and property damage. In the wake of New Haven's economic resurgence, West

Haveners grew even more dependent upon the new city for their livelihoods. When a group of prominent villagers joined in the rush of surrounding areas seeking independence from New Haven in 1784, they received the town's initial approval. But in truth, there was little real support to fend off Milford's historic objections, especially since the proposed new town would include present-day Orange. As suppliers of livestock, produce and manpower to the burgeoning City of New Haven, most West Haveners were simply too busy or worn out to bother with politics. Town status meant a separate government, likely higher taxes and potentially the loss of their inside track to New Haven's growing markets. Once again, Yankee practicality outweighed the long-held Puritan dream of village self-rule.[15]

Practicality also helped to recast West Haveners' attitudes towards each other. In the crucible of war, they found more common ground than not through their shared suffering and experiences. The war now over it was the future, not the past, that the villagers turned to with a sense of optimism and industry that would prove to be far out of proportion to their numbers. That future was no longer defined as Anglican or Puritan, Loyalist or Patriot. It was now clearly American with a Yankee accent.

By design, but more often by circumstance, these simple farmers, seamen and tradesmen had always displayed a level of ingenuity in seizing new opportunities and solving current problems that inexorably pushed them further away from their traditional saintly pursuits. Through trial and error they embraced innovation on the edge of an expansive frontier that historian Paige Smith described as "brand new, fresh, and in the process of becoming, but not yet complete."[16]

With the dawn of a new century, West Haveners took stock of their small New England village on the edge of the sea. In years to come it would prove to serve them and their descendants as it always had — as a harbinger of good and bad, but mostly good, in opening their minds and providing a gateway to the world and the future.

II

I t is ironic that one of Connecticut's earliest settlements was also its last to win incorporation as an independent town in 1921. Nearly a century and a half after its entry into the American Revolution, and nearly 300 years after it struggled to gain a measure of autonomy as a separate parish, West Haven finally achieved the right to call itself an independent town.

By 1961 West Haven was "Connecticut's Youngest City." As a boy I helped deliver campaign flyers for West Haven's last First Selectman and first Mayor, Gregory Morrissey. Before launching his political career Morrissey worked the soda fountain at Liggett's Drug Store on the corners of Campbell Avenue and Center Street. At the time, I was more interested in his victory celebration at the ice cream shop than reading into any significance concerning his election. Nearly a half century later I now realize what it really meant. Not unlike Thomas Painter two centuries before, Morrissey was a local up-and-comer from a small town who made good because he represented West Haven's future. It was 1959 — the same year the Thomas Painter House disappeared from West Haven forever.[17]

Perhaps it was poetic justice that old house vanished as it did. In a way it symbolizes the town's colonial past slipping out of our collective sight. Those who came before us now seem so remote — wooden, cold, almost one-dimensional. They predicted as much.

At a New Haven town meeting held in March 1784, it was duly recorded that:

> "... while the Distresses and Calamaties of the Late war are fresh in our Recollection, we may consider a persecuting Spirit as Justifiable[.] We must, when reason assumes her empire, reproach such a Line of Conduct and be Convinced that future generations ... will form their Ideas of our Character from those acts which a faithful Historian Shall have recorded and not from our passions of which they can have no History....[18]

The aging Samuel Bishop penned those words into the public record as if he were writing a self-fulfilling prophecy. Such passions are gone to the grave. All that remains of the visible saints are their words and deeds. And it is a legacy well worth remembering for the lessons can teach us.

Despite having one eye seemingly always cast heavenward, colonial West Haveners were driven by the same motivations that have defined human nature throughout history. Love and hate. Anger and revenge. The drive to succeed and their pursuit of life, liberty and happiness. All played their part in a community made up of people who, in the final analysis, were not very different from ourselves. Fiercely independent, outspoken, at times blatantly biased, brave, sometimes contentious, merciful and always passionate, they were also ultimately accepting of inevitable change. Each successive generation put its unique stamp on their idea of freedom. Collectively and ever so imperceptibly, they moved that fragile and precious idea ahead a very narrow path. What began as a Puritan experiment in the wilderness evolved into a living, breathing laboratory that bred the practical freedoms we now all take for granted. They did not come cheaply nor should they ever be forgotten.

Some were true giants to whom we owe much. Most were like ourselves. All deserve our gratitude for what the poet James Russell Lowell summed up best about these visible saints:

> "The English Puritans pulled down church and state to re-build Zion on the ruins, and all the while it was not Zion, but America, they were building."

We still are.

Appendix
Officeholders
1640 - 1798

Since the publication of Carl Bridenbaugh's ground-breaking study *Cities in the Wilderness*, historians have argued persuasively that a relatively small number of the "better sort," – mostly well-to-do merchants, businessmen and the Congregationalist clergy – ruled over colonial Connecticut and New Haven in particular. Even through the turbulent years of the American Revolution and the early national period that followed, Connecticut's leadership, they argued, remained largely unchanged. But does an analysis of colonial office holding in New Haven through those years actually support those claims or paint a different picture?

The answer is surprising. In the course of researching this study, I have compiled a list of some 603 adult men living in the New Haven area over a 150-year period from 1640 - 1798. Many, but not all, were residents of West Haven. Suffice it to say that the majority of New Haveners were not mentioned in the public records. Of the estimated 35,000 individuals who lived in the New Haven area throughout the 17th and 18th centuries, more than half were women, slaves, indentured servants and a number of other residents without property who were never officially recorded. That distinction was limited to those who attained at least "town status," a precursor to being voted a freeman of the town, which further required an adult male to be in good community standing and have property worth at least 40 shillings.

Based on those criteria, between the years 1640 - 1798, there were some 2,000 freemen mentioned in the town records, or roughly 29 percent of the estimated total number of adult males based on an arbitrary 1:5 ratio of the 35,000 total population. For purposes of this study, the following list contains 603 of those 2,000 individuals, or 30 percent of the total.

These 603 individuals were then matched to the various public offices they held in hopes of learning more about the nature and composition of local government in the New Haven area. Was it as tightly controlled a community as long thought or was it more "democratic" in the sense that holding a public office, even of some minor nature, was considered part of the social contract?

To simplify the task of analyzing the data, three general levels of offices were created: 1.) Lower-level positions, such as fenceviewers, hay wardens, surveyors, sealers, tythingmen, listers and tax collectors; 2.) Medium-level offices, such as grand jurymen, constables, marshals, town meeting moderators and minor committee members; and 3.) Higher-level offices, including selectmen, major committee members (including committees of inspection during the Revolution), town treasurers and deputies to the General Assembly.

The results were then further divided into three distinct time periods: 1640 – 1770; 1770 – 1784; and 1784 – 1798. This was done to see how public office holding may have changed through the years and especially during the period leading up to and including, and immediately following the American Revolution.

The resulting trends proved to be enlightening. Over the entire 150-year span, for example, New Haven appeared to be more democratic in nature in selecting low-level public officials who oversaw the daily affairs of the town. In all three periods analyzed, the majority of adult men who attained town status or above served in at least one if not multiple lower-level public offices. In fact, it seemed as if individuals were universally expected to claim a public stake in the community if they ever hoped to be fully accepted into New Haven society. And unless excused for good reason, refusing to serve resulted in hefty fines.

Not surprisingly, mid-and higher-level offices were more restrictive with no more than 10 percent of New Haveners holding these positions throughout the colonial period. The reason is easily explained. First, there were simply fewer of these offices available. More significantly, they were usually occupied by men of means, breeding, education or social standing, which repeatedly earned them election by affirmation at the annual town meetings. With no paper ballot, votes were cast by a show of hands, and woe to the brave soul who cast a dissenting vote against a pillar of the community. In many respects, it was tyranny by majority rule.

The exception proved to be the Revolutionary years. The war's drain on local talent and manpower, as well as the political leanings of some of those holding office, caused a noticeable spike in the number of adult New Haven men holding more important offices during the Revolutionary era. Some well-known individuals with Loyalist leanings fell out of favor and public office, such as the Ingersolls, Prindles and Chandlers. Others left town entirely. In either case, it created opportunities for a new generation of leaders, including Roger Sherman and two West Haveners, the firebrand Patriot Lamberton Smith and the ever-ambitious Thomas Painter. If considered on its own merits, the Revolution seemed to positively embrace the idea of a broadened leadership base in town. In fact, over half of the New Haven freeman tracked in this analysis during those years held a locally significant public office between 1770 – 1784. As revolutionary as that might seem, New Haven's experiment with a more democratic approach to local government proved to be short-lived.

By 1784, less than a year following the end of the Revolution, the number of residents holding a significant public office in New Haven dropped by half. That lends credence to contemporary and lingering complaints that a newly reconstituted merchant class in New Haven – drawn largely from the ranks of conservative merchants and former Loyalist businessmen who had been pro-actively invited to town by pledges of official support and tax breaks – regained control of New Haven politics at the expense of middle- and lower-class residents. It also goes a long way to explain why so many surrounding areas sought separate town status through the remaining decades of the 18th century. They were in search of self-representation.

In the case of West Haven, its bid for separate town status was repeatedly rejected and a significant number of its citizens continued to hold lower-level public offices in New Haven. But far fewer of its residents were now elevated to higher-level positions as the "better sort" consolidated their control over the town. Opening the floodgates to a truly democratic society was something New Haven's leaders never intended through the Revolution.

Ironically, this trend of the few ruling over the many is hardly new. In his ground-breaking study of Middletown, Robert Lynd pointed to the same phenomenon whereby the few, despite universal suffrage, controlled the community. American urban history is ripe with examples of political and social cliques dominating local, county and occasionally state politics. It is no stretch of the imagination to suggest that the seeds of modern-day machine politics were first sown in the Puritan soil of New England.

Why so many 18th-century New Haveners accepted the *status quo* is intriguing to ponder. Some political scientists suggest that the vast majority of residents throughout the colonial era enjoyed a progressively comfortable lifestyle best described as middle class. As residents progressed through their lives, usually as self-sufficient farmers, tradesmen or artisans, they married, reared children, expanded their personal holdings and wealth and gradually gained stature in the community. If a handful of men rose to the top of New Haven's socioeconomic ladder, there really were few true impediments to prevent anyone else from doing the same thing.

West Haven's Thomas Painter is a perfect example. The local teen was first a militiaman and then a privateersman during the Revolution, mixing patriotism with adventure and "get-rich-quick" schemes. By his mid-twenties he was a ship master and by his thirties he was a well-respected member of New Haven's ruling class, serving as selectman for a number of terms, leading the effort to establish West Haven's first public library, then spearheading the drive for West Haven independence through the early years of the nineteenth century. When it was finally won with the creation of Orange in 1820, Painter was among the new town's first selectmen.

What, then, does this analysis of colonial office holding actually tell us about 18th-century politics and Connecticut society? Public office holding during the colonial period was more commonplace than some historians have thought. West Haven and New Haven certainly remained part of a tight-knit Congregationalist society that controlled all aspects of the town's administration. But they also proved to be more open in sharing the day-to-day responsibilities of running the town, at least in low-level and mid-level positions. Ironically that became less prevalent in the early national period. As the greater New Haven population grew to over 8,000 residents by 1775, fewer adult males qualified as freemen while others who did simply never held public office. Ezra Stiles noted that approximately 600 adult men lived within the boundaries of the city in 1784. Of those, Stiles noted that 343 qualified as freeman, or 57 percent. As the city grew larger so did the franchise, but the levels of public service diminished significantly after the Revolution.

The exception was the Revolutionary era. More than half of New Haven adult townsmen and freemen held public office during those crisis years. Doing so not only fulfilled a public responsibility, it affirmed

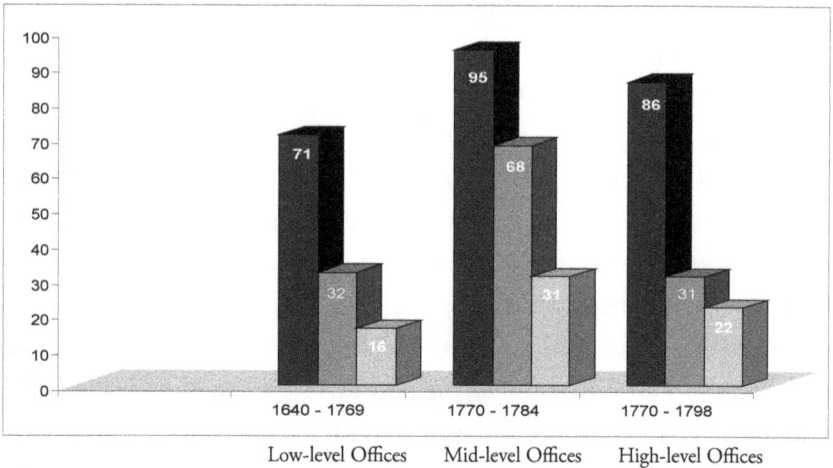

The above chart represents the percentage of New Haven townsmen and freeman noted in the public records as holding public office from 1640 - 1798. Black represents the years 1640 - 1769, grey represents1770 - 1784 and light grey represents the years 1784 - 1798.

their sense of local patriotism. From overseeing the town's defenses and prosecuting Loyalists and illicit traders to promoting local manufacturing and raising money, supplies and manpower for the war, most New Haveners continued to answer the call to public service. Why that level of participation fell in the post-war years is likely the return of normalcy to the town's traditional conservative bent. It is an area ripe for further study by political scientists, but falls outside the scope of this history.

II

What follows is a listing of New Haven men appearing in the New Haven Records between 1640 - 1798. The listing is not intended to be a definitive but instead is a sampling of approximately nine percent of all male inhabitants over the 150-year period. Where possible birth and death dates are provided along with an account of which offices they held and whether they had attained freeman status.

Officeholders

Name	General Assembly	Selectman	Town Treasurer	Town Clerk	Grandjuryman	Justice of Peace	Major Committeeman	Minor Committeeman	Constable	Surveyor	Freeman	Rate Collector/Lister	Brander/Sealer/Keykeeper	Hayward	Fenceviewer
Alcock, John (1675-1722)															2
Alcock, John (1705-1777)									1		Y	1		1	6
Alcock, Philip (ca. 1680)		1							2					1	3
Alcock, Thomas (1677 - 1757)		6		2					2		Y	5		1	1
Alling, Abram									1						
Alling, Abraham (1754 - 1837)						2						2			4
Alling, Amos (1764 - 1820)															
Alling, Caleb (1694 - 1756)					1						Y	2		1	
Alling, Caleb Capt. (1764 - 1827)															
Alling, Charles (1724 - 1808)															
Alling, Chauncey (1767 - 1842)															
Alling, Christopher (1735 - 1799)											Y	1			
Alling, Daniel (1688 - 1756)		2			1				1		Y	2		2	1
Alling, Daniel (1728 - 1821)									1						
Alling, Daniel (1758 - ?)															
Alling, Ebenezer (1687 - 1734)					1				1		Y	2	1	6	3
Alling, Ebenezer (1712 - 1744)								1			Y				
Alling, Edward (1768 - 1815)											Y				
Alling, Elisha											Y				
Alling, Elisha											Y				
Alling, Elisha (1751 - ?)											Y				
Alling, Enos (1719 - 1779)	1				1	8	1			3	Y				
Alling, Ichabod (1756 - 1809)															
Alling, Issac (1755 -1818)															
Alling, James (1756 - 1817)															
Alling, John (1647- 1717)	12	12	22	2				3			Y	2	1		6
Alling, John, Jr. (ca. 1690)								2	2				2		
Alling, John, Jr. (? - 1770)				1			1								
Alling, John (1743 - 1809)															
Alling, Jonathan (1683 -1775)	13	3		2					1		Y	5		5	4
Alling, Jonathan Jr. (1716 - 1771)							1						1		
Alling, Lemuel (1746 - 1809)									1						
Alling, Nathan (1729 - 1812)				1											
Alling, Roger (1612 - 1674)		6		3	6	3						2			3
Alling, Roger (1708 - 1770)					4	1			1		Y	14	2		
Alling, Samuel (1645 - 1709)					1			1			Y	2	2	1	6
Alling, Samuel (1669 - 1744)					1		2				Y	1		3	3
Alling, Samuel Jr.				3			1					2			
Alling, Silas (1734 - 1817)							2			3		2			
Alling, Silas, Jr. (1771 - 1805)															
Alling, Rev. Timothy (ca. 1738)											Y				
Allsop, Joseph, Sr. (? - 1698)					4				1		Y				
Allsop, John Jr. (1648 - 1691)						1									

Visible Saints

Name	General Assembly	Selectman	Town Treasurer	Town Clerk	Grandjuryman	Justice of Peace	Major Committeeman	Minor Committeeman	Constable	Surveyor	Freeman	Rate Collector/Lister	Brander/Sealer/Keykeeper	Hayward	Fenceviewer
Allsop, Philip (1648-1715)															1
Andrews, Nathan (1662-1713)	4							2			Y				1
Atwater, Abel (? - 1822)											Y	1			
Atwater, David Jr. (1756 - 1803)												1		2	4
Atwater, Eldad				1		1									
Atwater, Elnathan											Y				
Atwater, Jacob (1720 - 1799)										1					
Atwater, Jeremiah (1734 - 1811)	10			2				9		6					
Atwater, Jeremiah Jr. (1767 - 1832)											Y				
Atwater, Jeremiah 3rd (1773 - 1858)											Y				
Atwater, Jeremiah 4th											Y				
Atwater, Joel (1728 - 1794)				1				1				4			
Atwater, John				1		1									
Atwater, Jonathan											Y				
Atwater, Medad											Y				
Atwater, Moses (1729 - 1805)															
Atwater, Samuel (1739 - 1788)	3					3	3					2			
Atwater, Stephen (1720 - 1806)				2							Y				
Atwater, Thomas (1733 - 1805)											Y				
Atwater, Timothy (1751 - 1820)						1					Y				
Atwater, Ward											Y				
Baker, John (ca. 1770)											Y				
Ball, John (1649-1713)	8	2		1							Y	1		2	4
Ball, Glover (1748 - ?)										4	Y				
Ball, Hezekiah (1741 - ?)												1			
Ball, John , Jr. (1685-1731)	3			1				1		2	Y	1			
Ball, Stephen (1726 - 1799)	3			1	1					2	Y	1			
Ball, Stephen, Jr. (1762 - 1842)															
Ball, Timothy (1724 - 1786)								5		1	Y	1			
Ball, Timothy Jr.(1751 - 1832)											Y	1			
Beecher, Caleb (1724-1784)				1	1	6	1	3			Y	4			
Beecher, David (1738 - 1805)						1					Y	1			
Beecher, David, Jr. (1773 - 1834)											Y				
Beecher, Ebenezer (1686-1763)	2			4						4	Y	4			3
Beecher, Ebenezer (1714-1780)				1						1	Y				1
Beecher, Eleazer (1655-1725)				1							Y				6
Beecher, Eli (1747 - 1789)												1			
Beecher, Hezekiah (1703-1751)									1		Y				2
Beecher, Isaac (?-1690)									3						11
Beecher, Isaac (1698-1784)				6							Y	1			
Beecher, Isaac Jr. (1726-1814)	4			1	2					1		2			
Beecher, Isaac Jr, (1650-1708)											Y			1	2
Beecher, John (1646-1712)											Y				

Name	General Assembly	Selectman	Town Treasurer	Town Clerk	Grandjuryman	Justice of Peace	Major Committeeman	Minor Committeeman	Constable	Surveyor	Freeman	Rate Collector/Lister	Brander/Sealer/Keykeeper	Hayward	Fenceviewer
Beecher, John (1744-1786)										2		1	1		
Beecher, Joseph (? - 1728)									1		Y			7	5
Beecher, Joseph (1698-1763)											Y	2	1		
Beecher, Medad (1750 - ca. 1815)															
Beecher, Nathaniel (1681-1768)		1								3					
Beecher, Nathaniel (1706-1786)		1									Y	2			3
Beecher, Reuben (1742 - 1788)															
Beecher, Samuel (1687-1760)										1		1			1
Beecher, Stephen (1742 - 1795)															
Beecher, Thaddeus (1749 - 1823)															
Beecher, Thomas Jr.													1		
Beecher, Thompson (1768 - 1792)															
Beecher, Titus (1740-1803)										2					
Belden, Aaron (ca. 1770)															
Belden, Jared (1716-1796)															
Belden, Jared (? - 1778), Loyalist											Y				
Belden, Samuel (? - 1778), Loyalist															
Benham, David (?)										1	Y	1			
Benham, Gamiel (1738 - 1811)										1	Y				
Benham, Japhet (1697-1778)															
Benham, John, Sr. (?-1691)															3
Benham, John (1664-1744)										1	Y				1
Benham, John (1710 - 1777)				1		1									
Benham, Samuel															
Benham, Silas (1753? - 1777)															
Benham, Thomas		1										1			
Blakeslee, Abraham (1727 - 1785)										2					
Blakeslee, Archibald (1752 - 1830)															
Blakeslee, Ebenezer (1711 - 1771)										1	Y	1			
Blakesley, Isaiah (1751 - ?)											Y				
Blakesley, James (1735 - ?)				1			1					1			
Blakeslee, Job (1744 - 1823)				2						1	Y				
Blakeslee, Joel (1750 - 1814)						3									
Blakeslee, Jotham (1768 - ?)										1		3			
Blakesley, Obed (1754 - ?										1	Y				
Blakeslee, Oliver (1741 - 1824)										1					
Blakesley, Philamon (1760 - 1841)											Y				
Blakeslee, Samuel (1662 - 1732)										1					2
Blakeslee, Seth										2				9	
Blakesley, Zealous (1756 - 1829)											Y				
Blakeslee, Zopher (1730 - 1798)										1					
Blakesley, Tilley (1728 - 1811)						1	1	7				1			
Boykin, Nathaniel (1641 - 1705)									1		Y				7

179

Visible Saints

Name	General Assembly	Selectman	Town Treasurer	Town Clerk	Grandjuryman	Justice of Peace	Major Committeeman	Minor Committeeman	Constable	Surveyor	Freeman	Rate Collector/Lister	Brander/Sealer/Keykeeper	Hayward	Fenceviewer
Bradley, Aaron (1757 - 1828)											Y	1			
Bradley, Abijah (1769 - ?)						1									
Bradley, Abner (1695 - 1778)	1				3					4	Y	4		2	3
Bradley, Abraham 3rd															
Bradley, Abraham (1741 - 1817)					3	1					Y	3			
Bradley, Abraham Jr. (1746 - 1825)															
Bradley, Abson					1										
Bradley, Alexander (1758 - 1807)											Y				
Bradley, Alvin (1734 - 1810)											Y				
Bradley, Aner (1753 - 1824)					1										
Bradley, Amos (1746 - 1819)												3			
Bradley, Andrew	1				1	4		1	2		Y				
Bradley, Asa (1748 - 1816)											Y				
Bradley, Azariah (1734 - 1812)					2	5					Y	1			
Bradley, Azariah Jr.															
Bradley, Benjamin (1657 - 1728)								1	2		Y			1	1
Bradley, Caleb (1700 - 1784)					2			2	3		Y				
Bradley, Charles (1743 - 1799)											Y	2			
Bradley, Ebenezer (1726 - 1802)											Y				
Bradley, Edmund (1757 - 1828)											Y				
Bradley, Eli (1736 - 1811)													3		
Bradley, Elisha (1732 - 1815)													6		
Bradley, Erastus (1741 - 1808)	4				1	1				4	Y	1			
Bradley, Gamaliel (1733 - 1803)											Y				
Bradley, Gurdon (1738 - 1821)															
Bradley, Hezikiah (1731 -1777)					3		1				Y				
Bradley, Isaac (1722 - 1784)					1				1						
Bradley, Jabez (1733 - 1798)						1									
Bradley, Jacob (1734 - 1795)	1		1		1	3	2								
Bradley, James (1739 - 1817)						2					Y	1			
Bradley, Jared (1760 - 1814)															
Bradley, Jason (1740 - 1819)						2					Y	2			
Bradley, Joel Jr. (1738 - 1801)			1					1							
Bradley, John (1702 - 1772)									1		Y	2	4		1
Bradley, John, Jr. (1739 - 1779)											Y				
Bradley, Jonah (1732 - 1814)		1													
Bradley, Jonathan (1741 - 1771)												1			
Bradley, Joseph (1707 - 1787)	4	4				6	1				Y				
Bradley, Joseph Jr. (1742 - 1787)						1		1	2		Y				
Bradley, Josiah Capt. (1760 - 1822)	3				1	2	1	1			Y	1			3
Bradley, Lemuel (1759 - 1832)	1		2												
Bradley, Obed (1752 - 1776)					1	2					Y				
Bradley, Phineas (1745 - 1797)	1				1	13					Y	2			

180

Name	General Assembly	Selectman	Town Treasurer	Town Clerk	Grandjuryman	Justice of Peace	Major Committeeman	Minor Committeeman	Constable	Surveyor	Freeman	Rate Collector/Lister	Brander/Sealer/Keykeeper	Hayward	Fenceviewer
Bradley, Reuben (1750 - 1827)										2					
Bradley, Samuel (1731 - ?)														1	3
Bradley, Simeon (1731 - 1802)						1						6			
Bradley, Stephen (1726 - 1800)				1						2	Y	1	32		
Bradley, Timothy (1721 - 1803)	2					5					Y	1			
Bradley, Titus (1744 - 1811)										1	Y	3			
Bradley, Wilmont (1751 - 1814)										2	Y				
Bradley, Zina (1747 - 1802)											Y				
Bristol, Daniel (1671 - 1728)															
Bristol, David (1742 - ?)				5							Y	3			
Bristol, David, Jr. (1767 - 1817)												2			
Bristol, Eliphalet (1679 - 1757)										1	Y	3		1	
Bristol, George (1762 - 1813)								2			Y				
Bristol, Henry (? - 1695)															
Bristol, Henry (1683 - 1750)										1	Y				2
Bristol, John (1659 - 1735)										1	Y	2		1	
Bristol, Samuel (1651 - 1692)															
Bristol, Samuel (1706 - 1774)															
Bristol, Simeon (1739 - 1805)	2					4			5	1	Y				
Bristol, Stephen (1707 - 1785)				1						1	Y				
Brockett, Benjamin (1762 - ?)															
Brockett, Hezekiah (1727 - 1797															
Brockett, Lewis (? - 1828)															
Brockett, Miles (? - 1820)															
Brockett, Sidney (? - 1820)															
Brockett, William (1765 - 1794)															
Brown, David (? - 1726)											Y				
Brown, Ebenezer (1647 - 1714)										1	Y				1
Brown, Ebenezer (1670 - 1707)											Y				
Brown, Eleazer (1731 - 1799)															
Brown, Francis (1743 - 1810)											Y				
Brown, George (1702 - ?)															
Brown, James (1746 - 1770)															
Brown, Nathaniel (1701 - 1751)															
Brown, Nathaniel (1751 - ?)															
Brown, Robert (1736 - 1807)						1	1					1	2		
Brown, Thomas															
Brown, Timothy (1744 - 1823)										1	Y				
Brown, William (1768 -1811)											Y				
Budd, John (ca. 1655)															
Buell, Samuel															
Bunnell, Benjamin (1679 - 1749)											Y				
Bunnel, Israel (1689 - 1757)	5			1							Y				

Visible Saints

Name	General Assembly	Selectman	Town Treasurer	Town Clerk	Grandjuryman	Justice of Peace	Major Committeeman	Minor Committeeman	Constable	Surveyor	Freeman	Rate Collector/Lister	Brander/Sealer/Keykeeper	Hayward	Fenceviewer
Burwell, John															
Burwell, Samuel (1661 - 1719)				1							Y	1			
Burwell, Stephen (1696 -1784)				1								1			
Candee, Albert															
Candee, Caleb (1722- 1777)											Y	1			
Candee, Ezra (1731 - 1762)															
Candee, Gideon (1712 - 1748)											Y	1			
Candee, Job (1760 - 1845)															
Candee, Samuel (1664 - 1749)	2			2				1	1		Y	2		4	3
Candee, Samuel 1707 - 1773	4			2	1	1			5		Y	5	8		1
Candee, Samuel Jr. (1738 - 1821)										1		1	4		
Candee, Zaccheus (1640 - 1720)											Y				
Candee, Zaccheus (1743 - 1804)				1					1		Y	3			
Catlin, John (1715 - 1792)				1							Y	2			
Catlin, John (1759 - 1790)															
Catlin, Nathaniel (1749 - 1795)															
Clark, Caleb (1732 - ?)									3		Y	2			
Clark, Daniel (1737 - ?)											Y				
Clark, David (1742 - 1778)									1		Y		1		
Clark, Edmund (1750 - 1828)											Y				
Clark, James (? - 1712)						1	1								
Clark, Jehiel (1756 - 1816)															
Clark, John (1637 -1718)															
Clark, Joseph (1668 - 1703)															1
Clark, Merrit (1745 - 1823)				1							Y	2			2
Clark, Nehemiah															
Clark, Oliver											Y	1			
Clark, Parsons				1					2		Y	2			
Clark, Raphael				1			1								
Clark, Richard (1753 - 1793)															
Clark, Russel	3				3						Y	1			
Clark, Samuel (1666 - 1712)											Y			2	1
Clark, Samuel (1723 - 1778)					2	2					Y	2			
Clark, Samuel Jr. (1769 - 1817)											Y				
Clark, Thaddeus (1731 - 1813)	1			1			2	1			Y				
Clark, Thompson (1765 - 1792)															
Clinton, Anson (ca. 1665)															
Clinton, Anson (1764 - 1813)															
Clinton, Daniel (															
Clinton, David															
Clinton, George (? - 1776)									2		Y	5			
Clinton, Henry (1734 - ?)															
Clinton, Levi (1732 - 1782)				1					1		Y	1			

Officeholders

Name	General Assembly	Selectman	Town Treasurer	Town Clerk	Grandjuryman	Justice of Peace	Major Committeeman	Minor Committeeman	Constable	Surveyor	Freeman	Rate Collector/Lister	Brander/Sealer/Keykeeper	Hayward	Fenceviewer
Clinton, Shubael															
Clinton, Thomas (? - 1761)											Y				1
Downs, Benjamin (1734 - 1793)										1		2			
Downs, Ebenezer (1667 - 1711)														1	3
Downs, Ebenezer (1727 - 1790)															
Downs, Job					1							2			
Downs, John (n.d.)															2
Downs, Joseph (1732 - ?)										1		1			
Downs, Nathaniel (1701 - 1786)											Y	3			
Downs, Nathaniel, Jr. (1731 - 1801)															
Downs, Samuel (1696 - 1776)		1									Y	3		4	3
Downs, Samuel (1662 - 1711)		1									Y	1		3	2
Downs, Samuel (1720 - 1801)										2		2			
Downs, Seth (1704 - 1767)		1													
Downs, Seth (1730 - 1795)		1								2		3			
Downs, Thomas (1699 - 1785)		1								2	Y	2			
Eaton, James (ca. 1660)															
Ford, Matthew (1675 - 1751)										1	Y		1	7	4
Ford, Matthew (? - 1694)															2
Ford, Nathan (1733 - ?)		1								1	Y	2			
Ford, Samuel (1640 - 1712)											Y				
Ford, Stephen (1712 - 1776)										3		1			
Ford, Stephen (1749 - 1843)															
Ford, Timothy (1715 - ?)										2	Y				1
Gourley, James (? - 1787)															
Harges, Ebenezer (1760s)															
Hatch, John (1750s)											Y				
Hatch, Zephamiah (1706 - 1792)															
Higgins, Abraham (1770s)															
Hine, Isaac (1743 - 1807)															
Hodge, Benjamin (1770s)															
Hodge, Daniel (? - 1777)															
Hodge, Daniel, Jr. (1729 - 1787)															
Hodge, Jesse (1780 - 1856)															
Hodge, Thomas (1692 - ?)															
Hodge, William (1770s)															
Humphreville, Benjamin															
Humphreville, Ebenezer (1726 - 1802)															
Humphreville, Eliphalet (1703 - 1730)															
Humphreville, John (1690s)															
Humphreville, John (1702 - 1751)										1	Y				1
Humphreville, Joseph (1759 - 1830)															
Humphreville, Lemuel (1770 - 1828)															

Visible Saints

Name	General Assembly	Selectman	Town Treasurer	Town Clerk	Grandjuryman	Justice of Peace	Major Committeeman	Minor Committeeman	Constable	Surveyor	Freeman	Rate Collector/Lister	Brander/Sealer/Keykeeper	Hayward	Fenceviewer
Humphreville, Moses (1763 - 1829)															
Humphreville, Samuel (1666 - 1748)					1					1	Y	4		1	6
Humphreville, Samuel (1724 - 1790)										2	Y				
Humphreville, Thomas (1704 - 1738)										1	Y				
Johnson, Abraham (1694 - 1775)										3	Y				2
Johnson, Asahel (1736 - 1811)															
Johnson, Ebenezer (1737 - 1818)										1	Y		1		
Johnson, Eliaphlet (1668 - 1718)					1					1		2			
Johnson, Eliphlet (1742 - ?)										1					
Johnson, Enos (1725 - 1801)										1	Y				
Johnson, Enos (1766 - 1809)															
Johnson, Issac (1672 - 1750)	1				2	5				1	Y	2		1	1
Johnson, Jesse (1733 - 1822)										2					
Johnson, John (1665 - 1742)															
Johnson, John, Jr. (1665 - 1742)		1			2				1	3	Y	3		12	4
Johnson, John (1696 - 1774)										2		1		1	2
Johnson, John (1731 - 1791)					2						Y				
Johnson, John (1754 - 1837)															
Johnson, Joseph										2					
Johnson, Nehimah											Y				
Johnson, Obed (1744 - 1789)					1						Y	2			
Johnson, Peter (1745 - 1813)		1			5	3	1		2		Y				
Johnson, Samuel (1678 - 1755)										3	Y			3	5
Johnson, Samuel (1715 - 1788)												1			
Johnson, Thomas (1724 - 1784)										2		1			
Johnson, William (? - 1716)		1					1			1	Y	1			12
Johnson, William (1665 - 1742)		1					3			1	Y	5		3	5
Jones, Benjamin (1688 - 1752)															1
Jones, Issac (1694 - 1732)										1	Y				4
Jones, Isaac (1738 -1812)										1	Y	5			
Jones, Isaac Jr. 1775 - 1850)											Y				
Jones, John (1737 - 1802)															
Jones, Nathaniel (? - 1691)															2
Jones, Timothy (1696 - 1781)					3				5	1	Y	2		1	2
Jones, Timothy (1737 - 1800)								2			Y	2			
Kimberly, Agrippa															
Kimberly, Azel (1752 - 1802)		2			1					2	Y	5	10		
Kimberly, Eleazer (1639 - 1709)	1	1									Y				
Kimberly, Eliakim (1772 1854)															
Kimberly, Gideon (1765 - 1815)															
Kimberly, Gilead (1755 - 1831)						1	1			1	Y				
Kimberly, Israel (1724 - 1768)		2				2			7		Y	2			
Kimberly, Israel										1		1			

184

Name	General Assembly	Selectman	Town Treasurer	Town Clerk	Grandjuryman	Justice of Peace	Major Committeeman	Minor Committeeman	Constable	Surveyor	Freeman	Rate Collector/Lister	Brander/Sealer/Keykeeper	Hayward	Fenceviewer
Kimberly, John (1738 - before 1767															
Kimberly, Leverett (1772 - 1801)															
Kimberly, Linus (? - 1775)															
Kimberly, Nathaniel (? - 1705)									1	1	Y	4			
Kimberly, Nathaniel (? - 1720)															
Kimberly, Nathaniel (1700 - 1780)		8		2						4	Y	4	4		3
Kimberly, Nathaniel (1743 - ?)						1					Y	3			
Kimberly, Nathaniel (1759 - 1804)											Y				
Kimberly, Silas (1743 - 1803)				1		6	1		1	5	Y				
Kimberly, Thomas (? - 1672)		14							1	1	Y			2	4
Kimberly, Thomas, Jr.															
Kimberly, Zuriel											Y				
Kirby, Joseph (1705 - 1725)															
Lamberton, George (? - 1646)	6										Y				
Laboree, David (? - 1801)															
Leek, Philip (? - 1676)									2						
Leek, Thomas (1648 - 1720)														1	15
Mallory, Daniel (1687 - 1760)				1					1		Y			2	
Mallory, John (1705 - 1777)											Y			1	2
Mallory, Joseph (1666 - ?)															1
Mallory, Peter (? - 1698/99)															
Mallory, Peter, Jr. (1653 - 1720)											Y	1			2
Mallory, Thomas (1723 - 1805)											Y				
Meaker, William (ca. 1660s)															
Mix, Amos											Y				
Mix, Caleb (1750 - 1802)						1			1		Y				
Mix, David (1744 - 1790)											Y				
Mix, Diodate (1765 - ?)											Y				
Mix, Eldad (1733 - 1806)				1											
Mix, Elisha (1752 - 1813)											Y				
Mix, Hezikiah											Y				
Mix, John (1649 - 1712)		1							2	4	Y	4		3	14
Mix, John (1720 - 1796)		10			5				6	8	Y	6			11
Mix, John Jr. 1751 - 1820)															
Mix, Jonathan (1729 - 1779)								11		1	Y				
Mix, Joseph (1684 - 1757)	2	12		2			2			1	Y	5		1	7
Mix, Joseph (1740 - 1813)				1							Y				
Mix, Joseph											Y				
Mix, Nathaniel (1749 - 1781)				1							Y				
Mix, Samuel (1730 - 1813)		1		2	1						Y				
Mix, Stephen (1753 - 1784)											Y				
Mix, Thomas (1755 - 1810)										1					
Mix, William (1779 - 1803)											Y				

Name	General Assembly	Selectman	Town Treasurer	Town Clerk	Grandjuryman	Justice of Peace	Major Committeeman	Minor Committeeman	Constable	Surveyor	Freeman	Rate Collector/Lister	Brander/Sealer/Keykeeper	Hayward	Fenceviewer
Moss, John (1698 - 1777)				7											
Moss, Joseph (1643 - 1727)		7								9	Y	3			3
Moss, Joseph (1679 - 1732)	3										Y	1			
Mullinier, Thomas (1660s)															
Nash, John (1615 - 1687)				5		1									
Osborne, Benjamin															
Osborne, Daniel (1715 - ?)					2					1	Y	2			
Osborne, David (1746 - 1786)											Y				
Osborne, Elijah (? - 1814)											Y				
Osborne, Jeremiah (1656 - 1713)	10	2				2	11	4			Y	5			2
Osborne, Jonathan (1692 - 1750)															
Osborne, Joseph (1667 - 1735)					1				1	1	Y				13
Osborne, Medad (1753 - 1814)		4			1					4	Y	1			
Osborne, Samuel		2			1				3	1	Y	1			
Painter, Deliverance (1701 - 1781)		2			1										
Painter, Elisha (1736 - 1781)					1										
Painter, Joseph (1731 - 1766)					1				3	1	Y	1			
Painter, Lamberton (1741 - 1795)		1					2			1	Y	1			
Painter, Shubael (1697 - 1785)									7		Y	4		1	5
Painter, Thomas (1670 - 1747)		1			1				1		Y	3		2	2
Painter, Thomas (1696 - 1760)					1	1					Y	3			
Painter, Thomas (1760 - 1847)		4					6			1	Y				
Peck, Amos (1749 - 1838)					1						Y				
Peck, Benjamin (1746 - 1812)					1						Y	2			
Peck, Daniel													2		
Peck, Ebenezer		2													
Peck, Henry (1755 - 1802)					1				1		Y				
Peck, Hezikiah (1767 - 1840)									1						
Peck, James (1708 - 1794)		11			2			2	2	3	Y				
Peck, John										1		4			
Peck, Joseph (1647 - 1720)										2	Y	11	3		
Peck, Joseph (1718 - 1788)					2					4	Y	1	13		
Peck, Joseph Jr. (1749 - 1800)							1		13	1	Y				
Peck, Moses (1753 - 1837)											Y				
Peck, Roger (1746 - 1808)											Y	2	3		
Peck, Seth (1747 - 1831)					2						Y	4			
Peck, Stephen (1730 -1778)					2					4	Y	1			
Peck, Thomas Jr.											Y				
Peck, Timothy (1737 - 1807)									1		Y				
Peck, Titus (1742 - 1776)					1				1		Y				
Perkins, Edward (? - post 1688)															
Perkins, Jonathan (1694 - ?)											Y			5	7
Phipps, David															

Officeholders

Name	General Assembly	Selectman	Town Treasurer	Town Clerk	Grandjuryman	Justice of Peace	Major Committeeman	Minor Committeeman	Constable	Surveyor	Freeman	Rate Collector/Lister	Brander/Sealer/Keykeeper/Drummer	Hayward	Fenceviewer
Phipps, Solomon (1745 - 1813)											Y				
Phipps, Timothy											Y				
Platt, Ebenezer (1770s)													5		7
Platt, Josiah					1					1	Y	1			
Platt, Richard (1650s)					2							1			2
Preston, Edward (1619 - 1699)															
Prindle, Asahel (1759 - 1785)															
Prindle, Charles (1733 - 1806)					1						Y	1			
Prindle, Charles (1763 - 1841)											Y	1			
Prindle, Elijah (1744 - 1803)					4					1	Y	3			1
Prindle, Joel (1695 - ?)															
Prindle, John (1730 - 1806)						1			1	1	Y	2			
Prindle, Joseph (1663 - 1737)		2								1	Y				
Prindle, Joseph (1704 - 1771)					1	3				1					
Prindle, Joseph (1731 - 1814)					1					1	Y				
Prindle, Joseph (1757 - 1824)															
Prindle, Stephen (1765 - 1822)											Y	1			
Prindle, William (? - 1690)															
Punderson, John (1644 - 1781)		4									Y		4		5
Punderson, Thomas (1713 - 1781)				2							Y	3	4		
Roberts, Eli (? - 1693)															
Rosewell, Lydia (1666 - 1732)			1												
Rosewell, Richard (1652 - 1702)			1			5		1				2			2
Sabin, Hezekiah, Jr. (1750 - ?)			1			10	1			2	Y				
Sherman, Samuel (1673 - 1769)		2		1						4	Y	3	7		5
Sherman, Samuel (1704 - 1769)	7									1	Y	1	1		
Smith, Agrippa (1753 - 1783)	(Died aboard British prison ship)														
Smith, Andrew (1702 - 1789)					1					1	Y				
Smith, Andrew Jr. (1740 - 1796)					1					1	Y				
Smith, Asa (1728 - 1782)					1					1	Y	2			
Smith, Austin (1711 - 1797)										1	Y	1			1
Smith, Benjamin (1723 - 1792)					1			1			Y	2			
Smith, Benjamin (1753 - 1796)	(Lost at sea)														
Smith, Burrell									3						
Smith, Caleb															
Smith, Chauncey (1744 - 1778)															
Smith, Daniel (1693 - 1771)											Y		1		
Smith, Daniel (1710 - 1757)										2	Y	1			
Smith, David (1747 - 1809)					1						Y	3			
Smith, Deliverance (1719 - 1785)															
Smith, Deliverance (1755 - 1802)															
Smith, Ebenezer (1688 - 1767)		3									Y				
Smith, Ebenezer (1730 - 1808)															

Visible Saints

Name	General Assembly	Selectman	Town Treasurer	Town Clerk	Grandjuryman	Justice of Peace	Major Committeeman	Minor Committeeman	Constable	Surveyor	Freeman	Rate Collector/Lister	Brander/Sealer/Keykeeper	Hayward	Fenceviewer
Smith, Edward (1731 - 1813)															
Smith, Elihu (1749 - 1775)															
Smith, Ezra (1763 - 1841))						1									1
Smith, George (? - 1662)															
Smith, George (1681 - 1741)											Y				
Smith, George (1717 - 1794)					1					1	Y	4	11		
Smith, Gideon (1720 - 1776)															
Smith, Gold (1764 - 1800)		3			2						Y	2			
Smith, Hezikiah		1			1					1	Y	2			
Smith, Isaac										1	Y				
Smith, Jacob															
Smith, Jared (1766 - ?)															
Smith, Jeremiah (1754 - 1834)		3									Y	8			
Smith, John, Sr. (1647 - 1711)											Y	2			4
Smith, John, Jr. (1673 - 1768)										1	Y	2			8
Smith, John (1748 - 1777)	(Lost at sea)										Y				
Smith, John (1756 - 1777)										2	Y	2			
Smith, Jonathan (1692 - 1759)		2						1		2	Y	5		2	5
Smith, Johnathan (1716 - 1784)		2			2	1					Y	3			
Smith, Johnathan (1758 - ?)															
Smith, Joseph (1655 - 1697)															1
Smith, Joseph (1667 - 1713)															
Smith, Joseph (1680 - 1749)		2			2					2	Y	4		1	4
Smith, Joseph (1751 - 1797)															
Smith, Justin									2						
Smith, Justus (1754 - 1817)		2								2	Y	3			
Smith, Lamberton (1701 - 1779)					1	1				2	Y	2			
Smith, Lamberton Jr.(1734 - 1791)									7	1	Y	2			
Smith, Nathan (1656 - 1726)											Y	1			5
Smith, Nathan (1713 -1787)										2	Y	1			
Smith, Nathan (1733 - 1807)					1					2	Y				
Smith, Nathaniel (1758 - 1806)					1			1		2	Y	2	3		
Smith, Nehemiah (1730 - 1808)		6			2	12	2	1		2	Y	7			
Smith, Oliver (1735 - 1804)					1	1				7	Y	7			
Smith, Phileman (1748 - 1808)					1				4	1	Y	5			
Smith, Samuel (1651 - 1726)	1	5			1						Y	5			3
Smith, Samuel (1678 - 1753)	6				1					1	Y	2			2
Smith, Samuel (1717 - 1784)															
Smith, Samuel (1738 - 1784)					1						Y				
Smith, Samuel (1757 - 1794	(Lost at sea)														
Smith, Silas															
Smith, Stephen															
Smith, Thaddeus (1767 - 1800)	(Lost at sea)														

Officeholders

Name	General Assembly	Selectman	Town Treasurer	Town Clerk	Grandjuryman	Justice of Peace	Major Committeeman	Minor Committeeman	Constable	Surveyor	Freeman/Proprietor	Rate Collector/Lister	Brander/Sealer/Keykeeper/Drummer	Hayward	Fenceviewer
Smith, Thomas (1759 - 1807)											Y	2			
Smith, Titus (1756 - 1804)				1						3	Y	2			
Smith, Warham (1760 - 1805)															
Sperry, Aza (1736 - 1822)										2					
Sperry, Daniel (1665 - 1750)				2						1	Y				
Sperry, Ebenezer (1739 1815)										1	Y				
Sperry, Elihu (1746 - ?)											Y	2			
Sperry, Ezra (1737 - 1803)				1						1	Y	2			
Sperry, Ezra (1767 - 1838)										4	Y		1		
Sperry, Hezekiah (1746 - ?)				1				2		1	Y	1			
Sperry, Lemuel (1751 - 1840)											Y				
Sperry, Lent (1742 - 1823)											Y				
Sperry, Nathaniel (1656 - 1735)										1	Y	3			
Sperry, Nathaniel (1727 - 1776)										4	Y				
Sperry, Reuben (1735 - 1795)										2					
Sperry, Richard (1652 - 1734)											Y				
Sperry, Richard (1681 - 1740)		1								1	Y	1			
Sperry, Simeon (1738 - 1805)											Y				
Sperry, William (1740 - 1829)										1	Y	2			
Stevens, Thomas (1677 - 1777)	1			2							Y			1	2
Stevens, Thomas (1713 - 1752)											Y				
Thomas, Amos (1743 - 1797)									1	1	Y				
Thomas, Benajah												1			
Thomas, Charles				1							Y	1			
Thomas, Daniel (? - 1694)											Y				
Thomas, Daniel (1676 - 1760)				1						1	Y	2			
Thomas, Daniel (1710 - 1757)											Y				2
Thomas, Gershom (1760s)										1		1			
Thomas, Israel (1720 - 1784)				1							Y				
Thomas, John (1672 - 1712)											Y				7
Thomas, John (1675 - 1747)				1							Y	1			
Thomas, Joseph (ca. 1685)														4	5
Thomas, Samuel (1651 - 1711)											Y			1	2
Thomas, Samuel (1688 - 1726)														1	2
Thompson, Abraham				1						1	Y				
Thompson, Abraham Jr.															
Thompson, Anthony				2						3	Y	1		1	
Thompson, Ebenezer											Y				
Thompson, Elijah (1790s)										1	Y				
Thompson, Isaac				2							Y	3	1		
Thompson, Jacob											Y	1			
Thompson, James (1721 - 1803)				1				1		1	Y	2	7		
Thompson, Jared				1											

Visible Saints

Name	General Assembly	Selectman	Town Treasurer	Town Clerk	Grandjuryman	Justice of Peace	Major Committeeman	Minor Committeeman	Constable	Surveyor	Freeman	Rate Collector/Lister	Brander/Sealer/Keykeeper	Hayward	Fenceviewer
Thompson, John (? - 1707)	1					3					Y				1
Thompson, John (1657 - 1711)	6	1							1		Y	1			6
Thompson, John (1721 - ?)											Y	2			
Thompson, Jonathan (1732 - 1784)					1					1	Y	3			
Thompson, Joseph (1703 - 1745)								2			Y	2		1	2
Thompson, Joseph (1730 - 1794)					1		3				Y				
Thompson, Juduthan (? - 1779)	(killed in British invasion of New Haven)														
Thompson, Samuel (1743 - 1767)											Y				
Thompson, Stephen (1705 - 1746)					1				3	1	Y	1		1	1
Thompson, William (1674 - 1717)															3
Thompson, William (? - 1741)	1	4					12		2	48	Y	4	8	1	5
Tolles, Ebenezer ((1669 -1751)					1					1	Y				
Tolles, Henry (1736 1810)										1	Y	1			
Tolles, Nehemiah										1					
Tolles, Samuel										1	Y				1
Trowbridge, David											Y				
Trowbridge, Ebenezer					1				6		Y	3		2	2
Trowbridge, John (1684 - 1739)									1		Y	1			2
Trowbridge, Stephen (1688 - 1734)	1				1				1		Y	1			2
Trowbridge, Thomas (1663 - 1711)			1								Y	3		1	2
Trowbridge, William (1700 - 1793)					1					3	Y	3			4
Tuttle, Joseph (1640 - 1690)											Y	1		2	2
Ward, Ambrose (1735 - 1808)					2										
Ward, John (? - 1785)	(Died at sea)														
Ward, Thomas (1760 - 1830)															
Ward, William (1736 - 1829)															
Williston, Noah (1734 - 1811)											Y				

Selected Bibliography

Connecticut is blessed with an abundance of historical resources pertaining to its colonial history. From its voluminous public records to its many newspapers and wealth of primary and secondary sources, information on every aspect of Connecticut history is readily available at the state's public and private libraries and increasingly through the Internet.

There is no better place to start the study of Connecticut history than with a visit to the Connecticut State Library and its Web site (www.ctlib.org). The library's site provides a wealth of bibliographic and resource information on Connecticut as well as access to the statewide library catalog system. Its collection of Connecticut archives pertaining to both colony and state are unrivalled.

For any work available prior to 1982, Christopher and Bonnie Collier's *The Literature of Connecticut History* (Middletown, CT: Connecticut Humanities Council, 1982) is a treasure trove of information compiled by two of the state's leading scholars. Whether a serious historian or interested reader, any serious undertaking into Connecticut's past should start here.

Other "must-visit" repositories include The Connecticut Historical Society, the New Haven Museum, as well as Southern Connecticut, Wesleyan, UCONN and Yale universities.

With the advent of the Connecticut Card, the collections of virtually every public library in the state are now at researchers' fingertips. Much of the periodical literature is also available on-line, often in complete form. In compiling this study, I have included a brief mention of those resources at the end of this essay that I found to be the most helpful. Far from complete, it is meant to serve as a starting point for further research into West Haven, Connecticut and American colonial history in general.

Primary Sources: Manuscripts

Annual Army Lists, 1754 - 1874, British National Archives, London, England.

> A listing of British officers serving in the military through the latter half of the 18th Century into the 19th Century is helpful in tracing the service dates of specific officers but is not meant to be comprehensive.

British Headquarters. Orders, New York, September 11 - October 24, 1778. Early American Orderly Books, 1748-1817. New York Historical Society. Microfilm. Reel 3: No. 40.

> Copies of orders issued by the Commander in Chief of the British forces in North America, Sir William Howe, most regarding court martials and promotions.

British Regiment Footguards. Orders, New York and New Jersey, August 14, 1776 - January 28, 1777. Early American Orderly Books, 1748-1817. New York Historical Society. Microfilm. Reel 3: No. 37.

> Contains general, brigade and regimental orders including notice of Nathan Hale's execution.

Christ Church Episcopal Records, West Haven, Connecticut, 1788 - 1903. 6 vols. Hartford: Connecticut Archives, 1953, Connecticut State Library.

> The information contained in these volumes deals primarily with the normal events of the church, including vestry notes, marriages, deaths, and baptisms. They provide a vital source of information concerning the church's early years and membership.

Christ Church Register, 1851 - 1879. Hartford: Connecticut Archives, 1953, Connecticut State Library.

> Particularly significant are the few pages in this volume which recap Christ Church's 1740 budget, including amounts paid out for the construction of the first church.

Civil Officers of Connecticut 1669 - 1756. 3 vols. Hartford: Connecticut Archives, 1913, Connecticut State Library.

> Compiled by town, deal with the appointment of Connecticut individuals to various colonial

offices; important in tracing the rise of a select few to the highest offices in the colony.

Commissary General of Musters Office and Successors: General Muster Books and Pay Lists (WO12), British National Archives, London, England.

Essential resource in tracing the specific service dates and rank of individual British soldiers, often providing a brief description of the individual, his occupation ,and home town.

Crimes and Misdemeanors in Connecticut 1662 - 1789. 12 vols. Hartford: Connecticut Archives, 1913, Connecticut State Library.

These well-indexed volumes provide the particulars of celebrated crimes and misdemeanors throughout the colonial period and make for fascinating reading.

First Battalion of Guards. Orders, New York, January 1, 1779 - December 28, 1779. Early American Orderly Books, 1748 - 1817. New York Historical Society. Microfilm. Reel 6: No. 65.

Indispensable in learning the daily details of the Foot Guards in America, including official notice of William Campbell's death.

First Ecclesiastical Society Records in the Parish of West Haven 1724 - 1913. 12 vols. Hartford: Connecticut Archives, 1916, Connecticut State Library.

Of paramount importance in the study of the local Congregational church and the parish struggle to survive through its first 75 years.

Howe, Sir William. Orders, September 26, 1776 - June 2, 1777. Early American Orderly Books, 1748 - 1817. New York Historical Society. Microfilm. Reel 3: No. 40

Contains general orders of Sir William Howe, Commander in Chief of the British forces in America. Concerns the Westchester Campaign and the Battle of White Plains, the capture of Fort Washington, the New Jersey Campaign, and the Battles of Trenton and Princeton. Also a discussion of Loyalist troops.

Johnson, Samuel. "On Doubts of the Congregational Faith." New York: Columbia University Archives.

In his own words, the Reverend Johnson tells of his inner crisis of faith which led to his subsequent conversion to Episcopacy, along with a quarter of West Haven's Congregational parishioners.

New Haven Town Records 1769 - 1807. New Haven: New Haven Colony Historical Society.

> Chronicling the town's affairs during the Revolution and early national periods, the records trace the evolution of New Haven from a small colonial town to a major American city and its zenith as an American seaport. An annotated version of the records is in the possession of the author.

Pemberton, Ebenezer. "The Knowledge of Christ Recommended." Sermon Delivered At Yale College (April 19, 1741). New Haven: Yale University Archives.

> A fine example of its type, this sermon captures the emotions of revivalism and the Great Awakening's impact on the New Haven area.

Smith, Philemon. Record of Deaths From Aunt Lucena's List, 1774 - 1861. Hartford: Connecticut Archives, 1930, Connecticut State Library.

> A unique mortality listing of West Haven residents undertaken by an early resident and continued by the village clerk for nearly a 90-year period. An invaluable resource for the genealogist and local historian.

Stiles, Ezra, Papers. Beinecke Rare Book Library, New Haven: Yale University.

> A seminal resource by Yale president and leading clergyman that contains correspondence, itineraries, literary diaries, weather journals, miscellaneous papers, and sermons. A microfilm version of the Stiles papers also exists accompanied by a printed guide by Harold E. Selesky.

Travel Highways, Ferries, Bridges, and Taverns. Hartford: Connecticut Archives, 1913, Connecticut State Library.

> An essential resource for anyone interested in the developing infrastructure of the colony, from native footpaths to intercolonial travel.

Trinity Church Parochial Register, New Haven, Connecticut, 1767 - 1814. Hartford: Connecticut Archives, 1941, Connecticut State Library.

> Disappointing in its lack of details concerning Revolutionary events, the register does contain vital statistics of West Haven's Episcopal parish.

Weeks, Joshua. "Journal of Reverend Joshua Weeks, Loyalist Rector of St. Michael's Church, Marblehead, 1778 - 1779." Essex Institute, *Historical Collections*, 1915.

> Offers an incisive analysis of the American revolutionary movement and its methodology to convert Loyalists to the American cause.

Printed Primary Materials

Dexter, Franklin B., and Powers, Zara. Editors. *Ancient Town Records of New Haven*. 3 vols. New Haven: Tuttle, Morehouse and Taylor, I, II, 1919. The Quinnipiac Press, III, 1962.

> These volumes are indispensable in the study of West Haven's colonial history. The information is well documented, particularly in the third volume, and ranges from the incidental to the monumental.

Dexter, Franklin B. Editor. *Extracts from the Itineraries of Ezra Stiles 1755 - 1794*. New Haven: Yale University Press, 1916.

> An excellent reference compiled by one of America's most astute colonial observers. Topics cover a wide range of subjects, from traits of the Quinnipiac to the Royal Academy of Science.

_____, ed. The Literary Diary of Ezra Stiles, D.D., L.L.D. 3 vols. New York: Scribners' Sons, 1901.

> Notably important in the study of New Haven in the Revolution, Stiles's diary complements the town's official records with insightful information concerning social and political events throughout the Revolutionary period

Hoadley, Charles and Trumbull, Jonathan. Editors. *Public Records of the Colony of Connecticut*. 15 vols. Various publishers, 1850 - 1890.

> An indispensable resource in tracing the development of colonial affairs affecting both the colony and its various towns.

Hoadley, Charles, *et.al. Public Records of the State of Connecticut 1776 - 1792*. 7 vols. Hartford: Case, Lockwood and Brainerd, 1894 - 1948.

> A continuation of the affairs of official Connecticut as a state through the beginnings of the early national period.

Hoadley, Charles, editor. *Records of the Colony and Plantations of New Haven 1638 - 1665*. 2 vols. Hartford: Case, Tiffany and Company, 1858.

The primary source of information concerning New Haven's years as a separate colony.

Knight, Sarah K. *The Private Journal of Sarah Kemble Knight*. Norwich, Connecticut: The Academy Press, 1801.

> Although only briefly mentions New Haven, Knight's journal paints an interesting picture of life in colonial America as seen through the eyes of one of its keenest observers.

Painter, Thomas. *Autobiography*. Washington, D.C. Printed for private circulation, 1910.

> A West Haven resident who was prominent in the West Indies trade, Painter's recollections of the 1779 invasion of West Haven are among the few extant eyewitness accounts. Written many years after the fact, Painter 's version of the attack needs to be read with a tempered eye.

Sabine, William Henry Waldo, ed. *Historical Memoirs of William Smith, 1778 - 1783*. Manchester, NH: Ayer Publishing, 1971.

> Invaluable first-hand observations of the Revolution by a leading New York lawyer and Loyalist. Smith records some items pertaining to the British invasion of New Haven, including a report on casualties.

Secondary Works (Unpublished)

Boaz, Roy. "A Study of the Faith and Practice of the First Congregational Church of West Haven, Connecticut, 1719 - 1914." Ph.D. dissertation, Yale University, 1938.

> An admirable study of the First Society and its development as a religious entity. Boaz makes use of numerous sources and presents a well balanced thesis. Unfortunately, there is little documentation concerning the social and political evolution of the village, as its emphasis is primarily religious.

Chapin, Alonzo. "A Sermon Delivered in Christ Church, West Haven, Connecticut." Paper presented at the 100th Anniversary of Christ Church, West Haven, Connecticut, 1839. New Haven: Yale University Archives.

> The earliest years of Episcopacy in West Haven are sketchy at best. However, Chapin discusses the foundations of the church from its founding to the ministry of Reverend Bela Hubbard.

Colton, Erastus. "Discourse: Historical of West Haven Congregational

Church and of the Old Parsonage." Sermon presented at the 120th Anniversary of the First Congregational Church, West Haven Connecticut, 1839. West Haven, Connecticut: First Congregational Parish House.

> Most important for its genealogical information, this work also provides an historical sketch of West Haven's First Society through the Revolution.

Thompson, Harry Ives. West Haven, Connecticut, History and Genealogy Working Papers. Unpublished notes, Hartford: Connecticut Archives, 1938. Connecticut State Library.

> A prolific researcher and talented artist, Thompson developed what remains the most comprehensive source of information on early West Haven and its people. As working papers they are, at times, difficult to decipher. In reviewing Thompson's research, the reader should be mindful of his tendency to play fast and loose with dates.

Secondary Works (Published)

Atwater, Edward E. Editor. *History of the City of New Haven to the Present Time.* New York: Munsell and Company, 1887.

> Typical of its period, Atwater's work contains a host of commercial advertisements, biographies of New Haven luminaries, and a wealth of historical information pertaining to New Haven's social, religious, business, and professional development.

Bacon, Leonard. *New Haven One Hundred Years Ago.* New Haven: F.P. Shanley, 1876.

_____. *Thirteen Historical Discourses, on the Completion of Two Hundred Years, from the beginning of the First Church in New Haven.* New Haven: Durrie and Peck, 1839.

> Of particular significance is the description of New Haven's original theocracy prior to its union with Connecticut.

Baldwin, Alice. *The Clergy of Connecticut in the Revolutionary Days.* Connecticut Tercentenary Pamphlets. New Haven: Yale University Press, 1938.

Barber, John W. *History and Antiquities of New Haven from the Earliest Settlement to the Present Time.* New Haven: J.W. Barber, 1831.

> An accomplished artist, Barber illustrated most of the towns he visited and therein lies

its richest rewards. Barber's work also provides valuable insights to uncovering important source materials for the study of early New Haven.

Beals, Carleton. *Our Yankee Heritage*. New Haven: Bradley and Scoville Incorporated, 1951.

Beardsley, Eben E. *The History of the Episcopal Church in Connecticut*. 2 vols. New York: Hurd and Houghton Company, 1865 - 1869.

The best church history of the period, this work contains sketches of several leading figures who had a major impact on the Anglican mission in West Haven.

Bradstreet, Howard. *The Story of the War with the Pequots Retold*. In Connecticut Tercentenary Pamphlets. New Haven: Yale University Press, 1933.

A concise account of the war with references to the initial English discovery of the Quinnipiac.

Boardman, Roger S. *Roger Sherman, Signer and Statesman*. Philadelphia: University of Pennsylvania, 1938.

An adequate but dated study of New Haven's leading revolutionary figure. Should be supplemented by Christopher Collier's *Roger Sherman's Connecticut: Yankee Politics and the American Revolution*. Middletown, CT, 1971.

Bronson, Henry. "A Historical Account of Connecticut Currency, Continental Money and the Finances of the Revolution." In New Haven Colony Historical Society *Papers*. New Haven: Thomas Stafford, 1866.

Breton, Benjamin, "The Quinnipiac: New Haven's First Inhabitants," in *Communication on Contemporary Anthropology*, published online, http://comonca.org/2008012.aspx, December 2008.

A welcomed and much-needed study of the Quinnipiac people written by the director of education for the New Haven Museum.

Brown, Lloyd A. *Loyalist Operations at New Haven*. Ann Arbor: The Clements Library, 1938.

A collection of maps on the British raids in New Haven in 1779 and 1781.

Brown, Wallace. *The Good Americans: Loyalists in the American Revolution*. New York: William Morrow and Company, 1969.

A meticulous presentation of the Loyalists and their failure to organize a strong counter-revolutionary movement.

Bushman, Richard L. *From Puritan to Yankee*. Cambridge: Harvard University Press, 1967.

> A superb analysis of Connecticut's Great Awakening and its subsequent impact on the social and political developments of the Connecticut colony.

Calder, Isabel. *The New Haven Colony*. New Haven: Yale University Press, 1934.

> This often cited study of New Haven's early years is useful for a general overview in providing leads for further study.

Chidsey, Donald. *The Loyalists: The Story of Those Americans Who Fought Against Independence*. New York: Crown Publishers, 1973.

Collier, Christopher. *Roger Sherman's Connecticut: Yankee Politics and the American Revolution*. Middletown, Connecticut: Wesleyan University Press, 1971.

> Among the best biographies of Connecticut's foremost Revolutionary statesman and New Haven's first mayor.

DeForest, John W. *History of the Indians of Connecticut from the Earliest Known Period till 1850*. Hamden: Archon Books Reprint, 1972.

> Although dated, this work remains a standard resource in the study of Connecticut's native Americans, including details in the socio-political makeup of various tribes.

Dexter, Franklin B. *Biographical Sketches of the Graduates of Yale College with Annals of the College History, 1703 - 1812*. 6 series. New York: Henry Holt and Company, 1885 - 1912.

> Indispensable resource on Yale graduates, including many West Haveners.

East, Robert. *Connecticut's Loyalists*. Connecticut Bicentennial Series VI. Chester, Connecticut: Pequot Press, 1974.

> In line with the objective of the series, this enlightening monograph is written for a general audience, but does not sacrifice scholarship in its telling.

Ford, George. "The Defense of New Haven and Resistance made Against Invading Troops Along the West Shore, July, 1779." In *Revolutionary Characters of New Haven*. Edited by the Sons of the American Revolution. New Haven: Price, Lee and Adkins Company, 1911.

Offers one of the first accounts of the 1779 British attack on New Haven.

Farnham, Thomas J., "The Day the Enemy Was in Town." The British Raids on Connecticut, July 1779," *Journal of The New Haven Colony Historical Society*, New Haven: Volume 22, Number 2, Summer 1976.

The most comprehensive and professional account of the British invasion of New Haven, fully documented and well written.

Fowler, William. "Ministers of Connecticut in the Revolution." *Centennial Papers of the General Conference of Congregational Churches of Connecticut.* Hartford: Case, Lockwood and Brainerd Company, 1887.

An important resource to the Congregational clergy, especially Noah Williston of West Haven and his close friend Benjamin Trumbull of North Haven.

Gipson, Lawrence H. "Connecticut Taxation, 1750 - 1775." In *Connecticut Tercentenary Pamphlets*. New Haven: Yale University Press, 1933.

A proponent of the imperial school, Gipson presents an in depth study of Connecticut's fiscal development on the eve of the Revolution.

_____. *Jared Ingersoll, American Loyalist*. New Haven: Yale University Press; reprint edition, 1971.

An excellent treatment of an American Loyalist. Valuable for its insights into the Stamp Act crisis and the Loyalist issue. It is here that West Haven was found to be a community vehemently opposed to internal taxation as evident in the protest of 1765.

_____. *The Coming of the Revolution 1763 - 1775*. New York: Harper and Row, 1954.

This classic study delves into the complex and various aspects of imperial relations on the eve of the war. A well-balanced and objective study, it is of great help in understanding the strained relationship between the Empire and the growing sense of nationalism in the colonies.

Goodrich, Chauncey. "Invasion of New Haven by the British Troops, July 5, 1779." In New Haven Colony Historical Society *Papers*. New Haven: Tuttle, Morehouse and Taylor, 1877.

Another in the plethora of New Haven invasion studies, this work is among the first to look at the invasion through an historian's eye.

Graham, Marguerite M. *The Invasion of New Haven, July 5, 1779*. West

Haven: West Haven Bicentennial Commission; reprint edition, 1975.

Greene, Lousie M. "New Haven Defenses in the Revolution." *Connecticut Quarterly*, Vol. IV (September 1898) pp. 272 - 290.

Haller, William. *The Puritan Frontier: Town Planting in New England Colonial Development 1630 - 1660*. New York: Columbia University Press, 1951.

A seminal study in town development, following the Germanic town platt format.

Hayward, Marjorie. *The East Side of New Haven Harbor*. New Haven: Yale University Press, 1938.

A charming if unpolished account of East Haven's history. There are numerous bits of information pertaining to the demographic and social aspects of a Connecticut village, not unlike West Haven in its origins.

Hegel, Richard. *Nineteenth-Century Historians of New Haven*. Hamden, Connecticut: Archon Books, 1972.

Particularly important in placing a number of New Haven historians into historical perspective. Emphasis is placed on technique, viewpoint and thoroughness.

Hindle, Brooke. *Editor. America's Wooden Age*. Tarrytown, New York: Sleepy Hollow Restorations, 1975.

Written by seven specialists on the technology of wood, Hindle has compiled an excellent study of this natural resource and its importance to the colonial economy.

Hinman, Royal R. Editor. *Historical Collection of the Part Sustained by Connecticut During the War of the Revolution*. Hartford: Gleason Company, 1842.

Hinman provides an important primary resource, especially useful for the 1779 invasion of New Haven.

History of Christ Church West Haven, Connecticut 1723 - 1945. West Haven: Church Press, 1945.

Primarily a restatement of Alonzo Chapin's work in dealing with the church's earliest years, it carries the history of Christ Church into the twentieth century.

Jarvis, Lucy C. *Sketches of Church Life in Colonial Connecticut*. New Haven: Tuttle, Morehouse and Taylor, 1902.

Supplements the story of West Haven's Episcopal mission and growth of Christ Church.

Jenkins, Stephen. *The Old Boston Post Road.* New York: G.P. Putnam's Sons, 1913.

Full of historical gems on one of the country's first "highways."

Johnston, Henry P. Editor. *The Record of Connecticut Men in the Military and Naval Service During the War of the Revolution 1775 - 1785.* New Haven: Case, Lockwood and Brainerd Company, 1889.

Includes specific references to the men involved and the damages incurred by the series of invasions at West Haven, including the Assembly's actions to compensate residents.

Katz, Stanley, editor. *Colonial America: Essays in Politics and Social Development.* Boston: Little, Brown and Company, 1971.

Designed to supplement a survey of colonial America, this volume is especially valuable in detailing family structure, themes underlying the witchcraft hysteria of the seventeenth century, and the Great Awakening in Connecticut.

Kurtz, Stephen and Hutson, James, editors. *Essays on the American Revolution.* Chapel Hill: The University of North Carolina Press, 1973.

Offers controversial interpretations of the causes and long-range effects of the American Revolution.

Lambert, Edward R. *History of the Colony of New Haven.* New Haven: Hitchcock and Stafford Company, 1888.

Noteworthy for its discussion of New Haven geography and its earliest years as an independent colony.

Langdon, William. *Everyday Things In American Life 1607 - 1776.* New York: Charles Schribner's Sons, 1937.

From the clothes they wore to the taverns they drank in, colonial Americans are described in everyday terms that humanize their social lives.

Levermore, Charles H. *The Republic of New Haven: A History of Municipal Evolution.* Port Washington, New York: Kennikat Press, 1884.

The most scholarly of nineteenth-century New Haven histories, Levermore's work stresses New Haven's distinctive features in tracing its political evolution.

Loveland, Clara O. *The Critical Years: The Reconstruction of the Anglican Church in the United States of America 1780 - 1789.* Greenwich, Connecticut: Seabury Press, 1956.

Traces the crisis of loyalty to the king and the Anglicans' eventual readjustment as a nonaligned religion.

Main, Jackson Turner. *Society and Economy in Colonial Connecticut.* Princeton, New Jersey: Princeton University Press, 1985.

Drawn from thousands of colonial records, Main's quantitative study provides important research on the make up of Connecticut's colonial society.

Malia, Peter J. *The Invasion of West Haven, July 5, 1779.* West Haven: privately printed, 1979.

Retells the story of the 1779 British invasion from a West Haven perspective.

Menta, John. *The Quinnipiac: Cultural Conflict in Southern New England.* New Haven: Yale University Publications in Anthropology, No. 86.

Originally developed as the author's M.A. thesis, this is among the best studies of the Quinnipiac and their interactions with the English.

Mead, Nelson P. *Connecticut as a Corporate Colony.* Lancaster, PA: The New Era Printing Company, 1906.

Middlebrook, Louis F. *History of Maritime Connecticut During the American Revolution 1775 - 1783.*

Considered a seminal work in the study of the Revolution, Middlebrook's provides exhaustive research on the state's considerable role in naval affairs, especially in outfitting privateers against the British. Contains collaborative evidence concerning the Thomas Painter's naval exploits and imprisonment.

Middlekauf, Robert. *The Glorious Cause: The American Revolution, 1763 - 1789.* New York: Oxford University Press, 1982.

An excellent overview of the period which chronicles the growing colonial crisis that eventually led to war. This is the first in a series of volumes in the Oxford History of the United States.

Nelson, William H. *The American Tory.* Oxford, England: The Clarendon Press. 1961.

Presents an intriguing, alternative approach to the American Revolution as a New England plot against the empire.

New Haven Colony Historical Society. *Papers.* 10 vols. New Haven: various publishers, 1865 - 1951.

A collection of miscellaneous and highly regarded essays dealing with a variety of topics concerning New Haven and Connecticut history. Well worth consulting.

Norton, Mary Beth. *The British-Americans: The Loyalist Exiles in England 1774 - 1789.* Boston: Little, Brown and Company, 1972.

> Portrays the crisis of Loyalism and those who proved unwilling to remain in a country hostile to their cause. A general but adequate introduction to the subject of Loyalism.

Osterweis, Rollin G. *Three Centuries of New Haven, 1638 - 1938.* New Haven: Yale University Press, 1953.

> Encompasses 300 years of New Haven history and is presented in a fluid style that makes it a perennial favorite among historians and general readers alike.

Parrington, Vernon L. *The Colonial Mind, 1620 - 1800.* New York: Harcourt, Brace & World, Inc. Reprint edition, 1954.

> A sweeping study of Puritanism and its evolution toward democracy.

Peale, Arthur L. *Uncas and the Mohegan-Pequot.* Boston: Meador Publishing Company, 1939.

Randall, William Sterne. *Benedict Arnold: Patriot and Traitor.* New York: William Morrow and Company, 1990.

Schneider, Herbert W. *The Puritan Mind.* New York: Henry Holt and Company, 1930.

> Traces the evolution of the Puritan mentality from Jonathan Edwards to Chauncy. Important in gaining an understanding of the theological repercussions of the Revolution.

_____. *Samuel Johnson, His Career and Writings.* 4 vols. New York: Columbia University Press, 1929.

> Considered a definitive study of the clergyman who founded Christ Church and went on to become the president of Columbia College.

Simmons, William S. *Spirit of the New England Tribes: Indian History and Folklore, 1620 - 1984.* Hanover, NH: University Press of New England, 1986.

> Provides a scholarly view of Native American religions.

Sprague, William. *Annals of the American Pulpit.* 9 vols. New York: R. Carter and Company, 1857 - 1869.

> A series of biographical sketches of Connecticut clergymen and particularly important for information concerning Reverend Bela Hubbard, Anglican minister in West Haven

during the Revolution.

Starr, Harris E. *Second Company of the Governor's Foot Guard, 1775 - 1950.* New Haven: M.H. Davidson, 1950.

> A general treatise on the Foot Guard's origins and involvement in American wars.

Sons of the American Revolution. Editors. *Revolutionary Characters of New Haven.* New Haven: The Price, Lee and Adkins Company, 1911.

> A collection of addresses and essays, this publication is useful for its listing of all known
>
> New Haveners who fought in Patriot ranks in the Revolution.

Townshend, Charles H. *The British Invasion of New Haven.* New Haven: Tuttle, Morehouse and Taylor, 1879.

> Written as the centennial commemorative, this is the most complete and detailed study
>
> of the 1779 invasion.

_____. "The Quinnipiac Indians and Their Reservation." New Haven Colony Historical Society *Papers*, VI. New Haven: Tuttle, Morehouse and Taylor Company, 1900.

> An excellent companion piece to DeForest, this essay remains among the best in a field
>
> that is sadly understudied.

Trumbull, Benjamin. *A Complete History of Connecticut Civil and Ecclesiastical from the Emigration of its First Planters from England, in the Year 1630, to the Year 1764.* 2 vols. Hartford: Hudson and Goodwin Company, 1797 - 1818.

> As Connecticut's first historian, Trumbull spent many years researching and writing what
>
> continues to be an excellent study of the colony's history.

Tucker, Louis L. *Connecticut's Seminary of Sedition: Yale College.* Connecticut Bicentennial Series VIII. Chester, Connecticut: Pequot Press, 1974.

> The emphasis of this short monograph is on Yale's critical role as the seedbed of Revolution.
>
> It provides an competent overview of a little known chapter in Connecticut history.

Van Dusen, Albert. *Connecticut.* New York: Random House, 1961.

> Though dated, Van Dusen's work remains the standard history of Connecticut from its
>
> earliest settlement to modern times.

Vaughan, Alden T. *New England Frontier Puritans and Indians 1620 - 1675.* Boston: Little, Brown and Company, 1965.

Ver Steeg, Clarence. *The Formative Years 1607 - 1763.* New York: Hill and Wang Company, 1964.

An excellent general study of the colonial experience once used as a course text.

Weaver, Glenn. *Jonathan Trumbull: Connecticut's Merchant Magistrate.* Hartford: Connecticut Historical Society, 1956.

The biography of colonial merchant, politician, war governor and patriarch of the Trumbull clan is well documented in this important if now dated study.

Wright, Robert K., Jr. *The Continental Army.* Washington, D.C.: Center of Military History, 1983.

The last volume in a trilogy of works on the Revolutionary army, this study provides important details on its organization from militia to a professional fighting force.

Zeichner, Oscar. *Connecticut's Years of Controversy 1750 - 1776.* Virginia: The University of North Carolina press, 1949.

A solid account of Connecticut's developing troubles over the Loyalist issue on the eve of revolution.

Newspapers

Connecticut Courant, 1764 - 1820. Hartford: Connecticut Historical Society.

Connecticut Gazette, 1759 - 1768. New Haven: Yale University

Connecticut Journal and New Haven Post Boy, 1767 - 1820. New Haven: Yale University Microcard Collection.

New York Gazette, November 22, 1764. New Haven: Yale University Microcard Collection.

West Haven Journal, November 15, 1873, April 1, 1874. Connecticut State Library.

Online Resources

Although still in its infancy, online research is already redefining the historian's role. With the number of online resources growing exponentially, the traditional search for pertinent materials is now more of a sort through the literally thousands of references that online queries can generate. Still, the basic principles of sound historical research remain unchanged: patience, persistence, discretion, creativity and attention to scholarship are the critically important components of good history. When applied liberally to the online world, following this prescription can reap rewards that past historians never thought possible. Innumerable primary and secondary resource materials from around the globe are now literally only key strokes away and are often available in complete form.

This, however, does not make the historian's task any easier. Online research is only as meaningful as its interpreter and the evaluative process used to sort the proverbial wheat from the overabundant amount of chafe online. While the Internet may be the world's largest repository of human knowledge, it is also its largest dumping ground of junk passing as history. As in any archival repository, its gems need to be mined carefully and subjected to the same rigorous standards that define good scholarship in medium.

That said, for the study of Connecticut history, the Internet is an invaluable research tool. Readers might well begin with a visit to several key sites that include: the Library of Congress (http://www.loc. gov/index.); The Smithsonian (http://www.si.edu/); New York Public Library Digital Collection (http://www.nypl.org/digital); the British National Archives (http://www.nationalarchives.gov.uk/); The Church of the Latter Day Saints (http://www.familysearch.org/eng/default. asp); The New-York Historical Society (https://www.nyhistory.org/ web) and more specialized sites, such as various British regimental histories, parish registers available through http:// www.Scotlandspeople. gov.uk, and a host of other sites pertaining to colonial America and the American Revolution.

Online listings are so extensive it is impractical to note beyond a handful of key sites that anyone interested in Connecticut history would do well to consult. Among these are the Connecticut State Library (http://www.cslib.org/); Connecticut Heritage Gateway (http://

www.ctheritage.org/);Yale University (http://www.library.yale.edu/); The University of Connecticut Libraries (http://www.library.yale. edu/); The Connecticut Historical Society (http://www.chs.org/); The University of Connecticut Library (http://www.lib.uconn.edu/); The New Haven Museum and Historical Society (http://www.newhaven-museum.org/); the Google Digital Books project and Google Scholar as well as local public library sites that provide access to an expansive collection of online holdings, including WorldCat, which provides access to nearly 1.5 billion records.

As brave a new world as the Internet may be, a final word of caution is necessary: While it is tempting to rely on Web-based encyclopedias, these should be consulted as merely starting points, not final destinations. Many of these sites are maintained by volunteer contributors, are occasionally wrong and are by no means authoritative. Still, many also contain valuable references for further research, and the collaborative model is fast becoming the 21st century's online reference of choice. For an interesting discussion of these sights and their impact on the historical profession, see, Roy Rosenzweig, "Can History be Open Source? Wikipedia and the Future of the Past," *The Journal of American History* Vol. 93, Number 1 (June, 2006): 117-46, also available online at the Center for New Media and History's Web site, http://chnm.gmu.edu/resources/essays/d/42.

Personally, I look forward to a time when all of the world's knowledge is at our fingertips for the asking. I likely will not see that in my lifetime. But it is still worth the dream.

Notes

Chapter 1: Original Settlers

1. Mathias Spiess, *The Indians of Connecticut, Tercentenary Commission of the State of Connecticut* (New Haven: Yale University press, 1933), 26 - 27. See also, Quinnipiac Tribal Council Web site, http://acqtc.org/Maweomi/Legacy09, and http://en.wikipedia.org/wiki/Quinnipiac#Quinnipiac_Settlements_and_Self-Identity.

2. William S. Simmons, *Spirit of the New England Tribes: Indian History and Folklore, 1620 - 1984* (Hanover, New Hampshire: University Press of New England, 1986), 10.

3. *Ibid.*, 10 - 14, 41. See too, Quinnipiac Tribal Council Web site, http://acqtc.org/Maweomi/Legacy08.

4. *Ibid.* See also, http://en.wikipedia.org/wiki/Quinnipiac#Quinnipiac_Settlements_and_Self-Identity.

5. Benjamin Trumbull, *A Complete History of Connecticut, Civil and Ecclesiastical*, 2 vols. (New London: H.D. Utley, 1898) I:26 - 27.

6. Simmons, Spirit, 11. See also, Neal Salisbury, *Manitou and Providence: Indians, Europeans, and the Making of New England* (New York: Oxford University Press, 1982), 23, 25.

7. Simmons, 12 - 15.

8. *Ibid*, 38, 40.

9. *Ibid*, 45.

10. *Ibid*, 38 - 41.

11. Howard S. Russell, *Indian New England Before the Mayflower* (Lebanon, NH: University Press of New England, 1980), 11 - 12. See also, William S. Simmons, "Cultural Bias in New England Puritans' Perception of Indians," *William and Mary Quarterly*, 3rd series, 1: 56 - 72.

12. Simmons, *Spirit*, 38 - 41.

13. Edward H. Spicer, *A Short History of the Indians of the United States* (New York: Van Norstrand Reinhold Company, 1969), 32 - 34. Additionally see, Simmons, *Spirit*, 11 - 12, and John Menta, *Cultural Conflict in Southern New England: A History of the Quinnipiac Indians* (New Haven: Yale University Press, 2003), *passim*. Finally, an excellent introduction to the Quinnipiac appears on Wikipedia, http://en.wikipedia.org/wiki/Quinnipiac#Language.2C_Religion.2C_and_Folklore.

14. Simmons, *Spirit*, 11 - 12; Katherine J. Bragdon, *Native People of Southern New England* (Norman, OK: University of Oklahoma Press, 1999), 25.

13. Rollin G. Osterweis, *Three Centuries of New Haven, 1638 - 1938* (New Haven: Yale University Press, 4th printing, 1975), 10 - 11.

15. Simmons, *Spirit*, 12 - 13. See too, Iron Thunderhorse, "The Cultural Nature of the Central Council," at http://acqtc.org/Maweomi/HomePage. See also, Alan Taylor and Eric Foner, *American Colonies, Penguin History of the United States* (New York: Penguin Books, 2002), I: 188 - 189.

16. Charles Hervey Townshend, "The Quinnipiack Indians," *Papers of the New Haven Colony Historical Society* (New Haven: New Haven Colony Historical Society, 1900), VI: 151 - 219, *passim*. See also, Salisbury, 14.

17. Samuel Eliot Morrison, *The European Discovery of America: The Northern Voyages* (New York: Oxford University Press, 1971), 277 - 313, *passim*. Roodeberg, or red mountain land, referred to the reddish hue of West and East rocks.

18. Spicer, 15, and Osterweis, 9. See Also, William Wier, "Archaeological Dig in Branford Raises Settling Questions," in *The Hartford Courant*, July 10, 1998 as well as John Kirby, "The Branford Area in the Decade Before English Settlement: 1635 - 1644, at http://www.branford-ct.gov/History/Branford%20Before.htm.

19. Among the best overall treatments of the Pequot War (1637 -

38) is Alden T. Vaughan, *New England Frontier: Puritans and Indians, 1620 - 1675* (Boston: Little Brown, 1965) and Laurence M. Haptman and James D. Wherry, eds. *The Pequots in Southern New England*, (Norman, OK, University of Oklahoma Press, 1993). For an overall views of the Pequots, see www.pequotmuseum.org/. For details on the fate of the Swain sisters captured by the Pequot, see, Arthur L. Peale, *Uncas and the Mohegan - Pequot* (Boston: Meador Publishing Company, 1939), 33 - 35. Some recent research suggests that the English goaded the Pequot into war with an eye towards expansion. See, for instance, David W. Ditzer, "The Causes of the Pequot War," *The Connecticut Review* (April 1967). See also, http://www.connhistory.org/peq_rdgs.htm. For a Native view of the war see, Alfred A. Cave, *The Pequot War* (Amherst: The University of Massachusetts Press, 1996) and http://www.pequotwar.com/.

20. George Leon Walker, *Thomas Hooker* (New York: Dodd, Mead and Company, 1891), 99.

21. For an excellent overview of Puritan - Pequot misconceptions and biases that led to war see, Alfred A. Cave, *The Pequot War* (Amherst: University of Massachusetts Press, 1996), 13 -49.

22. See, Paul Tice, ed., *Indians in the Americas: The Untold Story by William Marder* (San Diego, CA: The Book Tree, 2006), 92. Also see, (http://www.aaanativearts.com/article31.html and http://www.brown.edu/Facilities/John_Carter_Brown_Library/jcbexhibit/Pages/exhibAfricans.html#anchor.

23. Osterweis, 5 - 13; Sarah Day Woodward, *Early New Haven* (New Haven: The Edward P. Judd Company, 1929) 3 - 6.

24. Osterweis, 437 -8; Edward Atwater, *History of the Colony of New Haven to Its Absorption into Connecticut* (New Haven: Printed by the author, 1881), 63. See also, Edward R. Lambert, *History of the Colony of New Haven, before and after the Union* (New Haven: Hitchcock & Stafford, 1838), 42.

25. Some estimates of original settlers in New Haven range from 450 to 800. See, Woodward, 8. One fact is certain. New Haven's first

permanent settlers arrived in September of 1637, fully seven months before the main body of the Davenport-Eaton Company.

26. Osterweis, 10. See also, Peale, 10; Woodward, 5 - 6. See also, Carleton Beals, *Our Yankee Heritage* (New Haven: Bradley and Scoville, 1951), 28.

27. The "great shippe" refers to the ill-fated voyage of Captain George Lamberton. Departing from New Haven harbor in 1646 with a cargo estimated to have been worth £5,000, the ship and its crew were lost at sea. See, Osterweis, 46 - 49; Atwater, 537 - 541. See, too, Roland Hooker, *The Colonial Trade of Connecticut* [in Connecticut Tercentenary Pamphlets] (New Haven: Yale University Press, 1936), 7.

28. Charles J. Hoadley, ed., *Records of the Colony and Planation of New Haven from 1638 to 1649*, 2 vols. (Hartford: 1857 - 1858), I: 61.

28. On land divisions, see, Charles J. Hoadley, ed., *Records of the Colony and Plantation of New Haven from 1638 to 1649*, 2 vols. (Hartford: 1857 - 1858), I: 91 - 92, and Peale, 12 -15.

29. Woodward, 22 - 23; Workers of the Writers' Program of the Works Progress Administration in the State of Connecticut, *History of West Haven, Connecticut* (West Haven: Church Press, 1940), 7. Hereafter cited as Writers' Program.

30. The 10 men who figured prominently in the Davenport and Eaton Company included Richard Mansfield, Robert Seeley, Thomas Jeffrey, William Preston, John Budd, Richard Hull, William Jean, Roger Alling, William Wilke and Edward Hitchcock.

31. Hoadley, I: 91 - 92.

32. Writers' Program, 7

33. Leonard W. Laboree, *Milford, Connecticut, The Early Development of a Town as Shown in Its Land Records,* Tercentenary Commission of the State of Connecticut (New Haven: Yale University Press, 1933), 4 - 5.

34. Early roads were primitive at best, many simply being expanded versions of native footpaths. See, Travel Highways, Ferries, Bridges and Taverns (Mss., Hartford: Connecticut State Archives), I: 12; 101. See also, Harry Ives Thompson. West Haven, Connecticut, History and Genealogy Working Papers (Mss., Hartford: Connecticut Archives, 1938). For a vivid description of how such roads were constructed, see, Eric Sloane, *Our Vanishing Landscape* (New York: Ballantine Books, 1974), 57 - 70.

35. Although the colonial records do not indicate permanent residents in West Haven prior to 1648, its lands were divided six years earlier, giving rise to the strong possibility that settlement of the village predated the commonly accepted date of 1648. See, Writers' Program, 7. For a partial listing of these first residents see, Thompson, Working Papers.

Chapter Two: In The Shadows Of New Haven

1. Osterweis, 13 -21
2. Albert Van Dusen, *Connecticut: A Fully Illustrated History of the State of Connecticut from the Seventeenth Century to the Present* (New York: Random House, 4th printing, 1968), 66.
3. *Ibid.*, 66. See also, Jackson Turner Main, *Society and Economy in Colonial Connecticut* (Princeton: Princeton University Press, 1985), 6.
4. Osterweis, 183. In 1790, the U.S. Census showed that Connecticut still contained 2,000 slaves, 30 of whom resided in the New Haven area. See too, www.slavenorth.com/connecticut.htm.
5. Alice Morse Earle, *Home Life in Colonial Days* (Middle Village, New York: Jonathan David Publishers, 1975), 252 - 280.
6. Main, 367 - 384.
7. *Ibid.*, 367 - 384.
8. Hoadley, *New Haven Colony Records*, I:133.

9. Osterweis, 18 - 21, 38; Van Dusen, 59 - 60.

10. Main, 4; Woodward, 20 - 21.

11. Main, 367 - 384.

12. See Appendix A, which provides a breakdown of colonial office holding.

13. Hoadley, *New Haven Colony Records*, I:193.

14. *Ibid.*, I:212.

15. *Ibid.*, I:155.

16. *Ibid.*, I:122. See also, Lambert, 27 - 28.

17. Lambert, 35.

18. Beals, 29. Seeley was a seasoned solider having been second in command to John Mason in the attack on the Pequot nation. During the battle Seeley was severely wounded with an arrow to his head just above his eye. He later served against the Dutch in New Amsterdam as a captain. He eventually became one of the founders of Elizabeth, New Jersey. See, Seeley Genealogical Society, 1997, available at http://www.seeley-society.net.

19. Lambert, 35.

20. Hoadley, *New Haven Colony Records*, I:122. See, too, Charles H. Livermore, *The Republic of New Haven* (Baltimore: Johns Hopkins University Press, 1886), 60 - 61; http://www.colonialwarsct.org/1675.htm.

21. Lambert, 35, 38.

22. *Ibid.*, 37 - 38.

23. Franklin B. Dexter and Zara Powers, eds., *Ancient Town Records 1664 - 1769*, 3 vols. (New Haven: Tuttle, Morehouse and Taylor, 1919; The Quinnipiac Press, 1962), III: 73 - 74.

25. http://en.wikipedia.org/wiki/Quinnipiac.

26. John Shy, *Toward Lexington: The Role of the British Army in the Coming of the American Revolution* (Princeton: Princeton University Press, 1965), 43 - 44. See also, Edward E. Atwater, *History of the City of New Haven to the Present Time* (New York: Munsell and

Company, 1887), 27 - 31.

   27. *Ibid.*, 44.

Chapter Three: The Rise of Self-sufficiency

   1. Steven H. Ward, "A Nest of Vipers: Expansionist Policies of the New Haven Puritans from 1637 to 1667," *Journal of The New Haven Colony Historical Society*, 31, No.1 (Fall 1984): 3 - 12.

   2. *Ibid.*, 3 - 12; Osterweis, 22 - 31.

   3. Van Dusen, 73 - 74. Osterweis, 62.

   4. Osterweis, 46 - 49. See also, Lamberton, 57 - 58 and Woodward, 22 - 23.

   5. Lambert, 58. See also, Woodward, 21.

   6. Thomas J. Farnham and Thomas J. Watts, *New Haven: The Earliest Years, The Bicentennial Radio Series* (New Haven: The New Haven Bicentennial Commission, 1976) I: 33 - 34.

   7. Main, 368 - 369.

   8. The original estimates of the average size of farms failed to take into account land received in the third and fourth land divisions, which took place in1704. For an excellent discussion of property and wealth see, Main, 28 - 114.

   9. Charles Carroll, "The Forest Society of New England," in Brooke Hindle, ed., *America's Wooden Age: Aspects of its Early Technology* (Tarrytown: Sleepy Hollow Restorations, 1975), 13 - 36.

   10. *Ibid.*, 10. Injuries were also commonplace. See, Majorie F. Hayward, *The East Side of New Haven Harbor, 1644 - 1868* (New Haven: Yale University Press, 1836), 29 - 30.

   11. Hoadley. *New Haven Colony Records*, I: 358.

   12. Thompson, Working Papers.

   13. Carroll, 21

14. Erastus Colton, "Discourse: Historical of West Haven Congregational Church and of the Old Parsonage (a sermon presented on the 140th An-

12. Thompson, Working Papers.

13. Carroll, 21

14. Erastus Colton, "Discourse: Historical of West Haven Congregational Church and of the Old Parsonage (a sermon presented on the 140th Anniversary of the Congregational Church, West Haven, 1859), 13.

15. Information on Allcock can be found in Franklin P. Dexter, ed., *Ancient Town Records* (New Haven: Tuttle, Morehouse and Taylor, 1919), II: 415. For a fascinating, if somewhat self-serving account of Painter's life in the Revolution see, Thomas Painter, *Autobiography* (Washington, D.C.: Printing Printed, 1910), 6 - 78, *passim*. Also available online under Papers of the New Haven Colony Historical Society.

16. Sarah Kemble Knight, *The Private Journal of Sarah Kemble Knight* (Norwich, Connecticut: The Academy Press, 1801), 49.

17. Mary Jeanne Anderson Jones, *Congregational Commonwealth: Connecticut, 1636 - 1662* (Middletown, CT: Wesleyan University Press, 1968), 149 - 151.

18. Kai T. Erikson, *Wayward Puritans: A Study in the Sociology of Deviance* (New York: John Wiley and Sons, 1966), 139 - 141.

19. The witchcraft trial of William Meaker was one of five such trials in New Haven, which resulted in two acquittals, two executions, and one imprisonment. A short time after the Meaker trial, both the accused and the accuser left New Haven, but not before Mulliner firmly established himself as a rogue, documented by his continual appearances before the New Haven court. Hoadley, *New Haven Colony Records*, II: 29, 77 - 78, and 224 - 226.

20. John Demos, "Underlying Themes in the Witchcraft of New England" [in Stanley N. Katz, ed., *Colonial America: Essays in Politics and Social Development*] (Boston: Little, Brown and Company, 1971), 125.

21. Cotton Mather, "Wonders of the Invisible World," 1693 [in Samuel G. Drake, ed., *The Witchcraft Delusion in New England* (Roxbury, MA: W. Elliot Woodward, 1866), 80 - 81.

22. Besides the conversion experience, proving that you were in the

covenant of grace was considered an essential requirement in becoming one of God's elect. Proof, of course, was largely subjective and based on one's exemplary behavior, including the acquisition of worldly goods through hard work and gain. See, Roy Boaz, "A Study of the Faith and Practice of the First Congregational Church of West Haven, Connecticut, 1719 - 1914" (Ph.D. dissertation, Yale University, 1938), 69.

23. Zara Powers, *Ancient Town Records: New Haven Town Records, 1684 - 1769* (New Haven: New Haven Colony Historical Society, 1962), III: 94 - 95.

24. Erikson, 136.

25. Clarence Ver Steeg, *The Formative Years, 1607 - 1763* (New York: Hill and Wang, 1964), 85 - 86.

26. Powers, III: 276.

27. Boaz, 12. See also, Ecclesiastical Affairs, 1658 - 1820 (Mss., Hartford: Connecticut State Archives), II.

28. Powers, III: 163 - 273, *passim.*

29. *Ibid.*, II: 381.

30. Boaz, 15 - 20. See also, Ecclesiastical Affairs, II.

31. Jonathan Trumbull and Charles Hoadley, eds., *The Public Records of the Colony of Connecticut,* 15 vols. (Hartford, CT: various publishers, 1850 - 1890), V: 494.

Chapter Four: Challenge To Permanence

1. Erikson, 139 - 141. Also see, George McKenna, *The Puritan Origins of American Patriotism* (New Haven: Yale University Press, 2007), pp. 32 -42.

2. McKenna, pp. 39 - 43.

3. Thompson notes that the Green had been a problem to all its owners, since fencing had to be maintained around the area as early as 1665 without its being workable land. From 1665, the property was owned by Henry Lions (Lyons), John Budd, John Morris, Henry Bristol

and Eliphalet Bristol, respectively, until its transfer to the committee in 1710. In this transaction, Lieutenant Samuel Smith, Ensign Samuel Burwell, Joseph Thompson, Eliazer Beecher, Joseph Prindle and Samuel Smith, Jr., acted as the committee and exchanged an equal amount of sequestered property with Eliphalet Bristol for the rights to the property. See, Thompson, Working Papers.

4. Apparently, there was little choice as to the location of the meetinghouse since the southern portion of the Green was filled marshland.

5. Powers, III: 384, 390.

6. First Ecclesiastical Society Records in the Parish of West Haven, 1724 - 1913, 12 vols. (Mss., Hartford: Connecticut State Archives) I: 138 - 141.

7. Lamberton Smith was such an individual, as he became involved in the Tory issue in 1776. See, Charles Hoadley, et. al., eds., *Public Records of the State of Connecticut, 1776 - 1792*, 7 vols.(Hartford: Case, Lockwood and Brainerd Company, 1894 - 1948), I: 34 - 35.

8. Boaz, 41.

9. Thompson, Working Papers.

10. Colton, 20. The General Assembly allowed West Haven to form its own militia unit in May 1706. See, Hoadley, *Public Records of the Colony of Connecticut*, IV: 538.

11. A West Haven resident, Browne would sail with Johnson to England and be ordained an Anglican minister. *History of Christ Church* (West Haven: Church Press, 1945), 51.

12. Boaz, 21.

13. Samuel Johnson, "On Doubts of Congregational Faith" (Ms., New York: Columbia University Library Archives).

14. Joining Johnson and Browne in this declaration were Yale President Timothy Cutler, John Hart, Samuel Whittlesey, Jared Elliot and James Westmore. See, Eben E. Beardsley, *History of the Protestant Episcopal Church in Connecticut*, 2 vols. (New York: Hurd and Houghton

Company, 1865), I: 38.

15. The actual number of persons leaving the church is unknown, but it is safe to assume their numbers approached 15 percent of the total congregation. Among the founders of the Anglican Church in West Haven were Samuel and David Browne, Daniel Browne, Joseph and Mary Prindle, Samuel and Sarah Clark, Rebecca Clark, Merrit Clark, John and Rebecca Humphreyville, John and Sybil Thomas, Eunice Thomas and Mehatebel Smith. See, West Haven Christ Church Episcopal Records, 1788 - 1903, 6 vols. (Mss., Hartford: Connecticut State Archives, 1953 - 1956), I: 150 - 151. See also, Whitney Hobart, *Christ Church Yearbook, 1888 - 1889* (New Haven: Tuttle, Morehouse and Taylor, 1889), 4, as well as Thompson, Working Papers.

16. The term "widowed" was often used to denote a congregation without a residing minister.

17. Boaz, 40.

18. *Ibid.*, 41. Contract terms for the Reverend Mr. Arnold are in the First Society Records of West Haven, I: 1. Concerning the increase in the minister's property, 50 acres were set aside for a West Haven parsonage to be located near the Milford line in 1722. Powers, III: 488.

19. Beardsley, I: 156.

20. *Ibid.*, I: 156.

21. First Society Records of West Haven, I: 12.

22. Boaz, 50.

23. Ecclesiastical Affairs, V: 269.

24. Arnold was given title to the property by William Gregson, no doubt a descendant of Thomas Gregson of the New Haven Colony. See, *History of Christ Church*, 53 - 57.

25. *Ibid.*, 57.

26. Following his failed efforts in New Haven, Arnold secured title to the southern portion of the West Haven Green, which the Congregationalists previously thought was unusable marshland.

27. Contrary to reports that he was lost at sea, Arnold was reassigned

to Long Island in 1740. See, *History of Christ Church*, 57.

28. *Ibid*, 16.

29. William Langer, ed., *An Encyclopedia of World History* (Boston: Houghton, Mifflin Company, 1940), 430 - 431.

30. *History of Christ Church*, 61. See also, Alonzo Chapin, "A Sermon Delivered in Christ Church West Haven (West Haven: Christ Church, 1839), 11.

31. Johnson remarked that the West Haven mission had grown to approximately 40 families by 1749, no doubt helped along by the continuing discord of the First Church. See, Lucy C. Jarvis, *Sketches of Church Life in Colonial Connecticut* (New Haven: Tuttle, Morehouse and Taylor Company, 1902), 166 - 167.

32. Due to Punderson's lack of discretion and controversial behavior, the Episcopal Church in New Haven was said to have suffered a tremendous setback. See, Atwater, 132, and *History of Christ Church*, 67.

33. Franklin B. Dexter, *Biographical Sketches of the Graduates of Yale College*, 6 vols. (New York: H. Holt and Company, 1885 - 1912), II: 537 - 539.

34. Ekikson, 155 - 156.

35. Boaz, 62.

36. *Ibid.*, 62. For a biographical sketch of Allen, see, Dexter, I: 554.

37. Vernon L. Parrington, *Main Currents in American Thought: The Colonial Mind* (Norman, OK: University of Oklahoma Press, 1987), 150.

Chapter Five: Growing Pains

1. James Axtell, ed., *The American People In Colonial New England* (West Haven, Connecticut: The Pendulum Press, 1973), 9-10.

2. Dexter, *Ancient Town Records*, II: 406-407.

3. Powers, *Ancient Town Records*, III:418, 438; 460-465; also 620;

733; 785; and 800.

4. *Ibid.*, III: 800.

5. For an interesting essay on land competition as a cause of social unrest in colonial America, see, Kenneth Lockridge, "Land, Population and the Evolution of New England Society" [in Stanley N. Katz, ed., *Colonial America: Essays in Politics and Social Development]* (Boston: Little, Brown and Company, 1971), 467-491.

6. *Ibid.*, 469.

7. Hoadley, *Records of the Colony of Connecticut*, VII: 374.

8. Sperry's case is the only one that appears in the town records. However, the fact that New Haven authorized that a pesthouse be built indicated that there were many more cases of smallpox in town. See, Powers, *Ancient Town Records*, III: 593

9. For a brief history of New Haven's medical profession see, Atwater, 260-279.

10. Powers, *Ancient Town Records*, III: 693; 696; 707.

11. *Ibid.*, III: 733. Smallpox continued to claim the lives of West Haveners well into the 18th century, as in the case of Chauncey Smith, who died of the disease in 1778. See, Thompson, Working Papers.

12. Powers, *Ancient Town Records*, III: 733.

13. First Society Records of West Haven, I: 55-57; See also, Writers' Program, 11-12.

14. Boaz, 122. See also, William Fowler, "Ministers of Connecticut in the Revolution" [in *Centennial Papers of the General Conference of the Congregational Churches of Connecticut*] (Hartford: Case, Lockwood and Brainard Company, 1887), 85-95.

15. Atwater,151-155, *passim*.

16. Hoadley, *Public Records of the Colony of Connecticut*, V: 408. Rate increases averaged 2d. on the pound, based on the school tax rate of 1746. First Society Records of West Haven, I: 55-57.

17. Atwater, 151-152.

18. *Ibid.*, 148; Osterweis, 92; Atwater, 148.

19. Atwater, 152; Hoadley, *Records of the Colony of Connecticut*, I: 520 - 521; 554 - 555.

Chapter Six: Testing The Limits Of Authority

1. In founding their own parish, West Haveners were willing to challenge the traditional authority of New Haven to gain a desired end. That precedent would come back to haunt them when fellow communicants founded Christ Church only a few years later.

2. Trumbull, I: 354. See also, Glenn Weaver, *Jonathan Trumbull, Connecticut's Merchant Magistrate, 1710 - 1785* (Hartford: Connecticut Historical Society, 1956), 37.

3. From 1739 to 1749, the price of silver per ounce increased an average of 27s. See, Nelson P. Mead, *Connecticut as a Corporate Colony* (Lancaster, Pennsylvania: The New Era Printing Company, 1906). See too, Hoadley, *Records of the Colony of Connecticut*, VIII: 295-327, *passim*.

4. First Society Records of West Haven, I: 43-86, *passim*.

5. For the rector's salary see, Franklin B. Dexter, *Yale Biographies*, 538. The churches that were constructed were located in West Haven (1739) and New Haven (1755). A church account of 1740 indicates that monies were paid out on a regular basis for services rendered and materials used in the construction of Christ Church.

6. No doubt this land was the same 50 acres given to the parish by New Haven in 1722. See, First Society Records of West Haven, I: 48.

7. West Haveners donated £1500 to the bank. With the Assembly's grant, the bank's assets totalled £2500. See, Boaz, I: 75-77.

8. *Ibid.*, 76.

9. Interest rates were based on the difference between money loaned and returned. Therefore, £10 represented a seven percent return.

10. Hoadley, *Public Records of the Colony of Connecticut*, IX: 375.

11. First Society Records of West Haven, I: 48-55, *passim.*

12. Richard L. Bushman, *From Puritan to Yankee* (Cambridge, Massachusetts: Harvard University Press, 1967), 184. For a fascinating study of Whitefield's commercial approach to evangelism, see, Frank Lambert, *Peddler in Divinity: George Whitefield and the Transatlantic Revivals* (Princeton, New Jersey: Princeton University Press, 1994).

13. Russell B. Nye, ed., *The Autobiography of Benjamin Franklin* (Cambridge, Massachusetts: The Riverside Press, 1958), 98.

14. Louis B. Wright, *The Cultural Life of the American Colonies, 1607 - 1763* (New York: Harper and Row: 1957), 94. See also, Atwater, 113.

15. Ebenezer Pemberton, *The Knowledge of Christ Recommended* (New Haven: A Sermon Delivered at Yale College, April 19, 1741), 25.

16. New Lights were the radical advocates of the Great Awakening. Those unaffected by revivalism were dubbed Old Lights, a name which, in itself, denoted a sense of being out of touch and old-fashioned.

17. Herbert and Carol Schneider, eds., *Samuel Johnson, President of Kings College, His Career and Writings,* 4 vols. (New York: Columbia University Press, 1939), I: 106.

18. Hoadley, *Records of the Colony of Connecticut,* VIII: 438-439.

19. The Old Lights proceeded with the consociation concept in full knowledge that the New Lights were totally opposed to the concept of Congregational law being divinely sanctioned.

20. Trumbull, I: 483-487.

21. Boaz, 86.

22. Schneider, I: 106.

23. In 1742 Allen spoke with Mr. Munson about the latter's misconduct in New Haven. A full account of Allen's revivalist tendencies appear in the Consociation records. See, Boaz, 79-82.

24. *Ibid.,* 82; See also, *History of Christ Church,* 60.

25. First Society Records of West Haven, I: 36. Boaz, 82.

26. Boaz, 82.

27. *Ibid.*, 97.

28. First Society Records of West Haven, I: 88.

29. *Ibid.*, I: 144. Boaz, 152.

30. Osterweis, 88.

Chapter Seven: On The Eve Of Revolution

1. Levermore, 203.

2. Van Dusen, 102-103.

3. Lawrence H. Gipson, "Connecticut Taxation and Parliamentary Aid," in *The American Historical Review*, XXXVI, 731-733.

4. Ver Steeg, 292; Shy, 420.

5. Shy, 140-148.

6. Van Dusen, 70.

7. The decision to institute a boycott was voted at a town meeting of February 22, 1763. See, Levermore, 204; Osterweis, 115.

8. *New York Gazette*, November 22, 1764.

9. Merrill Jensen, ed., *Tracts of the American Revolution, 1763 - 1776* (New York: Bobbs-Merrill Company, Inc., 1967), xxi-xlviii.

10. Bushman, 263.

11. G. H. Hollister, *The History of Connecticut, from the First Settlement of the Colony to the Adoption of the Present Constitution* , 2 vols. (New Haven: Durrie, Peck and Company, 1855), II: 130-131.

12. *Connecticut Gazette*, September 13, 1765. See also, Gipson, *American Loyalist: Jared Ingersoll* (New Haven: Yale University Press, 1971), 173.

13. Powers, *Ancient Town Records*, III: 813. See also, *Connecticut Gazette*, September 20, 1765.

14. Bushman, 284-286.

15. Shy, 192, 214-217.

16. Gipson, *The Coming of the Revolution*, 1763 - 1775 (New York: Harper and Row, 1954), 114.

17. Atwater, 28.

18. Van Dusen, 128.

19. Powers, *Ancient Town Records*, III: 797-798. See also, *Connecticut Journal* March 4, 1768.

20. Page Smith, *A New Age Now Begins,* 2 vols. (New York: McGraw-Hill Book Company, 1976), I: 272-280.

21. Oscar Zeichner, *Connecticut's Years of Controversy, 1750 - 1766* (reprint ed., Hamden, Connecticut:1970), 45-47.

22. Schneider, I: 349.

23. Charles Francis Adams, ed., *The Works of John Adams,* 10 vols. (Boston: Little, Brown and Company, 1850-1856), X: 288.

24. *Connecticut Journal* December 7, 1770.

25. The Coercive, or Intolerable, Acts as Americans called them, were the Boston Port Act; the Massachusetts Government and Administrations of Justice Acts; the Quartering Act; and the Quebec Act, all passed into law in the early months of 1774. For a concise explanation of these acts and their impact on the coming revolution see, Gipson, *Coming of the Revolution*, 223-228; Osterweis, 123; and Smith, I: 385-413.

26. New Haven Town Records, 1769-1807 (Mss. New Haven Colony Historical Society, Hew Haven, CT), 19-44. Copies of the manuscript records are in possession of the author and will appear as volume four in the Ancient Town Records series.

27. Gipson, *Coming of the Revolution*, 230.

28. Smith, I: 442-449.

29. Atwater, 40-42.

30. Osterweis, 125.

Chapter Eight: Crisis of Allegiance

1. Van Dusen, 133.

2. Osterweis, 124-124. The New Haven Town Records make no mention of this meeting. Interestingly enough, Samuel Bishop duly

recorded a February meeting, then left about a third of the page blank. His next entry is for a November meeting. The reason why is as fascinating as it is relatively unknown. Shortly after hearing of the Lexington and Concord engagements, Bishop was one of a handful of New Haveners who secretly raised funds to launch expeditionary forces against the British at Ticonderoga, Crown Point and St. John's. Consequently, Bishop was probably not in New Haven to record the minutes of the April 21 meeting. Knowing full well that what he did record would possibly prove to be self-incriminating should the Patriot cause collapse, Bishop likely thought better than commit to writing any summary of the contentious April 21 meeting, an account of Arnold's now famous demand for the powder house keys, or even a whisper of his own secret role in helping to plan a northern invasion. See, Atwater, 42-44. See also, Christopher Collier, *Roger Sherman's Connecticut: Yankee Politics and the American Revolution* (Middletown, Connecticut: Wesleyan University Press, 1971), 103-105.

3. Atwater, 42; Osterweis, 124. See also, Bushman, 265.

4. Boardman, 127-128. See also, Zeichner, 67, 271.

5. Atwater, 42. See also, Willard Sterne Randall, *Benedict Arnold, Patriot and Traitor* (New York: William Morrow, Inc., 1990), 81-83, and Harris E. Starr, *Second Company, Governor's Footguard, 1775 - 1950* (New Haven: M.H. Davidson Company, 1950).

6. Smith, I: 548-550. See also Osterweis, 131-132.

7. Osterweis, 126-129. See also, David M. Roth and Freeman Myer, *From Revolution to Constitution: Connecticut, 1763 - 1818* (Chester, Connecticut: Pequot Press, 1975), 24-25.

8.Alice Baldwin, *The Clergy of Connecticut in the Revolutionary Days* [in *Connecticut Tercentenary Pamphlets*] (New Haven: Yale University Press, 1938), 28-29.

9. *Ibid.*, 28-29. See also, William Sprague, *Annals of the American Pulpit,* 9 vols. (New York: R. Carter and Company, 1857 - 1869), IV: 135.

Notes

10. Richard J. Purcell, *Connecticut in Transition: 1775-1818* (Middletown, Connecticut: Wesleyan University Press, 1963), 37.

11. New Haven Town Records, November 6, 1775. See also, Roth, 23-25; Atwater, 45.

11. New Haven Town Records, December 11, 1775. Samuel Seabury, an outspoken Anglican clergyman from New York and later the first Episcopal bishop of Connecticut, had been captured by New Haven's Sons of Liberty and imprisoned in New Haven in November.

12. Hoadly, *Records of the State of Connecticut*, I: 34-35. See also, Van Dusen, 140-143.

13. The two men Smith charged as Tory sympathizers were Ralph Isaacs and Abiather Camp, both prominent New Haveners. The men were declared enemies of the state, and Camp was sent to Glastonbury under guard. He later published a confession, which appeared in the *Connecticut Journal*, October 4, 1775. Eventually, Camp's Loyalist leanings forced him to leave New Haven and inevitably suffer the confiscation of his estate. See, Hoadly, *Records of the Colony of Connecticut*, XV: 411-415. See also, "List of Confiscated Estates in the County of New Haven," Connecticut Archives, Revolutionary War, XXXIV: 456. For a brief account of the Smith charges see, Gipson, 372-373.

14. Clara Loveland, *The Critical Years: The Reconstruction of the Anglican Church in the United States of America 1780-1789* (Greenwich, Connecticut: Seabury Press, 1956), 14-15. See also, Wallace Brown, *The Good Americans: The Loyalists in the American Revolution* (New York: William Morrow and Company, 1969), 36, 126. Chapin, 20-22.

15. Although unquestionably Loyalist in their leanings, the majority of Christ Church communicants remained in West Haven through the war. Chapin, 20-22.

16. Following the Battle of Long Island in 1776, New York City remained under British martial law throughout the war.

17. Loveland, 15. See also, Donald B. Chidsey, *The Loyalists: The Story of Those Americans Who Fought Against Independence* (New York:

Crown Publishers, 1973) 87.

18.Writers' Program, 15; and Levermore, 221. See also, Thompson, Working Papers, and Sons of the American Revolution, *Revolutionary Characters of New Haven* (New Haven: Price, Lee and Adkins Company, 1911), 99-114.

19. Joshua Weeks, "Journal of Rev. Joshua Weeks, Loyalist Rector of St. Michael's Church, Marblehead, 1778 - 1779," Essex Institute, *Historical Collections* (1916), 163.

Chapter Nine: A Dire Sense of Expectancy-

1. Osterweis, 131.

2. *Ibid.*, 136

3. *Ibid.*, 136; Ernest H. Baldwin, *Stories of Old New Haven* (Taunton, MA: C.A. Hack and Son, 1902), 163.

4. See, for instance, Robert Middlekauff, *The Glorious Cause: The American Revolution, 1763-1789* (New York: Oxford University Press,1982).

5. Edmund Morgan, "The American Revolution: Revisions in Need of Revising," *William and Mary Quarterly* (Vol. 14, 1957), 3 - 15.

6. *Ibid.*, 13-15.

7. Linda S. Luchowski, Sunshine Soldiers: New Haven and the American Revolution, (Ph.D. dissertation, New York University, 1976), 2.

8. *Ibid.*, 9.

9. Hoadley, *Public Records of the Colony of Connecticut*, 14:344; Osterweis, 481; Louis B. Tucker, *Connecticut's Seminary of Sedition: Yale College* (Pequot Press, 1974). See also, Benjamin Trumbull, An Address from the Civil Authority of the Town of New Haven to the Inhabitants of Said Town, November 27, 1772, Benjamin Trumbull Collection (Mss., Yale University Library).

10. Tucker, 39.

11. Gipson, *American Loyalist: Jared Ingersoll*, 172-173. See also, *The New London Gazette* September 6, 1765.

12. New Haven County Court Records (Mss., New Haven: New Haven County Court) VI: 81. See also, Leveritt Hubbard to Ezra Stiles, January 2, 1766, in Franklin B. Dexter, ed., *Extracts From the Itineraries of Ezra Stiles* (New Haven: Yale University Press, 1916), 509; *The Connecticut Gazette* February 7, 1766; and Roger Sherman Collection, Yale University Library.

13. *The Connecticut Journal,* September 15, 1769.

14. *Ibid.,* September 22, 1769.

15. Powers, *Ancient Town Records,* 786. See also, New Haven Town Records, December 14, 1772; and Bruce Bliven, *Under The Guns, New York: 1775 - 1776* (New York: Harper and Row, 1973), 59; 63-70.

16. Smith, I: 645-646.

17. Dexter, Stiles, III: 22.

18. Dexter, Stiles, II: .

19. Thomas Trowbridge, "History of the Ancient Maritime Interests of New Haven," *New Haven Colony Historical Society Papers* (New Haven: New Haven Colony Historical Society, 1882), 5 - 15.

20. *The Connecticut Journal,* October 29, 1777; Gibson, *American Loyalist: Jared Ingersoll,* 34.

21. Connecticut Archives, Revolutionary War Series, I, Vol. I: Part II: 396a-400. See also, Hoadley, *Records of the Colony of Connecticut,* XIV: 391-392.; XV: 53-54.

22. Luchowski, 334 - 338.

23. Henry P. Johnston, ed., *The Record of Connecticut Men in the Military and Naval Service During the War of the Revolution, 1775 - 1783* (New Haven: Case, Lockwood and Brainard, 1889), 116.

24. *Ibid.,* 156.

25. *Ibid,* 196. See also, Lorenzo Sabine, *The American Loyalists* (Boston: Little Brown, 1864), 194.

26. Johnston, 215; Sabine, 643.

27. Luchowski, 307.

28. New Haveners compiled a less-than-admirable record of attendance to militia duty throughout the war. Divided loyalties no doubt accounted for some of the militia's difficulties, but apathy was the most significant reason. See, for instance, An Account of Bills of Cost Allowed Against Delinquents of the Militia in the Town of New Haven, Chauncey Family Papers (Mss., Yale University Library).

29. Luchowski, 200; New Haven Town Records, 1775 - 1781, *passim*.

30. New Haven Town Records, December 29, 1777.

31. Luchowski, 201-202.

32. See, for example, Benjamin Trumbull, Sermon, May 6, 1779, Mss., Benjamin Trumbull Collection, Yale University Library.

33. For Yale student activities during the Revolution see, Tucker, 51 - 72. For details of the mob attack on Elijah and Archibald Austin, see, *The Connecticut Journal*, April 2, 1777. For a description of what happened to the Loyalists Abiather Camp and Ralph Isaacs, see, *The Connecticut Journal*, February 21, 1776.

34. Louis Middlebrook, *History of Maritime Connecticut During the American Revolution*, 2 vols. (Salem, Massachusetts: The Essex Institute, 1925), II: 61; 82-83.

35. *Ibid.*, II: 122; 132-133. Among New Haven merchants supporting privateers during the war were: Ebenezer Peck, Jesse Leffingwell, Samuel Perkins, John C. Ogden, Peter Colt, Abel Buell, John Mix, Jr., Michael Todd, Phineas Bradley and Pierpont Edwards, to name a few. Many others served as crew members. Middlebrook, II: *passim*.

36. Frederick G. Mather, *The Refugees of 1776 from Long Island to Connecticut* (Baltimore: Genealogical Publishing Company, 1972), 326.

37. *The Connecticut Journal*, April 30, 1780.

38. Mather, 220; Villers, 168.

39. Prudence Punderson, Diary of Prudence Punderson, Mss., Hartford: The Connecticut Historical Society.

Notes

40. Hoadley, *Public Records of the State of Connecticut*, III: 204.

41. Mather, 246.42. Middlebrook, II: 268.43. See also, Charles Hall, *Life and Letters of General Samuel Holden Parsons* (New York: n.p., 1968), 300 - 301;

44. Painter, *Autobiography*, 3 - 30, *passim*.

45. Middlebrook, II: 219 -224; *Rivington's Gazette*, August 28, 1779. Mather, 326; and Henry Onderdonk, *Revolutionary Incidents of Suffolk and Kings County, New York* (New York: Leavitt & Co.,1846), 64, 73.

46. *The Connecticut Journal*, December 19, 1782.

47. Hervey Garrett Smith, "Ebenezer Dayton: Patriot Peddler," http://www.longwood.k12.ny.us/history/bio/edayton.htm. Following the war, *The Connecticut Gazette* of April 5, 1787 reported that Dayton had drowned in the Housatonic River, but no body was ever recovered. It appears he staged his own death, as family records list Dayton as dying of yellow fever in 1802 in New Orleans. See too, Israel P. Warren, Chauncey Judd (Naugatuck Press, 1906), Chapter 8.

48. Local residents or Long Islanders, not British regulars, perpetrated most of the hostilities of the war in the New Haven area. In fact, the area suffered from notable enemy attacks on July 5, 1779; February 3, 1781; April 18, 1781; August 20 and 30, 1781; and September 17, 1781. Numerous smaller sorties also took place throughout the war. See, Dexter, Stiles, II: 552, 530; Louise Greene, "New Haven Defenses in the Revolution and the War of 1812," *The Connecticut Magazine*, IV (1898), 272 - 290. See also, New Haven Town Records, 1775 - 1783, *passim*; Charles Townshend, *The British Invasion of New Haven* (New Haven: Tuttle, Morehouse and Taylor, 1879); Peter J. Malia, *The British Invasion of West Haven* (West Haven: Privately Printed, 1976); Osterweis, 138 - 148. For damage claims see, Hoadley, *Public Records of the State of Connecticut*, II: 426 - 427; Connecticut Archives, Revolutionary War, Series 3, I: 61b; *The Connecticut Journal*, May 3, 1783.

Chapter Ten: The War Comes Home

1. Thomas J. Farnham, "The Day the Enemy Was in Town," *Journal of The New Haven Colony Historical Society* (Vol. 24, No. 2, Summer, 1976,), 11. See also, General David Wooster to New Haven, July, 1779. Mss., Nathan Pond family, Milford, Connecticut, and George Ford, "The Defense of New Haven and Resistance Made Against Invading Troops Along the West Shore, July, 1779," in *Revolutionary Characters of New Haven*, 33.

2. Farnham, 13.

3. *Ibid.*, 13. See also, Lord George Germain to Sir Henry Clinton, January 23, 1779, in William B. Wilcox, ed., *The American Rebellion: Sir Henry Clinton's Narrative of His Campaigns* (New Haven: Yale University Press, 1954), 397 - 399.

4. Henry B. Carrington, *Battles of the American Revolution, 1775 - 1781* (New York: A. S. Barnes and Company, 1876), 466.

5. Farnham, 15 - 16.

6. Commodore Sir George Collier and Major General William Tryon, Address to the Inhabitants of Connecticut (Mss., New York Historical Society).

7. Ferguson conducted a surreptitious survey of Connecticut defenses only weeks before the attack. The inventor of the Ferguson rifle, he allegedly once had Gen. Washington's back lined up in his sights but refused to fire. He was later killed in the Southern campaign. See, Lloyd A. Brown, "Loyalist Operations at New Haven," Ann Arbor, MI: University of Michigan, 1938), 12 pp. See also, Donald Norman Morgan, "Major Patrick Ferguson: The Sharp Shooter Who Almost Won the War for the British," http://www.americanrevolution.org/ferguson.html.

8. Farnham, 19; Carrington, 468 - 469.

9. Carrington, 469.

10. Farnham, 19.

11. West Haveners played a significant role in Connecticut's naval

war. Among those vessels on which West Haveners served included the *Firebrand*, captained by Caleb Trowbridge, *Wooster*, owned in part by West Haveners, and the *Hetty*. See, Middlebrook, II: 90 - 246, *passim;* Osterweis, 133. In addition, by 1778, each town was required to provide its soldiers in the field with "a hunting -shirt, two linen shirts, two pairs of linen overalls, one pair of stockings and two pairs of well-made shoes." See, Van Dusen, 147.

12. Hoadley, *XV: 178*. See also, Thomas Painter, "Personal Reminiscences of the Revolutionary War," in *Papers of the New Haven Colony Historical Society,* IV (New Haven: New Haven Colony Historical Society, 1888), 246.

13. Painter, *Autobiography*, 3 - 30. See also, New Haven Town Records, 83, and Louise M. Greene, "New Haven Defenses in the Revolution," *Connecticut Quarterly*, IV (September, 1898), 277. In West Haven, Lamberton Smith and Silas Kimberly were appointed to oversee the construction of defenses.

14. Thompson Working Papers; Hoadly, *Records of the State of Connecticut*, III: 180.

15. In 1778 a fleet of nearly 100 ships passed West Haven on its way to the infamous destruction of Newport, RI. In 1777 one of the most celebrated prisoner exchanges of the war took place off the West Haven - Milford shore when a British ship released its human cargo of more than 200 American prisoners, a quarter of whom died within a month of their release. See, Stephen Jenkins, *The Old Boston Post Road* (New York: G.P. Putnam's Sons, 1913), 211.

16. Charles H. Townshend, *The British Invasion of New Haven* (New Haven: Tuttle, Morehouse and Taylor, 1879), 38.

17. Sabin and Hillhouse were both in New Haven seeking recruits for another company of men. See, Greene, 277.

18. General David Wooster to New Haven, July, 1779. Mss., Nathan Pond family, Milford, Connecticut. New Haven also received reports of the fleet's progress from Stratford at approximately 10 p.m.

July 4, 1779. See, Ford, "Defense of New Haven," 33.

19. Painter, *Autobiography*, 45 - 60, *passim*.

20. R.R. Hinman, ed., *Historical Collections of Official Records of Connecticut in the Revolutionary War* (Hartford: Gleason Company, 1842), 264. See also, Hoadley, *Records of the State of Connecticut*, I: 129.

21. In the early morning hours of July 5, 1779, Joseph and Stephen Prindle were prompted by their father, Warden Joseph, Sr., of Christ Church, to carry fresh food and information to Collier's flagship. When word leaked out of the boys' activities, an angry mob descended on the Prindle home, but both boys escaped. In the aftermath of the invasion the incident went unreported to town officials. See, Writers' Program, 15. For information on Tryon's original instructions from Sir Henry Clinton see, Townshend, 33 - 34.

22. Painter, *Autobiography*, 45 - 60,

23. *Ibid.*, 45 - 60.

24. Townshend, 7.

25. Farnham, 18.

26. First Battalion of Guards, New York, January 1, 1779 - December 28, 1779, Early American Orderly Books, 1748-1817, (Woodbridge, CT: Research Publications, 1977), Reel 6, No. 77. See also, Ithiel Town, ed., *A Detail of Some Particular Services Performed in America* (New York: Ithiel Town), 91. Among the British troops were Lt. Col. Edmund Fanning, a Loyalist graduate of Yale, and William and Thomas Chandler, Tory brothers and sons of a New Haven attorney. Townshend, 5 - 7.

27. Sarah Day Woodward, *Early New Haven* (New Haven: The Edward P. Judd Company, 1929), 92 - 93. While enroute to the West Haven Green, the British alledgedly plundered the Thomas and Kimberly homes. In the latter residence, tradition has it that a British officer thrust his sword through the family Bible, which is believed to still be in the possession of the Kimberly family.

28. *Ibid.*, 92. General Tryon and 1,500 men launched their as-

Notes

sault against Black Rock Fort in East Haven and Garth had agreed to rendezvous in New Haven

29. The Campbell - Williston encounter has been retold many times in secondhand fashion. The only known primary source noting that Williston actually suffered a broken leg appeared in the Reverend Ezra Stiles' diary for July 25, 1779. "Lord's day. I preached at West Haven for Rev. Mr. Williston, who broke his leg in escaping from the enemy." See also, for instance, Erastus Colton, Discourse: Historical of West Haven Congregational Church and of the Old Parsonage. Sermon delivered at the 120th anniversary of the First Congregational Church, West Haven, CT, 1839 (Mss. West Haven, CT: First Congregational Parish House), 28 - 29. 37.

30. *Exercises at the Unveiling of the Monument to Adjutant William Campbell, Who Fell During the British Invasion of New Haven, July 5, 1779* (New Haven: Monument Committee, 1891),10. See too, Franklin B. Dexter, *Biographical Sketches of the Graduates of Yale College*, 4 vols. (New York: Holt, 1907), 315 - 316.

31. British Pay Lists and Musters, British Archives, London, England, WO12/1762 - 1784. For information on the role of adjutant, see, http://en.wikipedia.org/wiki/Adjutant. See also, Robert K. Wright, Jr., *The Continental Army* (Washington, D.C.: Government Printing Office, 1983), 32.

32. George Campbell to Peter J. Malia, Ms., May 13, 2009. Mr. Campbell is a distant descendant of Adjutant Campbell and an independent historian based in Scotland. For more information on the Battle of Culloden and its aftermath see, John Prebble, *Culloden* (New York: Atheneum, 1962); Stuart Reid, The Scottish Jacobite Army 1745 - 1746. Elite series No. 149 (Oxford, England: Osprey Publishing, 2006); http://www.nts.org.uk/Culloden/Home/

33. Robin May, *The British Army in North America 1775 - 1783* (Oxford, England: Osprey Publishing, 1998), 5 - 10. See also, Erastus Colton, Discourse: Historical of West Haven Congregational Church

and of the Old Parsonage. Sermon delivered at the 120th anniversary of the First Congregational Church, West Haven, CT, 1839 (Mss. West Haven: First Congregational Parish House), 37.

34. See, http://www.scotsguards.co.uk/history.htm. See too, Farnham, 18 - 19.

35. Five hours after the initial invasion of West Haven, General Tryon and 1,500 troops landed at East Haven and overran Black Rock Fort. Tryon and General Garth had agreed to march simultaneously on New Haven by 10:00 a.m. See, *The Connecticut Journal*, July 7, 1779. See also, Tucker, 61.

36. Goodrich, 42

37. *Ibid.*, 47 - 50; *Connecticut Journal*, July 7, 1779; Ford, "Defense of New Haven," 8 - 9; Farnham, 22 - 23. See also, Goodrich, 77.

38. Townshend, 45. See also, Osterweis, 144; and Farnham, 22 - 23.

39. Thompson, Working Papers, cites the Johnson home was located atop Milford Hill at the site of what is now The University of New Haven. This was the home of John Johnson (1732 - 1791), whose wife, Mabel, likely cared for the dying Campbell. Who actually shot the Adjutant, however, is a matter of debate. While the above-mentioned Johnson certainly lived on the scene and likely had the opportunity, there are no firsthand accounts of what actually occurred. What is known from second-hand accounts is that the shooter's name was, in fact, John Johnson. While Goodrich noted that Campbell was carried to a nearby home, he did not identify its owners nor did he provide any details beyond stating that, "When the enemy had passed on, and the people of the neighborhood returned, his [Campbell's] dead body was found entirely stripped of clothing." Some years after the Goodrich account, both Charles Hervey Townshend and Francis A. Cogswell added to the story. They identified the young John Johnson as a married man who returned home after the battle to find that his wife had cared for Campbell and the Adjutant's body remained in his home. As compel-

ling a tale as that might make, both Townshend and Cogswell may have gotten their John Johnsons mixed up. There was, in fact, another John Johnson (1754 - 1837) living in the Allingtown area at the time. His age better fits the description of "a young man," provided by all three accounts, but he was unmarried at the time of the invasion, so Campbell was not carried to his home, nor was the younger man related to the older John Johnson. Possibly the younger man was the shooter and the older Johnson was the owner of the home where Campbell died. Donald Lines Jacobus, *Families of Ancient New Haven* (West Haven: Donald Lions Jacobus, November, 1927), Vol. 5, No 1: 1044 - 1045. See also, Goodrich, 42 - 48; Townshend, 30; *Exercises at the Unveiling of the Monument to Adjutant William Campbell,* 1 -23.

40. Goodrich, 42; Townshend, 30.

41. *Exercises at the Unveiling of the Monument to Adjutant William Campbell,* 1 -23. Concerning the reported theft of Campbell's uniform, it is intriguing to consider that it may have served as a model for the Milford Grenadiers, founded shortly after the Revolution and populated by men all over six feet tall. Their uniforms were described as consisting of a scarlet coat with buff facings and lace trim, similar to the Guards, which coincidentally also favored tall men. See, John W. Fowler, *History of the Milford Grenadiers: Their Origin, Progress and Disbandment, With a List of the Officers and Members* (Milford: The Sentinel, 1876), 1 - 8. See too, William Howe Downes, "An Old Connecticut Town," in *New England Magazine An Illustrated Monthly* (Vol.1, Boston: New England Magazine Company, 1890), 273. See, too Farnham, 18.

42. Campbell's grave went unmarked until 1831 when John Warner Barber placed a small headstone on the grave after being shown its approximate location by Chauncey Alling, who witnessed the Adjutant's burial. That stone was eventually stolen by relic hunters and was replaced with the present memorial in 1891 in the vicinity of the original.

43. Farnham, 25. It is likely that William Chandler, a former student of Daggett, saved his life. See, Goodrich, 46; see also, Hoadly,

Public Records of the State of Connecticut, II: 545 - 553.

44. *Ibid.,* 25.

45. Farnham, 32 - 36.

46. Osterweis, 146 - 147.

47. Ford, "Defenses of New Haven," 36;

48. Osterweis, Chapter 16. Contemporary reports during the invasion lend credence to Osterweis' theory of a deal being made between the British and Americans. See, Lt. Col. Sabin's to Captain Caleb Alling, in the Caleb Alling Papers (Hartford: Connecticut Archives), No. 45. See also, Goodrich, 49; Farnham, 34 - 40.

49. Townshend, 11.

50. *Ibid.,* 11

51. Franklin B. Dexter, "Notes on Some of the New Haven Loyalists," New Haven Colony Historical Society *Papers* (New Haven: New Haven Colony Historical Society, 1918), 29 - 45.

52. Townshend, 30; Farnham, 36.

53. John Warner Barber, *Connecticut Historical Collections* (New Haven: Durrie, Peck and J. W. Barber, 1836), 71; Farnham, 37.

54. Estimates of British losses vary widely. Tryon's official report listed 9 killed, 40 wounded and 25 missing, which was likely underreported. Lt. Col. Kemble reported that as many as 47 had been killed with total casualties numbering close to 100. The Americans suffered 27 dead, 19 wounded and 22 taken captive. Townshend, 22 - 40; Goodrich, 52. See also, *Connecticut Journal,* July 7, 1779; New York Historical Society, *Journals of Lt. Col. Stephen Kemble,* 2 Vols.(New York: New York Historical Society, 1885), I: 179.

55. Washington remained in New York and was determined to regain lost ground in the Hudson Valley. By July 16, 1779, American troops had recaptured Stony Point, which effectively ended Clinton's master plan of isolating New England and drawing the Continental Army into a decisive, open battle. See, Townshend, 38. See also, Washington Irving, *The Life of George Washington,* 5 vols. (New York: G.P. Putnam's Sons, 1855 - 1859),

III: 495 - 509.

56. Apart from the two West Haveners known to have been killed in the invasion (Juduthan Thompson and Pomp), at least two dozen other residents reported damages to their personal property, totaling an estimated £25,000 (roughly $5 million in 2007 U.S. dollars).

57. Three families, the Chandlers, Botsfords and Camps left with the British in fear of what their neighbors might do. A number of prisoners were also taken. Townshend, 22.

58. In the first town meeting following the invasion, New Haveners appointed a committee to investigate those inhabitants who had refused to come to the defense of the town. On August 16, 1779, the final report was read charging a number of New Haveners with negligence, but then recommended leniency. Among those charged were five West Haveners, Stephen Ball, Thaddeus Beecher, Charles Prindle, Enos Alling and John Alling. See, New Haven Town Records, August 16, 1779; Atwater, 60.

59. Atwater, 62; Hoadly, *Records of the State of Connecticut*, II: 46 - 48.

60. Franklin B. Dexter, ed., *The Literary Diary of Ezra Stiles, D.D., L.L.D.*, 3 vols. (New York: Scribner's Sons, 1901), II: 508. Stiles noted that there were at least six whaleboats and 50 men involved in the West Haven attack.

61. The actual number of British troops involved is a matter of debate. While Erastus Colton puts the figure at approximately 150, Henry Johnston estimates their number to approach 500. Based on a contemporary newspaper account, Colton's figures appear to be more accurate. See, *The Connecticut Journal*, September 6, 1781. See also, Colton, 13; and Henry P. Johnston, T*he Record of Connecticut Men in the Military and Naval Service During the War of the Revolution 1775 - 1783* (New Haven: Case, Lockwood and Brainard, 1889), 626.

62. Among those West Haveners reportedly killed in the August 20th attack were Major Elisha Painter, Mrs. Hannah Kimberly and Philemon Smith. Among those taken prisoner and later said to have been drowned

in a storm were: Deliverance Painter, Captain John Catlin, Samuel Smith, Captain Silas Kimberly, Corporal Nathaniel Kimberly, James Alling, Samuel Trowbridge, Daniel Johnson, Alling Smith, Samuel Clark, Thomas Benham, Thaddeus Smith, David Trowbridge, Andrew Smith, John Picket, Eunice Ruslear and Mr. Willet. Some of these individuals, however, survived the storm. See, Colton, 13; Johnston, 626; Thompson, Working Papers. See also Jacobus, Ancient Families of New Haven, *passim.*

63. For Arnold's report on the battle see, http://www.patriotfiles. com/index.php?name=News&file=article&sid=81. See also, Carrington, 625 - 629.

64. Dexter, *Literary Diary of Ezra Stiles*, II: 557. See also, Louis L. Tucker, *Connecticut's Seminary of Sedition: Yale College* [Connecticut Bicentennial Series, VIII] (Chester: CT: Pequot Press, 1974), 70.

65. In the New Haven area, assessment values decreased from £72,395 in 1774 to £58,461, a drop of 19 percent. Van Dusen, 162.

66. Royal Hinman, ed., *Historical Collection of the Part Sustained by Connecticut During the War of the Revolution* (Hartford: Gleason Company, 1842), 626. Previous to this award for damages, West Haveners received the sum of £312 in May of 1780 to offset damages caused by Garth's invasion. See, Hoadley, *Public Records of the State of Connecticut*, III: 46 - 48.

Chapter 11: From Saints To Citizens

1. Boardman, 197 - 198.

2. New Haven Town Records, December 26, 1785.

3. Leonard Laboree, *Milford, Connecticut: The Early Development of a Town as Shown in Its Land Records* [Tercentenary Commission of the State of Connecticut] (New Haven: Yale University Press, 1933), 1 - 29, *passim*

4. Mary R. Woodruff, compiler, *History of Orange, North Milford, Connecticut 1639 - 1949* (New Haven: Payne and Lane, 1949), 17 - 36.

5. *Ibid.*, 17 - 36.

6. *Ibid.*, 60.

7. http://www.cityofwesthaven.com/

8. New Haven Town Records, August 14, 1786.

9. Osterweis, 165.

10. Van Dusen, 170 - 171.

11. David Hoeveler, *Creating the American Mind* (Lanham, MD: Rowman and Littlefield, 2002), 266 - 271.

12. Herbert Mitgang, *The Man Who Rode the Tiger: The Life and Times of Judge Samual Seabury* (New York: Fordham University Press, 1996), 10.

13. Osterweis, 163 - 169.

14. *Ibid.*, 169 - 173; 201.

15. Osterweis, 174 - 194, *passim.*

16. *Ibid.*, 174 - 194, *passim.*

17. Van Dusen, 170 - 171.

18. Michael Sletcher, *New Haven: From Puritanism to the Age of Terrorism* (Mt. Pleasant, SC: Arcadia Press, 2004), 36.

19. Paige Smith, *The Shaping of America: A People's History of the Young Republic,* 3 Vols. (New York: McGraw Hill, 1980, III: 23 - 37.

20. Osterweis, 170 - 178.

21. Van Dusen, 170

22. *Ibid.*, 176 - 178. See also Boardman, 281.

23. Osterweis, 175 -176; Collier, 203 - 205.

24. Van Dusen, 180; Page Smith, 38 - 49.

25. Osterweis, 176 - 178; Collier, 203 - 220, *passim.*

26. htttp://westhaven.org//lib_hist.htm. See also Dexter, *Biographical Sketches,* 501 - 505; Barber, *Connecticut Historical Collections,* 246.

27. Barber, *Connecticut Historical Collections,* 246. See too, Van Dusen, 178 - 179; Ronald H. Norricks, "To Turn Them From Darkess: The Missionary Society of Connecticut on the Early Frontier, 1798 - 1814" (Ph.D. dissertation., University of California, 1975).

Chapter 12: Dreams Of Their Fathers

1. Daniel Boorstein, The Americans: *The National Experience* (New York: Vintage Books, 1965), 3 - 9.

2. For additional information on the Episcopal Church in Connecticut see, Bruce E. Steiner, "Connecticut Anglicans in the Revolutionary Era: A Study in Community Tensions," (Bicentennial pamphlet XXVIII, 1978). See also, Louis Leonard Tucker, "The Church of England and Religious Liberty at Pre-Revolutionary Yale," *William and Mary Quarterly* 3rd series 17(July, 1960), 3:314-28; David H. Villers, "Connecticut Anglicanism and Society to 1783: A Review of the Historians," *Historical Magazine of the Protestant Episcopal Church,* Vol. 53 (March, 1984) 1: 45-59; and Glenn Weaver, "Anglican-Congregational Tensions in Pre-Revolutionary Connecticut." *Historical Magazine of the Protestant Episcopal Church* Vol. 26(1957), 269-85.

3. Alonzo B. Chapin, "A Sermon Delivered in Christ Church, West Haven," in Historical Notes About Christ Church West Haven, Connecticut Concerning Its Two Hundred Years of Existence, 1723 - 1923 (West Haven: Christ Church, 1923), 8.

4. See, Chapters 2 and 3.

5. By the time the Connecticut Assembly took steps to ban itinerant preachers in May 1742, The Great Awakening had already swept through the colony to cause a severe split between Old Light and New Light Congregationalists and fuel the growth of the Anglican Church. See, Van Dusen, 118.

6. An Old Light, Connecticut Governor Thomas Fitch proved too conservative and completely out of step with the ascending New Light political agenda. When he reluctantly supported the Stamp Act as an obligation to uphold the law, he and his administration lost the 1766 election. See, Oscar. Zeichner, *Connecticut's Years of Controversy, 1750-1776* (Hamden, CT: Archon Books, 1970), Chapters 2 and 3.

Notes

7. Richard Bushman, *From Puritan to Yankee, passim.*

8. Zeichner, chapters 2 and 3.

9. Division of Archives and History, ed., *The American Revolution in New York: Its Political, Social, and Economic Significance* (Albany: The University of the State of New York, 1926), 10, 15. See too, Roger J. Champagne, "New York's Radicals and the Coming of Independence," *Journal of American History* , Vol 51 (1964), 21-40; and Paige Smith, *A New Age Now Begins,* 2 Vols. (New York: McGraw-Hill, 1976), I: 189 - 219.

10. Herbert and Carol Schneider, eds., *Samuel Johnson, President of King's College: His Career and Writings* ,4 vols. (New York: Columbia University Press, 1929), I: 349. See also, Charles Francis Adams, *Works of John Adams,* 10: 288.

11. The religious origins of the American Revolution is the subject of voluminous scholarship. A sound starting point is James H. Hutson, *Religion and the New Republic: Faith in the Founding of America* (Lanham: Rowman & Littlefield, 2000), *passim.* See also, "Religion in the American Revolution," Part III, Religion and the Founding of the American Republic, Library of Congress exhibition, June 4 - August 29, 1998 (http://www.loc.gov/exhibits/religion/obj-list.html).

12. Osterweis, 129, 151; Atwater, 63.

13. Osterweis, 170 - 172

14. New Haven Town Records, 1785 - 1798, *passim.* See also, Painter, *Autobiography;* Osterweis, 202; Woodruff, 35.

15. Woodruff, 33 - 36; Osterweis, 164.

16. Smith, II: 1817.

17. The Thomas Painter House was relocated to Litchfield, CT in early 1959. See, Thomas Painter House, Historic Homes Research Folder, Litchfield Historical Society, Litchfield, CT.

18. New Haven Town Records, March 8, 1784.

Index

Adams, John, 86
Adjutant William Campbell Memorial, 133
Alcock, John (1675-1722), 177
Alcock, John (1705-1777), 177
Alcock, Philip (ca. 1680), 32, 177
Alcock, Thomas (1677 - 1757), 177
Algonquian, 1, 5
Allen, Rev. Jonathan, 64, 65
Allen, Rev. Timothy, 52 -53, 73 - 74, 223
Alling, Abraham (1754 - 1837), 176
Alling, Abram, 176
Alling, Amos (1764 - 1820), 176
Alling, Caleb (1694 - 1756), 176
Alling, Caleb Capt. (1764 - 1827), 176
Alling, Charles (1724 - 1808), 176
Alling, Chauncey (1767 - 1842), 177, 237
Alling, Christopher (1735 - 1799), 177
Alling, Daniel (1688 - 1756), 177
Alling, Daniel (1728 - 1821), 177
Alling, Daniel (1758 - ?), 177
Alling, Ebenezer (1687 - 1734), 177
Alling, Ebenezer (1712 - 1744), 177
Alling, Edward (1768 - 1815), 177
Alling, Elisha (1751 - ?), 177
Alling, Elisha, 177
Alling, Elisha, 177
Alling, Enos (1719 - 1779), 177, 238
Alling, Ichabod (1756 - 1809), 177
Alling, Issac (1755 -1818), 177
Alling, James (? – 1781), drowned, 238
Alling, James (1756 - 1817), 177
Alling, John (1647- 1717), 177
Alling, John (1743 - 1809), 177, 238
Alling, John, Jr. (? - 1770), 177
Alling, John, Jr. (ca. 1690), 177
Alling, Jonathan (1683 -1775), 177
Alling, Jonathan Jr. (1716 - 1771), 177
Alling, Lemuel (1746 - 1809), 177

Alling, Nathan (1729 - 1812), 177
Alling, Rev. Timothy (ca. 1738), 177
Alling, Robert, 23
Alling, Roger (1612 - 1674), 177, 212
Alling, Roger (1708 - 1770), 177
Alling, Samuel (1645 - 1709), 177
Alling, Samuel (1669 - 1744), 177
Alling, Samuel Jr., 177
Alling, Silas (1734 - 1817), 177
Alling, Silas, Jr. (1771 - 1805), 177
Allingtown, CT, 131 – 132
Allsop, John Jr. (1648 - 1691), 177
Allsop, Joseph, Sr. (? - 1698), 177
Allsop, Philip (1648-1715), 177
American Revolution, vii, 33, 42, 51, 77, 85, 87, 92, 101 - 115, 126, 161, 165, 166, 168, 171 - 175
Amity, CT, 104, 136, 145
Andrews, Nathan (1662-1713), 177
Anglicans, 49, 50, 52, 73, 75, 99, 100, 147, 158, 161, 162, 163, 165, 202, 241
Arnold, Benedict, 94, 95, 96, 101, 105, 142, 226, 240
Arnold, Rev. Jonathan, 46, 47, 48, 49, 217
Articles of Confederation, 101, 109, 149
Atwater, Abel (? - 1822), 177
Atwater, David Jr. (1756 - 1803), 177
Atwater, Eldad, 177
Atwater, Elnathan, 177
Atwater, Jacob (1720 - 1799), 177
Atwater, Jeremiah (1734 - 1811), 177
Atwater, Jeremiah 3rd (1773 - 1858), 177
Atwater, Jeremiah 4th, 177
Atwater, Jeremiah Jr. (1767 - 1832), 177
Atwater, Joel (1728 - 1794), 177
Atwater, John, 177
Atwater, Jonathan, 177
Atwater, Medad, 177

245

Index

Atwater, Moses (1729 - 1805), 178
Atwater, Samuel (1739 - 1798), 178
Atwater, Stephen (1720 - 1806), 178
Atwater, Thomas (1733 - 1805), 178
Atwater, Timothy (1751 - 1820), 178
Atwater, Ward, 178
Austin, Archibald, 230
Austin, Elijah, 230
Baker, John (ca. 1770), 178
Ball, Glover (1748 - ?), 178
Ball, Hezekiah (1741 - ?), 178
Ball, John (1649-1713), 178
Ball, John, Jr. (1685-1731), 178
Ball, Stephen (1726 - 1799), 178, 238
Ball, Stephen, Jr. (1762 - 1842), 178
Ball, Timothy (1724 - 1796), 178
Ball, Timothy Jr.(1751 - 1832), 178
Barber, John Warner, 197 - 198, 237
Battle of Culloden (Scotland), 130
Battle of Lexington, 92, 93
Battle of Long Island, NY, 227
Battle of Niagara, 77
Battle of Saratoga, 103
Beecher, Caleb (1724-1794), 178
Beecher, David (1738 – 1805), 178
Beecher, David, Jr. (1773 - 1834), 178
Beecher, Ebenezer (1686-1763), 178
Beecher, Ebenezer (1714-1790), 178
Beecher, Eleazer (1655-1725), 178, 218
Beecher, Eli (1747 - 1799), 178
Beecher, Hezekiah (1703-1751), 178
Beecher, Isaac (?-1690), 178
Beecher, Isaac (1698-1794), 178
Beecher, Isaac Jr, (1650-1708), 178
Beecher, Isaac Jr. (1726-1814), 178
Beecher, John (1646-1712), 178
Beecher, John (1744-1796), 179
Beecher, Joseph (? - 1728), 179
Beecher, Joseph (1698-1763), 179
Beecher, Medad (1750 - ca. 1815), 179
Beecher, Nathaniel (1681-1768), 179
Beecher, Nathaniel (1706-1796), 179
Beecher, Reuben (1742 - 1798), 179
Beecher, Samuel (1687-1760), 179
Beecher, Stephen (1742 - 1795), 179

Beecher, Thaddeus (1749 - 1823), 179, 239
Beecher, Thomas Jr., 179
Beecher, Thompson (1768 - 1792), 179
Beecher, Titus (1740-1803), 179
Belden, Aaron (ca. 1770), 179
Belden, Jared (? - 1778), Loyalist, 179
Belden, Jared (1716-1796), 179
Belden, Samuel (? - 1778), Loyalist, 179
Benham Hill Road (West Haven, CT), 16
Benham, David (?), 179
Benham, Gamiel (1738 - 1811), 179
Benham, Japhet (1697-1778), 179
Benham, John (1664-1744), 23, 55, 179
Benham, John (1710 - 1777), 179
Benham, John, Sr. (?-1691), 179
Benham, Samuel, 179
Benham, Silas (1753? - 1777), 179
Benham, Thomas (? – 1781), 179; repo-
erted drowned, 240
Bethany, CT 104, 136
Bill of Rights, 156
Birdseye, Nathan Rev., 74, 75
Bishop, Samuel, 158, 169, 225 – 226
Bissell, Israel, 93
Black Rock Fort (New Haven, CT), 113,
119, 124, 131, 139, 141, 235
Blakeslee, Abraham (1727 - 1795), 108,
179
Blakeslee, Archibald (1752 - 1830), 179
Blakeslee, Ebenezer (1711 - 1771), 179
Blakeslee, James (1735 - ?), 179
Blakeslee, Job (1744 - 1823), 179
Blakeslee, Joel (1750 - 1814), 179
Blakeslee, Jotham (1768 - ?), 179
Blakeslee, Oliver (1741 - 1824), 179
Blakeslee, Seth, 179
Blakeslee, Zopher (1730 - 1798), 179
Blakesley, Isaiah (1751 - ?), 179
Blakesley, Obed (1754 - ?, 179
Blakesley, Philemon (1760 - 1841), 179
Blakesley, Samuel (1662 - 1732), 179
Blakesley, Tilley (1728 - 1811), 179
Blakesley, Zealous (1756 - 1829), 179
Bleeding, as medical treatment, 57
Block, Adrian, 7

Index

Index

Index

15, 184, 210
Lamberton's Quarter (Plantation), 13, 14, 15
Landsgraf Jaegers, 118, 127
Leek, Philip (? - 1676), 185
Leek, Thomas (1648 - 1720), 185
Leffingwell, Jesse (merchant), 229
Levenworth, Jesse, 113
Long Island, NY, 108, 112
Long Wharf, 139, 149, 166
Loyalists, 96 - 99, 108, 109, 118, 120 - 121, 139, 140, 141, 152, 166, 167, 198, 227 230, 234, 239
Lumber, 30, 31, 32, 148
Lyons, Henry, 215
Lyons, James Rev., 49

Mallory, Daniel (1687 - 1760), 185
Mallory, John (1705 - 1777), 185
Mallory, Joseph (1666 - ?), 185
Mallory, Peter (? - 1698/99), 185
Mallory, Peter, Jr. (1653 - 1720), 185
Mallory, Thomas (1723 - 1805), 185
Mansfield, Richard Rev., 50, 212
Marriage, 19
Mason, John Capt., 8, 9, 214
Massachusetts Government and Administration of Justice Act, 224
Massachusetts, 1, 150
Mattabesec (Middletown, CT),
Meaker, Robert, 23
Meaker, Thomas, 35 - 36
Meaker, William (ca. 1660s), 185
Meaker, William, 216
Measles, 114
Meigs, Return J., 111
Meloy Road (West Haven), 16
Middletown, CT, 2
Miles, John, 109
Milford Grenadiers, 236
Milford Hill (West Haven, CT), 234
Milford, CT, 13, 18, 55, 117, 145, 146, 156, 159, 160, 167, 212, 219, 232, 233, 237, 245. See also North Milford
Military Service, 23 - 24, 26, 27

Mishimyaget, 1
Mix, Amos, 184
Mix, Caleb (1750 - 1802), 185
Mix, David (1744 - 1790), 185
Mix, Diodate (1765 - ?), 185
Mix, Eldad (1733 - 1806), 185
Mix, Elisha (1752 - 1813), 185
Mix, Hezikiah, 185
Mix, John (1649 - 1712), 185
Mix, John (1720 - 1796), 185
Mix, John Jr. 1751 - 1820), 185, 230
Mix, Jonathan (1729 - 1779), 185
Mix, Joseph (1684 - 1757), 185
Mix, Joseph (1740 - 1813), 185
Mix, Joseph, 185
Mix, Nathaniel (1749 - 1781), 185
Mix, Samuel (1730 - 1813), 108, 185
Mix, Stephen (1753 - 1784), 185
Mix, Thomas (1755 - 1810), 185
Mix, William (1779 - 1803), 185
Mohawk, 6
Mohican, 6 - 7
Molasses, 148
Morris, Amos, 132
Morris, John, 217
Morris, Theophilius Rev., 49
Morrissey, Gregory, 168
Moss, John (1698 - 1777), 186
Moss, Joseph (1643 - 1727), 186
Moss, Joseph (1679 - 1732), 186
Mount Carmel, CT, 145
Mulliner, Thomas (1660s), 35 - 36; 186, 216

Nancy (sloop), 166
Nash, John (1615 - 1687), 186
Native Americans, 6 - 7
Neck Bridge (New Haven, CT), 136
New Amsterdam, 7, 28, 214
New England Restraining Act, 92
New Haven Green, 48, 50, 77, 95, 101, 106, 136, 144
New Haven, CT, vix, 4, 8,16, 17,18, 19, 20, 21, 26, 27, 28, 29, 30, 31, 32, 34, 35, 36, 37, 38, 39, 40, 41, 42, 43, 46, 48, 50,

Index

5, 77; American Revolution, 103, 109, 168 - 169; Anglicans, 64; boycott, 79, 80, 87, 91; British relations, 77, 79, 89, 90, 91, 93, 94, 95, 96, 101, 104; city of, 146 - 147, 154, 158, 166, 171; civic improvements in, 148 - 149, 154, 166; defenses of, 119 - 120; disease in, 57, 58, 158; expansionist plans of, 21 - 30; finances, 143, 146, 167; franchise, 150, 170 - 175; invasion of, 103, 107, 108, 109, 115 - 140, 142, 236 - 237; land divisions, 15, 55; maps of, 102, 125; militia, 23; New Lights, 73, 75; Loyalists, 96 - 97, 98, 99, 106 - 108, 140 - 141, 143, 147, 150, 166; office holding, 171- 190; patriotism of, 108 - 110; privateers, 110 - 114; providing for troops, 232 - 233; seaport, 12, 41, 104, 148, 151, 160, 166; settlement of, 9 - 14, 210 - 211; schools, 60 - 61, 62, 159; slavery in, 211; smuggling, 106, 110 - 114; social classes in, 95, 104, 156; Stamp Tax, 79 - 80, 83, 84, 85; Tea Act, 88, 89, 90; violence in, 105 - 107, 110; and West Haven, 39 - 40, 146, 159

New Lights, 70, 71, 75, 81, 85, 147, 163, 165, 223, 242

New London, CT, 101, 117, 142, 148

New Tenor Bills, 64

Newfoundland, 92

Newgate Prison (Granby, CT), 112

Newport, RI, 121, 232

Nonimportation, 84

Norfolk, VA, 116

North Haven, 104, 145

North Milford, CT, 145, 146, 160

North Street (West Haven), 16, 32

Nova Scotia, 92

Office holding, 170 - 189

Ogden, John, merchant, 230

Ohio, 56, 60

Old Lights, 70, 71, 72, 75, 81, 86, 87, 147, 163, 223, 242

Orange, CT, 145, 156, 175

Osborne, Benjamin, 186

Osborne, Daniel (1715 - ?), 186

Osborne, David (1746 - 1786), 186

Osborne, Elijah (? - 1814), 186

Osborne, Jeremiah (1656 - 1713), 186

Osborne, Jonathan (1692 - 1750), 186

Osborne, Joseph (1667 - 1735), 186

Osborne, Medad (1753 - 1814), 186

Osborne, Samuel, 186

Oyster Point (New Haven), 58, 111, 120

Oyster River (New Haven, CT), 55, 121

Painter, Deliverance (1701 - 1781), 65, 185; reported drowned, 239

Painter, Elisha (1736 - 1781), 185, 239

Painter, Joseph (1731 - 1766), 186

Painter, Lamberton (1741 - 1795), 186

Painter, Shubael (1697 - 1785), 186

Painter, Thomas (1670 - 1747), 186

Painter, Thomas (1696 - 1760), 186

Painter, Thomas (1760 - 1847), xii, 19, 32, 100, 113, 120, 124, 148, 156, 157, 159, 162, 166, 168, 173, 175, 186, 203, 216

Paleo-Indians, 2

Palmer, Solomon Rev., 51

Papal Plot (1688), 49

Parliament, 78, 79, 80, 82, 83, 84, 85, 87, 88, 89, 90 - 91, 93,

Peace of Paris, 144

Peck, Amos (1749 - 1838), 186

Peck, Benjamin (1746 - 1812), 186

Peck, Daniel, 186

Peck, Ebenezer, 185 (merchant), 230

Peck, Henry (1755 - 1802), 186

Peck, Hezikiah (1767 - 1840), 186

Peck, James (1708 - 1794), 186

Peck, John, 186

Peck, Joseph (1647 - 1720), 186

Peck, Joseph (1718 - 1788), 186

Peck, Joseph Jr. (1749 - 1800), 186

Peck, Moses (1753 - 1837), 186

Peck, Roger (1746 - 1808), 186

Peck, Seth (1747 - 1831), 186

Peck, Stephen (1730 -1778), 186

Peck, Thomas Jr., 186

Peck, Timothy (1737 - 1807), 186

Peck, Titus (1742 - 1776), 186

Index

Index

Trowbridge, David (? – 1781), 190; 240
Trowbridge, Ebenezer, 190
Trowbridge, John (1684 - 1739), 190
Trowbridge, Samuel (? – 1781), 239
Trowbridge, Stephen (1688 - 1734), 190
Trowbridge, Thomas (1663 - 1711), 190
Trowbridge, William (1700 - 1793), 190
Trumbull, Benjamin Rev., 97, 154
Trumbull, Jonathan, 113, 147
Tryon, William Gen., 116, 117, 121, 128, 131, 234; failed strategy of, 140; Proclamation of, 136 - 138, 139
Tuttle, Joseph (1640 - 1690), 58, 190

Union Avenue School (West Haven, CT), 159
US Constitution, 153 - 154

Vermont, 158
Verplanck's Point (NY), 116
Verrazzano, Giovanni da, 7
Visible Saints, xv, 20, 27, 34, 35, 53, 161, 162, 164, 169, 216 – 217

Ward, Ambrose (1735 - 1808), 190
Ward, John (? - 1785), 190 (Died at sea)
Ward, Thomas (1760 - 1830), 190
Ward, William (1736 - 1829), 190
Ward-Heitman House (West Haven, CT), 32, 33
Washington, George, 57 - 58, 96, 101, 116, 117, 140, 142, 143, 232, 238
Waterbury (CT), 50
Wayward Puritans, 38
Weed, Samuel, 66
Welch Fusiliers, 118
West Haven Green, 42, 128, 133, 217, 219
West Haven, CT, 1; Anglicans in, 50, 52, 75, 81, 86, 97, 98, 99, 100, 147, 158, 161, 162, 163, 165, 202 - 203, 239; British invasion of, 115 - 140, 141, 142, 143, 239; Christ Church, 46, 48 -49, 64 -65, 72, 73, 97,98, 99, 122, 162, 163, 164, 166, 222, 227; colonial wars, 24 - 27; commerce of,

32, 149; defenses, 118 - 119, 120; education in, 59 - 62, 157, 159; farming, 30 - 31; franchise, 170 - 175; government of, 17; independence of, 38 - 40, 63, 66 -67, 75 - 76, 81, 144, 145, 156 - 160, 162, 163 - 169, 174; land disputes, 15 - 16, 55; library, 157; Loyalists, 96, 97, 98, 99, 108, 109, 118, 120 - 121, 139, 140, 141, 152, 166, 167; maps, 13, 155; officeholders, 171 - 190; provincialism, 49 - 50; religious schism, 71, 72, 218 - 219; roads, 16; seaport, 32, 84, 111, 118, 167; settlement of, 14, 16, 212; society in, 34, 54 -55, 67 - 68; Stamp Act, 80, 82 - 83, 105
West Indies, 30, 33, 77, 84, 148, 166
West River (West Haven, CT), 14, 15, 146
Western Reserve, 60, 152, 153. See also Firelands, Sufferers' Lands
Westmore, James, 217
Westmoreland, 152
Westville, CT, 135
Whitefield, Geroge Rev., 68, 69, 223
Whiting, John, 109
Whitney, Eli, 158 - 159
Whittlesey, Samuel, 218
Wilkes Riots (London), 131
Wilkie, William, 212
Willet, Mr. (? – 1781), drowned, 240
Williston, Noah Rev.(1734 - 1811), 75, 97, 121, 128, 129, 154, 156 - 157, 158, 162, 190, 200, 235 - 236
Williston, Payson Rev., 157
Winthrop, John, 41, 154
Witchcraft, 36 - 37, 202, 216
Woodbridge, CT, 12, 145
Woodhall, Richard, 107
Woodland Age, 2, 3
Wooster, David, 95, 101, 123, 232, 233
Wyoming Valley (PA), 151, 152

Yale College, 44, 45.48, 50, 51, 57, 62, 73. 74, 77, 79, 96, 101, 104 - 105, 107, 110, 113, 118, 126, 131, 135, 142, 191

About The Author

A native of West Haven, CT, Peter J. Malia received his graduate training in American History at Trinity College, Hartford, and Fordham University, New York. He has served as primary research historian at Sleepy Hollow Restorations, Inc., Assistant Editor of Sleepy Hollow Press, and Editor-in-chief of The Connecticut Historical Society. He currently resides in Monroe, CT with his wife, Celeste.